GROWING UP
BIDEN

GROWING UP
BIDEN

A Memoir

VALERIE BIDEN OWENS

CELADON
BOOKS

New York

Unless otherwise noted, all photographs are courtesy of the author.
Grateful acknowledgment is made for the use of photographs provided by Michael Connor,
Brad Glazier, Sue Goldstein-Rubel, Jim Harrison, Catherine McLaughlin, and Adam Schultz.

Library of Congress Cataloging-in-Publication Data

Names: Biden Owens, Valerie, 1945– author.
Title: Growing up Biden : a memoir / Valerie Biden Owens.
Description: First edition. | New York : Celadon Books, 2022.
Identifiers: LCCN 2021059429 | ISBN 9781250821768 (hardcover) |
    ISBN 9781250821775 (ebook)
Subjects: LCSH: Biden Owens, Valerie, 1945– | Biden Owens, Valerie,—
    Family. | Biden, Joseph R., Jr.—Family. | Women political consultants—
    United States—Biography. | Political consultants—United States—
    Biography. | Political campaigns—United States—Anecdotes.
Classification: LCC E918.B57 .A3 2022 | DDC 320.092 [B]—dc23/eng/20211209
LC record available at https://lccn.loc.gov/2021059429

Our books may be purchased in bulk for promotional, educational, or business use.
Please contact your local bookseller or the Macmillan Corporate and Premium Sales
Department at 1-800-221-7945, extension 5442, or by email at
MacmillanSpecialMarkets@macmillan.com.

First Edition: 2022

10 9 8 7 6 5 4 3 2 1

To my family

CONTENTS

INTRODUCTION

In late September 2021, when I sat down with my brother in the White House, Washington, DC, had just experienced one of its periodic late-summer thunderstorms. Loud bursts of thunder threatened to tear open the sky before finally giving way to a gentle rain. At last, the city bathed in calm. It was hard not to see a metaphor in that. Joe and I had certainly weathered our share of storms in the past seven decades.

Since Joe was elected to the presidency in November 2020, I have been to the White House many times. I am thrilled with the majesty of what it represents—power, diplomacy, and American values. Never once, not even for a moment, have I taken that honor for granted. I will never forget what it took to get here, the millions of people who put their faith in Joe, who devoted their financial resources, time, and effort. Nor have I forgotten those we lost along our improbable, seemingly impossible journey. I still feel them with us every day, their imprint on everything we do.

On this September night, I was here again, back in the home of

Jefferson, Lincoln, Roosevelt. And now Biden. The White House's thoughtful and professional stewards had left no detail to chance. Jill had requested that my favorite wine be chilled for my arrival. The stewards had already made sure that the specially created cookies, on which the White House pastry chef had piped "Valerie" in blue icing, awaited me in my room. Jill had gone home to Delaware earlier in the day. Joe had stayed for meetings and a speech he had to give the following afternoon.

When Joe arrived in the family residence, he and I walked into the dining room for a quiet dinner alone. We sat at a long mahogany table—Joe at its head, and me at his side. It was beautifully set with crystal, china, and the evening's entrée: salmon in a pastry shell with a medley of vegetables.

"Damn, she makes me eat this healthy stuff all the time," my brother said. Neither of us particularly likes salmon. But he ate it. So did I. Who were we to challenge the First Lady of the United States?

My daughter Missy stopped by later to visit with us, so the three of us moved to the living room to talk. After a few minutes, Joe, the President of the United States, excused himself to raid the refrigerator. He brought back some dessert for us—a delicious lemon pound cake with ice cream—only to go back an hour later for round two. This time, he appeared with a carton of Breyers chocolate chip ice cream that he proceeded to finish with nothing but a spoon. Our father, a stickler for table manners, undoubtedly would have commented: "Champ, put that in a bowl."

Eventually, the conversation turned to my book. Missy asked Joe his thoughts about our lives together. He praised my decency and loyalty, but then cut to the essence of our bond: "She's been my best friend since I was three years old," he said.

"Everyone knows that already," Missy reminded us. She was curious about what more we could share. We hadn't quite come up with anything, any big moment or anecdote that offered the key to understanding how we operate.

Trying again, Missy asked if we had ever had a major disagreement over all these years. We both drew a blank. Joe and I don't work that way. We don't hold grudges against each other. There's no long list of grievances, no scorecard.

The truth is, we never disagreed about much—especially on the important things. Don't get me wrong: he could drive me up the wall. And I had no problem telling any of my brothers when I thought they were being jerks. They did the same for me on those occasions when I was in the wrong.

But those were small things. On the big things, we shared a common worldview. In various profiles of Joe over the years, I have been called "the Biden Whisperer," and that isn't wrong. We intuitively understand each other. We can finish each other's sentences. With just a glance, we know what the other means. As his campaign manager, I could instantly tell whether a mailer, speech, logo, or TV ad was true to Joe or not. He needed me to do that. He trusted me to do that. Without question.

Well, except for once.

As we sat together in that spacious private living room on the second floor, flanked by grand arched windows, I reminded my brother of a tense moment many campaigns ago.

The year was 1996, and Joe was up for reelection to the Senate. I had approved a campaign ad that was running in the expensive Philadelphia media market, and someone who'd seen it complained to Joe. Joe was furious about what he'd heard, and he stormed into my campaign office with a look I'd seen before, but never directed at me—one of contained fury.

He leaned over my desk, reciting a litany of complaints about the ad. "Why the hell would you approve something like that?" he demanded.

I looked back at him. "Because it's the best ad I've ever seen."

"Why didn't you say that in the first place?" he asked. Then he came around my desk, kissed me on the forehead, and left.

Within seconds of that explosion, the storm had subsided. He had humbly backtracked, remembering that there was no way I would do anything that I didn't think was in his best interest.

Now, in 2021, as we relived that moment, I walked over to his chair and kissed him on the forehead.

The President of the United States leaned back. I saw the tears well up as he closed his eyes. I stayed quiet—no words were needed to explain total trust.

There we sat, filled with love and gratitude in recollecting that incident, reminded of our gift of understanding and rapid repair, grateful we were still a team.

"That's it," he said, his voice low. "That says it all."

We had found the elusive memory that explained us. And then I urged my brother, the leader of the free world, to finally go off to bed.

"I saw the angel in the marble and carved until I set him free." Maybe you've heard this quote before. Like a lot of resonant sayings, it's been passed around to the point that some people don't even know where it came from. As the legend goes, these were the great artist Michelangelo's immortal words when asked how he could have created a masterpiece like his *Angel* sculpture at the Basilica of San Domenico.

Whether or not that story is true, the message is powerful. We all carve and are carved. Sometimes we hold the chisel, and sometimes we are the marble.

There's still dust on my shoulders from the many Michelangelos in my life who saw the angel, that potential, in me—my parents, my brothers, my husband, so many teachers and family members, so many good friends. And I've tried to pass on the gift to be a Michelangelo to others around me who've looked over the years for advice, guidance, or unflinching love.

My three brothers and I grew up with many advantages. I'm not talking about wealth or status—we Bidens had neither. Rather, I'm referring to things that are far more valuable and precious—our family, our upbringing, our faith. Because of these values, our parents expected us not to squander what we had been given but to be change agents, to make a difference. And that's just what my brother Joe and I set out to be—agents of change—to share our ideas, and to invite others to engage with us on this journey toward a more just and equitable future.

Together—with me as campaign manager—we launched Joe's first US Senate race on a platform to advance Civil Rights, end the war in Vietnam, and protect our planet. He was twenty-nine years old. I was twenty-six. We had no pedigree, no established organization behind us, and no influence. But we had passion and commitment and hope. We were too idealistic and too young to know what we shouldn't be doing. So we made our own rules. We worked hard and scrambled—and, yes, sometimes we had small disagreements along the way. After all, it isn't easy raising an older brother.

I was the kid sister whose brother pulled up a chair for her at a table where there had been no room for women. All the political pundits were men, all the consultants were men, and most of the reporters covering Joe's campaign were men. They believed that a woman's rightful place in politics was answering the phones and sending out mailers. Women didn't manage Senate campaigns in 1972. But I did. So, sometimes I had to set the guys straight. I wasn't dubbed "the Hurricane" by happenstance.

I went on to manage Joe's next six Senate races and his first two campaigns for the Democratic presidential nomination. For the entirety of our professional lives, we have worked side by side: he as candidate or elected official; I as advisor, surrogate, media consultant, and confidante. But more than any formal role, we have been, first and foremost, brother and sister and best friends.

In many ways, our family story is not all that unusual. We are a middle-class, Irish Catholic family whose parents worked hard to raise healthy, kind, empathetic children. We went to church, to Catholic schools, and occasionally got into childhood mischief. We were surrounded by an extended family filled with great characters. We were encouraged to always stand up for ourselves and for one another. We faced setbacks as a team, and together we celebrated one another's victories. When Joe first decided to go into politics, politics became a family calling. That's just the way we did things as Bidens.

My story—of being an American woman in the latter half of the twentieth century and the first part of the twenty-first—is also a familiar one. The baked-in expectations of gender roles, the balancing of work and raising children, the breaking of professional barriers, the evolution of gender-related policy—all these social and legal currents ran through my own life, at home and in the workplace.

My experiences in the political world came first at my brother's side. But those experiences enabled me to eventually train other women to be political leaders, both in the United States and around the world, to find a seat at their own table. And the conversations and experiences I had, both on the campaign trail and in my consulting work, helped me offer my brother a deeper understanding of the challenges women face every day.

In writing all of this down, I've been intrigued by the vagaries of memory. I've consulted my own paper trail and other family members wherever I can, but there are details of my own life, it turns out, that elude even me. In reminiscing about my early days as a teacher at the same high school my younger brother Frankie attended, he surprised me by recalling that he had been in my class. "How could you not remember that?" he marveled, and we laughed. Nonetheless, I have attempted, to the best of my ability, to convey the essence of how each experience felt, and the joy of growing up Biden.

October 30, 2020

When we arrived at the Iowa State Fairgrounds for the last "Biden for President" rally, it felt as if we'd stepped into a ghost town: all the buildings vacant, the merry-go-round still, paper swirling across the empty fields and roads. It was a clear, crisp, blue-sky day, as late fall should be. COVID-19 was ravaging the country, and the bustling conviviality usually found here was a distant memory.

Over the next few hours, cars filled with supporters began to arrive. They lined up across the field, separated by rope dividers designed to create a safe distance between the vehicles while a makeshift parking lot began to take shape several hundred feet from the podium. The press pool was out in the open air—our team had cordoned off an area for them, situated on the asphalt surface closer to where Joe was to speak. Joe's granddaughter Maisy and I sat near them while we listened to the introductions, waiting for Joe to take the stage for his final appeal to voters, just four days before the election.

While some people stepped outside or sat on their hoods, most stayed in their cars so at this event, applause was expressed by the honking of horns. The fairgrounds took on the sound of a downtown city street at rush hour: horns blaring and people shouting through their car windows. "It was a great honkin' day" became our in-house rallying cry.

Midway through Joe's remarks, I was distracted by members of the press who had begun whispering and were looking up and pointing to the sky. Instinctively, protectively, I thought, Why aren't they listening to Joe? *One of the local campaign staffers who worked with the press came over to me and said, "Look, Val!" Maisy and I craned our necks to see where she was gesturing. Directly above us, an eagle was circling. It passed over Joe's head, soared back and forth a few times, and then flew off.*

"Hello, Beau—thanks for stopping by," I said aloud, and thought back to a difficult caucus day in Iowa nine months earlier. Several eagles had perched in the trees lining the road where my daughter Missy and I were campaigning that day. We felt protected under their watchful eyes and were so moved by the sight of them that we pulled over to take it in.

It had been a long and arduous journey since February 3, but we had come full circle. I felt in my heart and soul that we were heading for a smooth landing.

FORTY-EIGHT YEARS,
TO THE DAY

O n the night of Saturday, November 7, 2020, I waited for my brother amid a sea of jubilant voters at the Chase Center on the Riverfront, in Wilmington, Delaware. Loudspeakers were blasting upbeat music and lights glittered over the Christina River. Earlier that afternoon, four days after the election had been held, the Associated Press finally called the race: Joe had won Pennsylvania, giving us an insurmountable lead over the four-year nightmare that was Donald Trump. In a few minutes, Joe would come out and declare victory to the waiting crowd of supporters—despite the fact that his opponent had not conceded (nor would he ever), and despite the fact that there were still protesters chanting "STOP THE COUNT!" outside voting facilities. The worst was yet to come, though we could not have imagined it at the time. For this one moment, at least, none of that mattered.

My husband, Jack, and I took in the scene. Like the rest of the family, we were stationed in one of the Jeep Wranglers that the campaign had secured for the event. Jack was in the driver's seat; I was standing up on the passenger's seat, head and arms poking through the open sunroof. Looking around at the countless smiling eyes shining above BIDEN–HARRIS face masks, I felt a wave of gratitude and affection. These people knew Joe—had known Joe—for decades, ever since his first campaign for public office, a County Council race in 1970. Having been his campaign manager for that race and having run every Senate campaign and two presidential campaigns since, I knew them just as they knew Joe. They were our friends, our neighbors, our people—the people who'd brought Joe "to the dance," as he would say in his speech a few moments later.

We were just a five-minute drive from the Hotel Du Pont, the place where we had launched Joe's first Senate campaign in 1972. At the time, I was a twenty-six-year-old high school teacher; Joe was a twenty-nine-year-old lawyer.

That year, we campaigned in supermarket parking lots and snapped Polaroids with shopkeepers. I recruited my students to knock on doors and drop campaign literature throughout the state. We hit every small-town parade, block party, and parish festival from the day school let out for the summer to Election Day in November. The press called us "the Children's Crusade," because we did everything with throngs of middle and high school students—a combination of Joe's vision and the encouragement of their eighth-grade and social studies teachers (Joe's wife, Neilia, and I).

The Democratic Party saw us as sacrificial lambs—no one thought we had a chance in hell of winning the seat; others saw us as a nuisance. Our opponents didn't see us at all. I was flying by the seat of my pants—I hadn't the slightest clue what I was supposed to be doing. That didn't stop me, though. We were as scrappy as we were inexperienced.

When Joe won, by an astoundingly slim margin of 3,163 votes, he became the first US Senator either of us had ever known. And on top of that, he became one of the youngest Senators *ever*. On election day, he was too young even to be sworn in; he had to wait until November 20, his thirtieth birthday.

Between that first victory and this one, decades later, lay several lifetimes' worth of triumphs and disappointments, joys and heartbreaks, serendipity and loss. To that point, 2020 had been grueling and dispiriting: after a disappointing fourth-place finish in the Iowa caucuses on February 3, we were declared dead in the water. The *New York Times* called it "a damaging blow"; Joe called it "a gut punch." Joe's campaign was functioning on a shoestring, with the distinct possibility that he would have to take out a loan to cover expenses. People were beginning to talk about an exit strategy.

Meanwhile, the pandemic had turned campaigning norms—along with all other facets of American life—upside down. Joe thrives on person-to-person human connection, and suddenly the only new faces we saw were on Zoom, a communication medium combining the awkward pauses of a phone conversation with the discomfort of staring at yourself in a mirror. Nothing about the path of the campaign had been ideal. But Joe never lost his quiet confidence or his ability to soldier forward. He remained clearheaded and calm.

The night Joe clinched the Democratic nomination for President, June 5, 2020, he made a peculiar kind of history: no modern candidate had come from so far behind to win so decisively. Thinking back on that night, one might expect I would have felt *elated*. But that wasn't my experience. I remember thinking, *I should be shouting with joy right now*—but that elation didn't come.

Call it Irish superstition, but the truth is it isn't in my nature to celebrate before all is said and done. We were raised not to tempt the Fates. It's also not in my nature as a lifelong campaign manager, always on red alert, primed for the next catastrophe. But more than having a specific impact on me, the previous year had simply brought too much suffering for too many Americans, whether from COVID-19, racial injustice, or other losses. And the depredations our democracy had experienced over the previous four years had been too grave for any sense of victory to kick in.

But that night, November 7—as I stood in the Wrangler, watching the stage and waiting for Joe—our collective triumph was starting to sink in. I mused that it was exactly forty-eight years *to the day* since we burst onto the national scene after an astounding upset in the Delaware race for United States Senate.

My mind drifted to those who were no longer with us—Neilia, Joe's late wife; Naomi, Joe's daughter, whom the family called Amy; Mom and Dad; and now Joe's eldest child, Joseph R. Biden III, whom we called Beau.

Neilia and Amy died when an eighteen-wheeler plowed into the side of their car on December 18, 1972. Joe was not in the car, but Beau and Hunter were, and were seriously injured and hospitalized. For a moment, we weren't sure if we would lose them, too. Beau died in 2015 of an aggressive cancer, glioblastoma, at the age of forty-six. So much tragedy and darkness, but balanced by equally powerful light to throw those shadows into relief. It was enough to make anyone go still.

After their deaths, I got into the habit of talking to them. I was convinced Beau had his hand on his father's shoulder throughout the entire campaign. At times of great joy and great sorrow, my first thoughts went to them: *I wish Mom could see this. I wish Dad could be here. Beau would be so proud.*

I was lost in these thoughts when suddenly a roar went up. Joe walked out, his smile as wide and welcoming as always. In spite of myself, I hollered and cheered, waving my hands over my head to elongate my five-foot-four-inch frame. And just then, Joe spotted me in the crowd: "Val! We did it!" From sibling to sibling, those were the only words that needed to be said. Chills went through me, and I felt Beau's presence as my eyes filled with tears.

Joe's speech was pitch-perfect. He promised to "lower the temperature," to end the era of demonizing our fellow Americans. This was something he and I both felt strongly: politics, the art and science of living together peacefully while we tussle over the allocation of scarce resources, had become a degrading blood sport. President Trump brought out the worst of our human tendencies, and the nation's very soul had been battered by hatred, intolerance, and bigotry. That night, everyone craved healing. Joe radiated a bone-deep sense of understanding that comes from *truly* listening—in a word: empathy.

As fireworks exploded and the sound system boomed, Joe stood onstage with Jill, the future First Lady; their daughter, Ashley; her husband, Howard; Hunter and his wife, Melissa; and finally the grandkids: Naomi, Finnegan, Maisy, Natalie, Hunter, and Baby Beau. "A Sky Full of Stars," a song by Coldplay, one of Beau's favorite bands, rang out into the night. Newly elected Vice President Kamala Harris and her husband, Doug Emhoff, joined them. "You are Bidens now, whether you like it or not," Joe had joked in his speech, and at that moment, they did already feel like family.

After the speech, the family went inside to take turns lining up for a quick photo with Joe and Jill. It was nice, but also strange. Normally when we are together, we're like cubs: snuggled up close, joshing each other, hugging. But that night, like so many other families living through the threat of COVID-19, we did our best to adhere to the formalized protocol of social distancing. As a result, it didn't feel anything like a Biden family celebration.

After our photos, Joe and Jill went into their hold room at the Chase Center to gather their things, the day's pomp and circumstance finally over. I followed them in and sat down next to Joe, drained, and he and I stared at the television in silent wonder. The two of us sat alone, brother and sister. Just as always, he was at my side, and I was at his.

I was born on November 5, 1945, on a blustery Monday morning during rush-hour traffic. My parents always remembered it as a blizzard. I was two weeks early, and Mom and Dad were stuck in traffic en route to Boston's Lying-In Hospital; no matter, I was coming, ready or not. On the way to the hospital, Dad spotted a traffic cop, explained the situation, and convinced the officer to give them a police escort. Mom and Dad made it to the hospital just twenty minutes before I made my debut. I had to be there in time for my big brother Joey's birthday—after all, I was his present, his little sister.

Joe and I have always been together, whether as kids on the baseball diamond at Maloney Field in Scranton, Pennsylvania, or over the years on the campaign trail. I am told I was the first female campaign manager to run a modern US Senate campaign; I know I'm the first to have run a presidential one. And although I am also a teacher, a media consultant, a wife, and a mother of three beautiful children, it's fair to say that I lived the first forty years of my public adult life in Joe's shadow. This was a conscious choice I made when Joe first decided to run for public office, and I believe it is also mandatory for any successful campaign manager or political media consultant.

In truth, this decision came easily to me, as it did for all the Biden children. It might just have been birth order, but it seems a noncompete clause came embedded in our DNA. No sibling coveted what the other had. None wanted to be the other. We each had our own space and were comfortable with our roles. We reveled in one another's successes and shared in one another's disappointments.

Our parents drilled it into our heads from birth that we were to take care of one another. In my mom's words: "Family is the beginning, the middle, and the end. Period." They taught us that we were a gift to one another. "There is nothing closer than brothers and sisters," my mom would say. No matter what our disagreements might be, we had to straighten them out at home. God forbid if one of us turned on another. Once we were outside, we were Bidens, and nothing could come between us.

These dicta weren't written down anywhere—writing this book might be the first time I've seen them set down in black and white. But they didn't need to be transcribed. We all knew precisely what was expected of us.

We were expected to tell the truth—no matter what. The truth might be embarrassing or ugly or sometimes even shameful, but my parents made us understand that truth is the only option. They would be there for us, no matter what—so long as we told them the truth. If you're going to be late, call. If you are in trouble, call. If you want to get out of trouble, call. No questions asked.

We were expected to stand up to bullies. If we were getting pushed around, Mom told us to punch that bully right in the nose if we had to, so long as it was a fair fight. (These days, of course, we don't advocate for schoolyard fights, but in my parents' day, things were different.) Dad taught us that the greatest sin of all was the abuse of power.

We were expected to treat everyone with dignity. "No one is better than you, and you're no better than anyone else," Mom said. We knew to be kind to kids who wanted to be our friend, especially when that kid was "less than cool."

We were expected never to despair. "It's not how many times you get knocked down," my father used to say, "but how quickly you get up." Our family would have many opportunities to discover this truth on our own. Failure, darkness, tragedy were inevitable in life. But giving up? That was unforgivable.

This ethos taught us everything we knew about what it meant to be a Biden. And it was on our little shoulders to make our family proud.

Mom had some choice sayings that became something of a refrain through-out our childhood. One, "Beware the righteous," was a favorite back then and remains just as relevant.

As parents, Mom and Dad practiced what they preached: they never accused or lectured us. They never threatened to ground us. They simply loved us. And even when we were in grade school, we intuitively understood our responsibility to uphold our end of the bargain—and as a result, we were very hesitant to break their trust.

When we did, as all kids do at some point in their journey to adulthood, it weighed heavily on us.

To this day, I can count on one hand the number of times I did mess up. One such instance, which happened when I was about ten years old, is still seared in my mind.

When my family lived in Arden, we used to visit the neighborhood "pool" in the summer. The pool was cold, muddy, and natural—it was just a creek that had been backed up to create a swimming hole: no chlorine, no aqua-colored concrete, no fancy chaises, no dressing rooms.

Swimming lessons took place at 9:00 a.m. in the shallow end. I complained to Mom that it was freezing that early in the morning, but she wouldn't let me go to the pool at all unless I signed up. So reluctantly, I did.

At the far end of the pool, there was a diving board. Oh! I longed to jump off it like all the big kids—but Mom had forbidden me to do so. I remember thinking, Jeez, that is such a dumb rule. *You didn't even need to know how to swim, really, to make it to the ladder.*

I reasoned that she was making a big deal out of nothing. If I jumped off the side, it was just a few strokes. . . . I'd be on my way up and out, lickety-split. Not a big risk but a big reward: freed from the baby pool!

I was an obedient child by nature, and not a brat—but after scoping it out for days, my evil twin, Skippy, reared her head, and I decided to go for it. I climbed onto the board, and before I allowed myself to be slowed yet again by inner debate, I moved quickly to the edge.

Just as I lowered my head for the dive, I caught a glimpse of Mom, who didn't normally come back to get us that early, heading toward the pool. Uhh-ohh, *I thought, scrambling off, but the damage was done. My mother's thunderous eyes were upon me.*

Next thing I knew, Mom delivered the six most devastating words in her vocabulary: "I am so disappointed in you." I was crushed.

To disappoint is a terrible thing, and to know you have done so is even worse.

2

MOM AND DAD

When I was a child, I never thought of my mom and dad as individuals. To me, they were just Mom and Dad—that reality took up my whole universe. Maybe it's a generational thing—my own children know more about me than I ever knew about my own parents as I was growing up, and my kids understand and admire the fact that being a mom is only part of my identity. But for whatever reason, I have never stopped learning about my parents, even long after both of them have passed.

Dad, Joseph Robinette Biden Sr., was born in Baltimore, Maryland, in 1915, and grew up in Saint Thomas's parish in Wilmington, Delaware. In Catholic neighborhoods, the parish in which you lived was everything; you identified yourself by name first, parish second. Dad's family lived in a row house—had it ever gentrified, it would now probably be called a brownstone, but it hasn't and it isn't. He was the eldest of three children, and his father worked for the American Oil Company until he died suddenly in his midforties from a blood clot that broke off in his leg. I've never seen so much as a picture of my paternal grandfather. Everyone tells me he was the spitting image of our thirty-fourth President, Dwight D. "Ike" Eisenhower.

Dad's mom, Mame, dropped dead only a couple of years later. She was visiting my parents in Boston, went into the powder room, and never came out. Her death certificate reads "heart attack"; family lore deemed it a broken heart.

My dad never talked too much about his past. The few tantalizing hints I got just made me want to learn more. When Joe was accepted into Syracuse University College of Law, Dad let slip that he'd enrolled in Johns Hopkins University to study business—something we never knew. Years later, when my husband, Jack, and I were renovating our new beach cottage in Fenwick Island, Delaware, I mentioned that the floorboards had come from an old, now-defunct local joint called the Black Cat Saloon. "My God," Dad said. "We played there when I had my band." *What band? Played what?* Clarinet, we later learned, in a blues band. He was a man of few words, but when he spoke, we listened. I wish he had spoken more.

One of the very few stories Dad told me was that he had developed Saint Vitus' Dance when he was in grammar school. The proper name for the disease is Sydenham's chorea, or chorea minor, but it got the medieval moniker Saint Vitus' Dance for what it does to you. Caused by rheumatic fever, Saint Vitus' Dance manifests itself in jerky movements, face contortions, and occasional slurred speech. It usually resolves itself within three months. I try to imagine a young boy, unable to control his jerking limbs, frightened by his strange condition and drawing stares. I've sometimes wondered about the mark it must have left on my dad, unable to run and play with his friends—or even coordinate his body movements. Was he made fun of? I bet he was, but Dad never said. Perhaps that's why he was so tender with our insecurities, and why Dad chose solo sports; he was a graceful swimmer, diver, horseman, and skier. None of these activities involved teammates.

In keeping with the times, Dad was more of a father figure than a "daddy." When he got home from work, sometimes he would fall asleep the moment his head hit the easy chair, but not before offering a kind smile or an encouraging remark. Fifteen minutes later—after what we'd now call a power nap—he'd be bounding up again. The Energizer Bunny had nothing on our dad. I wish I, too, could nap on demand.

When I was a little girl, it never occurred to me to climb onto my dad's lap. He wasn't cold or distant, just a dad of a different generation. I did not feel the emotional side of my father until I had children of my own. When Dad became a grandfather, I watched in amazement as the grandkids crawled all over him, and he doted on them completely. Our kids would go as often to Dada, as they called him, as they would to my mom, Mom-Mom. I always knew my father loved me, but it wasn't until he held my children that I came to know his gentleness. It was a profound gift, to see this side of him.

My mom, Catherine Eugenia "Jean" Finnegan, was born in 1917, the only girl in a family of four brothers—three older, one younger—living in Scranton, Pennsylvania. Her father, Ambrose Finnegan, worked for the *Scranton Tribune*—not as a reporter, but on the business side. He ran a department with the morbid title of "the Morgue," where they stored old newspapers, not bodies. My grandmother, Geraldine, stayed home, raising their five children. They were a typical Irish Catholic family of their time, whose values were faith, family, country. Oh, and they were Democrats to the core.

Mom was cherished by her brothers. Her immediate older brother, Ambrose Jr., nicknamed Bosie, was her knight in shining armor. She was devastated when he went missing in action after his plane was shot down over the South Pacific near Guam in World War II. She never learned what happened to him. Was he captured and tortured? Eaten by sharks? Gruesome scenes played out over and over again in her mind. For years, she held on to the hope that he would be rescued or his body would be recovered. Eventually, she just had to let go. I am sure she talked to him and prayed for him every remaining day of her life.

Losing Bosie likely lent extra fierceness to her admonition to her own children: "No one is closer than your brothers and sisters—not even your parents. Love each other. Take care of each other."

Mom was a beacon of empathy, but she was also a tough woman, and Lord help you if you crossed her or her family. She was like the rose of Sharon: she was beautiful, but she had thorns. When she was eight or nine years old, she walked over to the playground to confront a boy who was picking on her youngest brother, Jackie. She punched him square in the nose and told him to stay away from her brother or she would be back. She was tiny but a huge force to be reckoned with, even then.

She would pass this lesson along to us, too. Once, when my younger brother Jimmy was about ten or eleven, a neighborhood kid had written something nasty about a neighborhood boy in a freshly poured square of concrete. There it was, hardening into permanence on our corner. Mom took Jimmy and me aside and asked us calmly if we knew who had done this. Jimmy did. Mom brandished a five-dollar bill: "Whoever comes back with bloody knuckles gets this five-dollar bill." Jimmy went over, knocked on the front door, asked for the boy politely, took him around the side of the house, and popped him right in the face.

Like I said, Mom didn't normally advocate violence or rough justice. But she knew that words were weapons, and that they could hurt as much as blows. Mom despised gossip and imprinted a deep aversion in all her kids to spreading rumors. "Gossip is like taking a down pillow, slicing it open, and then flipping it out the window to let the feathers fly," she used to tell us. "No matter how hard you might try, you will never be able to get all those feathers back in that case."

To Mom, it was just as important that we learn to stand up for ourselves as it was to look out for others. When I was five years old, I entered the first grade at Marywood Seminary, the all-girls Catholic school up the street from home. This was the same school Mom had gone to as a child. My teacher, who was a nun, insisted that all children be called by a saint's name. Apparently Valerie wouldn't do—so she called me Valeria. To make matters worse, she mispronounced my last name *Bidden*.

I told Mom. Though I was just three days into my first week of school, she insisted I correct the nun. The idea alone made me blanch. *Correct a nun? Is she nuts?* That day, when the nun went through roll call, I made my move: "My name is Valerie Biden." Sister stared at me for a beat and then moved on to the next name on the list. Later, when I raised my hand to answer a question, Sister struck again. "Yes, Miss Bidden?" I had failed.

I confessed to Mom that I simply couldn't face Sister again. "I can't go back there, Mom. I quit." Not a chance. Mom marched me up to Marywood, found my teacher, and threatened to "knock that bonnet right off" her head if she did it again. "If she mispronounces your name, don't stand up for roll call," Mom ordered. The message was crystal clear: I was a child, but my dignity mattered just as much as anyone else's, and I wasn't to tolerate disrespect.

Mom and Dad first met in Scranton in 1933, when Mom was a sophomore in high school. Dad had graduated from Saint Thomas the

Apostle School in Wilmington, Delaware, in 1936, and his father had just been transferred to Scranton. In Mom's telling, Dad was the hotshot who rode into town in his own car—tall, handsome, and a meticulous dresser. He was also the boy from out of town, and Wilmington was considered cooler than Scranton. Mom became best friends with Dad's sister, Mary Alice, who was also a sophomore at Marywood Seminary. When Mom and Dad fell in love, their attraction was strong enough to survive the combined objections of Mom's three overprotective older brothers. They married in Scranton on May 30, 1941, when Mom was twenty-four and Dad was twenty-six—and moved to Harrisburg, where my father worked for the American Oil Company, just like his dad. Their firstborn, Joey, arrived on November 20, 1942.

Soon after, Dad left the American Oil Company and went to work for his Uncle Bill, a businessman whom everybody called Old Man Sheen. William Sheen Sr. was an entrepreneur who owned the patent on a sealant that helped protect merchant marine ships from German U-boats patrolling the North Atlantic. The portrait I had of Old Man Sheen from family stories was of a bigger-than-life figure, the kind of profligate spender who made a million and lost a million in the same breath. He and his wife, my dad's Aunt Al, owned a big country house in Baltimore, with maids and butlers who set a formal dining table. Their son, Bill Jr., was not just Dad's first cousin but also his best friend.

When Dad was young, he would leave his family's Wilmington row house and spend part of his summer in Baltimore, riding horses on the estate with his cousins. My dad was always welcome, but the distinction between son and nephew was always clear. Where Old Man Sheen gave Uncle Bill a new Cadillac, he gave Dad a Ford.

Maybe this is where my father inherited his insistence on impeccable table manners. If one of my brothers came in from swimming in our aboveground backyard pool or from playing ball, God help him if he sat down at the table to eat without a shirt. Even now that my son, Cuffe, is an adult, he apologizes if he shows up at the table wearing a baseball hat, and immediately whips it off—"I know what Dada would say, Mom." My father worked for his uncle and cousin during the war. At that time, the business was divided up into ports. Old Man Sheen was in Norfolk; Bill Sheen Jr.'s family took New York; and Mom and Dad wound up in Boston, where I was born.

When Mom and Dad were living in Boston in the 1940s, they had more money than ever before. Mom had a fur coat, beautiful china, a nice car, and a comfortable home in the suburbs. But they were unable to enjoy the good life—Mom's brothers were overseas on active duty then, and Dad was fighting growing guilt that he was not active in the theater of war himself. He was portside in Boston because the government had deemed him an essential worker.

After World War II ended, so did the sealant business. The family relocated to Long Island, New York, for a spell. Dad and Bill Jr. went into business together, spraying crops from small planes. Dad knew how to fly an airplane—another surprise. I have no memories of this time—I was still a toddler—but in some ways, these early years shaped the course of our family's life.

The crop-dusting business went belly-up. There were many reasons, not the least of which was Bill Sr.'s and Bill Jr.'s alcoholism. Their profligacy got the best of them, and everything was lost. To regroup, Mom and Dad moved back to Scranton and rented an apartment a few miles from Mom's family home on North Washington Avenue.

Scranton was where my brother Jimmy was born—May 16, 1949. Then, two months later, our mom's mom died of colon cancer at sixty-three.

I believe these years solidified my parents' ironclad belief in the power of resilience. Dad had already been knocked back on his heels by the events with Uncle Bill, and now the entire family was learning in real time how to adjust to radically changed circumstances. Dad was unable to find suitable work in Scranton, so his younger brother Frank, who was in Delaware, encouraged him to come back home. "There's work here," he said.

Dad first got a job cleaning boilers for a heating and cooling company in Wilmington, which meant he was gone all week, only back in Scranton on the weekends. Mom, Joey, Jimmy, and I left the apartment and moved back in with Mom's dad—Pop—her brother, and her aunt on North Washington Avenue.

These transitional years had a more profound effect on Joey than they did on me. Joe remembers Dad telling him that he had to go to Delaware to get a new job, and that he would be home every weekend to see us. While he was gone, Joey had to be a big boy and help Mom take care of his little sister and brother. Dad's travels had no impact on me that I was aware of, probably because I had so many family members in the house. I missed him, but I felt secure.

Aunt Gertie lived in the Scranton house, too, with Pop and Uncle BooBoo. Aunt Gertie was Pop's sister-in-law. She never married, and today we would call her an agoraphobe. Back then, I just thought it odd that she never left the house. She had white hair that went all the way down her back, which she wore in a bun, and long fingernails perfect for scratching our little backs. She always wore a housedress with a full apron that had two front pockets, and when she wasn't in the kitchen, cooking our meals and making rice pudding for Jimmy, she was sitting in her rocking chair, guarding the front door and watching TV. Aunt Gertie watched all the game shows. She entered Mom's name in every quiz show in existence, and years later, Mom even participated on two of them via phone. I think one of them was *Let's Make a Deal,* where you had to figure out what was behind door number three. (Turned out: a washing machine.)

Aunt Gertie loved Joey and Jimmy the best, but she did fix me coffee and toast every morning. The coffee was two-thirds milk with two teaspoons of sugar. Quite a way to start the day for a five-year-old; I felt very grown-up.

The house had a single staircase leading to the second-floor bedrooms, but at the lower landing it split in two: the kitchen to the right, the living room to the left. I loved that landing—I could sit and hear conversations on both sides of the house. I don't recall what was said, but I remember soaking up all the sounds of our home.

There were only two places I wasn't allowed to go. One was the dormer room in the attic, where Aunt Gertie slept. The other was the cellar, with its coal-burning furnace and dimly lit stairs. Sometimes, if I wanted to test my bravery, I would sneak down to the cellar anyway to explore the coal bin—to make sure, I told myself, there were no bad men hiding there. I would emerge from the coal bin blackened, covered with soot, but feeling certain I had saved everyone in the house from harm.

Most of the time, I went down there to stand with Uncle BooBoo while he fed the furnace. Born Edward Blewitt Finnegan, he got hit with the nickname BooBoo because his eldest nephew couldn't say Blewitt, but he never seemed to mind the name. BooBoo was a bachelor, and I was his favorite niece. Heck, I was his favorite *anyone,* save his dog, Mr. Skip.

Uncle BooBoo sold Serta Perfect Sleeper mattresses, and I used to ride with him on his day trips to check in on his customers. He also sold the bunting for coffins, so I would go with him to the workshops where the coffins were made. I thought I was pretty cool, crawling into a coffin and having BooBoo take my picture. At the end of these day trips together, Uncle BooBoo and I would stop at Kovach's beer joint in downtown Greenridge, which was only about two miles from our house—I was the only five-year-old with her own barstool.

BooBoo was the smartest person I knew, and he was patient with all my questions. When I was a little girl, he could explain to me how all those people could get inside the car radio and talk to us, or why it rained on one side of the street and not the other. He taught my brother and me that when people used vulgarity to express themselves, it was because they were not bright enough to think of better, more appropriate words.

When I got older, he would fill me in on his view of current events. He always had a more jaded view of the world than my dad, who got up every day with an attitude that he was a winner. BooBoo thought he got the short end of the stick. He had a bad stutter that plagued him throughout his years and he blamed it for any misfortune. However, he showered me with whatever hopefulness and joy he had within him. It wasn't much, but it was plenty for me. I loved him.

BooBoo bought me my first everything, from roller skates to my prom dress. He bought me every Nancy Drew book the day it came out. She was the girl I admired most—brave, inquisitive, independent. She did everything a boy could do, and she brought her friends along, too. She was a leader, but not an obnoxious one.

Normally, my father would have been the one buying these things, but Dad was grand: he saw how much it meant to BooBoo to play an important role in my life and did not begrudge him that joy.

But with this love, I felt a tremendous responsibility. Uncle Boo-Boo was a functioning alcoholic and a lapsed Catholic. For the latter, the nuns said he was going to hell. When he opened the furnace door to shovel in the coal, the flames leapt into life and roared with a tremendous force, much like I imagined they did in hell.

I said my rosary every night for BooBoo, because when he died, I had to be sure to get him into heaven one way or another. When he returned to church, I would exult in my power and declare my mission accomplished; when he stopped showing up at Mass, I was despondent, wondering whether I could have saved him for sure if I'd just kept at my prayers a little longer.

I was never afraid of the dark as a child; I knew I could just flip on a light switch. But the inner darkness in the people I loved, like Uncle BooBoo—that was another matter. Inner darkness is not so easily banished. I was more afraid of the things I could not control, like BooBoo's drinking, than the things I could, like taking the lead in the school play. Our grade school, Saint Helena's, was one block away from a fire station. It seemed that the fire sirens went off at least once a day. Sister would stop whatever we were doing, and we would all say a Hail Mary to protect whoever was in trouble. My immediate thought was always, *Maybe that's our house on fire. Please, dear God, save our house.* To this day, whenever I hear a fire engine, I immediately slip into a Hail Mary.

I don't know exactly how old I was that summer. I know I was a little girl, but I thought I was much older because my big brother, Joey, took me everywhere with him.

One day we went into a field for a picnic. It was so sunny and hot—I remember the dragonflies skimming across the water by the creek. We brought lunch, peanut butter and jelly sandwiches, although mine was always just jelly. We rode our bikes—mine had a basket in front—and we met up with Janet and her brother, Mickey.

Janet lived in a house that had a tree growing in the middle of it. Janet's mom worked all day, so in the summer, Janet was like the mom— she stayed at home and took care of her younger brothers.

Janet was beautiful, and probably a year younger than Joey, which made her just right, and Mickey was a year or two younger than Janet— which he figured made him just right for me.

I was not a beautiful Janet. I was a straight-up-and-down tomboy whose girlish charms and body had yet to present themselves to me, let alone the world.

I still wonder after all these years how Mickey could have been so misguided.

Anyway, I was sitting on the big rock, drinking my Royal Crown soda, when up jumped Mickey to kiss me. I screamed for my brother, who had been planning to do the same thing to Janet down by the creek. My timing was a little off from his perspective.

After my bloodcurdling "Joey!" I was off that rock and running to my bike to get out of there. By the time Joey got home to find me, I had stopped crying long enough to want to punch him. "Why did you leave me with that creep?" I yelled.

Guess I already knew that answer: I had learned the hazards of being a tagalong when an afternoon kiss was the real reason for the trip.

3

THE MAGIC OF YOUTH

In the fall of 1951, when Joe was in third grade and I was in first, Dad drove us to Delaware to show us our soon-to-be new home in Claymont. The housing development, Brookview Apartments, was in a working-class neighborhood just across the Pennsylvania border, and Dad was full of eager trepidation as we arrived. He was going to give us a brand-new start. This was the first step.

To me, the place looked like a perfect playground—trucks, open buildings, big ditches, boards, nails, plenty of red mud to play in forever. It was a construction site.

But Mom was seeing a different place altogether—not only a place that was not Scranton but one without trees, paved roads, sidewalks, friends, or family.

"Mom," Joey said, "what's wrong? Why are you crying?"

"Because I am so happy," Mom said, wiping her eyes. "Isn't it beautiful? Isn't it beautiful?"

Indeed, it was beautiful—the love that I was not mature enough to understand until years later. Mom knew that Dad was almost ashamed that this was where he had landed the family. But there was no embarrassment for Mom, only respect for her husband's grit, determination, and gumption.

Our new home was a two-bedroom apartment with very little wiggle room for visiting family. This was the only time I remember not having relatives stay with us on a semipermanent basis. Mom and Dad had one room, where they also put Jimmy's crib, and Joe and I shared the other with our bunk bed.

We moved in when I was in the middle of first grade. My parents couldn't afford to buy me the new green uniforms the girls wore at Claymont's Holy Rosary School, so the nuns said I could wear my old blue one from Marywood for the rest of the year and get a fresh one at the start of second grade. As a result, I wasn't just the girl who came in the middle of the school year, but also the blue girl in a field of green. An awareness of that feeling of being singled out, left out, has always stuck with me.

I remember few things about our time in Claymont, but each is a nice memory: playing kick the can every night until dark in the horseshoe-shaped courtyard in front of the apartment building; eating navel oranges on the sidewalk, chomping the top of the rind off and squeezing the juice into our mouths; and Mom with the TV on, watching the McCarthy hearings and muttering to no one in particular about how that man was a disgrace to Irishmen everywhere.

Next, we moved to Arden, Delaware. It was originally an arts and crafts community, but I don't think that fact crossed my parents' minds even once. They chose a nice house at the right rental price, and in every way, it was very different from our home in Claymont. Here, the homes were clustered together on one-half of a 162-acre tract, with the rest of the land remaining open space. It was a beautiful wooded enclave surrounded by modern suburbia. Here, there were no concrete circle courts or stucco-coated pink apartments lined up in a row. It was a land of curving, shady roads leading to exotic places.

To Joey and me, it was a magical place, our very own personal Sherwood Forest, where I was sure I would one day come across Robin Hood and his band of Merry Men. Mom and Dad let us roam free. It was exhilarating. We couldn't wait to get up in the morning and get going.

Just down the lane and across two more was The Pig 'n' Whistle, a little cottage store where you could buy everything from penny candy to perfume for Mom on Mother's Day. It was covered with ivy, had a dirt floor and low ceilings and little sunlight inside. It sat catty-corner from a green expanse of trees—who knew what kind of animals lived in and around those trees?

In Arden, my dad's bachelor brother and our youngest brother's namesake, Frank Biden, came to live with us. Like my dad during this time, Uncle Frank was in the car business, and he always drove a sporty convertible. He was also a great dresser, like my dad. While my dad favored Hickey Freeman suits with a pocket square, wing tip cordovans, starched shirts, and cuff links, Uncle Frank was just as dapper, but more casual—preferring Madras sport coats, Bermuda shorts with knee socks, and loafers.

Mom would say that having Uncle Frank living with us was like having a teenager in the house. Mom talked to him the way she talked to us when she was mad. "Now, Frank—you come home tonight, and come home sober," she said. "I don't feel like waiting up and worrying about you."

Lots of women wanted to get their hands on this very eligible and jovial bachelor. I remember one woman who insisted, to our astonishment, that we refer to her as Aunt Connie, while the gin and tonic in her right hand steadily disappeared. *Yeah, right,* we thought as we fought to keep a straight face. *Call me Aunt Connie* immediately entered the Biden kids' private vocabulary. It was code for "you've got to be kidding me."

The most important event of the Arden years was the birth of our youngest brother, Frankie, on November 25, 1953—the night before Thanksgiving. Dad and Mom left early in the morning to go to the hospital. When Dad came home to tell us we had a new brother, I didn't listen—I was huddled under the dining room table, crying and screaming because Joey was trying to put Mercurochrome and a bandage on my bloody knee.

Joey and I had been out exploring in Arden. We were creek-hopping, and I had slipped on one of the rocks, leaving a deep gash. Joey had taken me home and tried to help clean it, but I was having none of it—and it turned out, neither was Dad. I think that evening was one of the only times Dad ever raised his voice at me. I quickly recovered, and have a scar on my left knee to commemorate the occasion.

Mom and Frankie came home two days later, and we all settled into a rhythm. Joey, Jimmy, and I were given the naming rights, and after much deliberation, we chose Danny. That was a "go," as far as we were concerned, until the morning of his baptism.

Uncle Frank pulled a fast one. He appealed to Mom's heart: "Jean, I will never marry and have a son of my own—there will never be another Frank Biden—would you consider naming him after me?"

Mom fell for it—and in a wink of an eye, "Danny" was hijacked by Frank. Oh, by the way, Uncle Frank eventually did marry and have a son—whom he named Jeff.

When I was in fifth grade, we moved from Arden to Mayfield. Dad tried to buy the house we'd been renting, but the landlord must not have been too fond of us, because he kept raising the sale price.

While Arden was an eccentric neighborhood, with no two houses or families alike, Mayfield was mostly uniform, with smooth, asphalt roads, good for roller-skating and performing tricks on bike handlebars. None of the yards had any trees, so the developer planted little saplings that looked like sticks near the sidewalks to simulate the effect. In Mayfield, everyone was Protestant; most families had only two children, and everyone's dad worked for the DuPont Company.

The company was synonymous with Delaware at the time. Working for the DuPont Company was a straightforward deal: you bought into the culture, and you would probably be able to work for them for the rest of your life. The company culture, for the most part, consisted of unblinking loyalty to DuPont. You wore your DuPont tie clip, you reported to work, you came home to your family, and you put on your steel-tip shoes when you tended your small patch of lawn.

It seemed that my dad was the only one who didn't work for DuPont. There were about seventy-five houses in the development, and we were one of a handful of Catholic families, along with the Mulrines, the Conleys, the Lewises, and the Rivers. I don't know how we slipped in. We were the "Catholic school kids."

We were among the first families to move into Mayfield, just as we had been in Claymont. Gray Magness was the construction company, and as far as the eye could see, there were houses being built. They were all split-level homes, with a rec room that frequently flooded and needed a sump pump. Joey and I used to go around with a wagon to all the construction sites, collecting empty soda bottles and hauling them to Bill's Gourmet Shop on Marsh Road for a refund of two cents apiece. We were in business for a couple of summers and thought we were pretty flush with cash.

Frankie was a toddler by then, and I would occasionally wheel him around the block in a little wagon. Mom never asked me to watch Frankie, so I never got stuck being a second mother to him, as so many big sisters did. But even if I had, I don't think I would have minded. He was a sweet boy, a gentle soul.

Our house was command central. Mom threw open the doors to all our friends, and when Dad got home at night, he would have to step over all the bodies that were stretched out across the living room floor.

It was in Mayfield that Joe first introduced the idea of the "family meeting." There were four of us in attendance: Joe, me, Jimmy, and Frankie. It was a democratic organization—an arbitration board, so to speak. Any of us kids could call a meeting for any reason. We would gather alone—our parents never interfered—and we would get right to the heart of the matter.

"You embarrassed me." "You hurt my feelings." "I am so mad." "You were mean." These were the typical squabbles of siblings, but we handled them in an atypical way. Our goal was to get the offense out in the open, explain how the transgression had made us feel, take responsibility for our actions, stop the hurt the action had caused, mend the rift, and move on. We didn't know it at the time, but we were learning to develop empathy. Those meetings helped me build an emotional muscle that I have used over and over again through the years.

We also had "family fights"—orchestrated matches consisting of water balloon fights, egg peltings, and mild forms of psychological torture, like scary sneak attack games in the night.

Jimmy and I were always on the same team against Joey and Frankie. Jimmy and I always won because they always underestimated us and because we always went for the jugular. We were masters of the first strike, and we tried to land it hard.

Sometimes retaliation was called for, family meeting or not. Jimmy and I were excellent at cooking up creative punishments when the circumstances demanded them. One day, Joe had ticked us off—about what, I swear to God I no longer have any idea, but I remember we were incensed. Big Joey needed to be taken down a peg or two, we decided.

I hatched the plan: I ordered Jimmy to grab some money from his bureau drawer—thanks to his booming lawn mowing and paper delivery businesses, he always had cash—and follow me on his bike up to the pet store about four blocks away.

We walked in and went right to the big glass case where the snakes lived. We picked out a cute little one—skinny, black, surely slimy—and carried him home in a box with tiny holes in the lid. We could hardly contain ourselves until it was time for bed.

As the only girl, I now had my own room. Jimmy, Frankie, and Joey shared the other kids' bedroom, which was separated from mine only by a thin wall. I crouched on my bed, my ear to the wall, tense with glee. Just before Joey got into bed, Jimmy slid the snake out of the box and into the sheets at the bottom of Joe's bed. Well, you can imagine what happened next. Mr. Snake found a nice warm leg and began to make his way up and up. Joe catapulted out of bed with a bloodcurdling scream, Jimmy fell out of his bunk, hysterical with laughter, and Frankie started to cry. On the other side of the wall, I grinned. *Game, set, match!*

Just like our Scranton home, our Mayfield house was multigenerational. It did not house the same relatives permanently, but it did permanently house relatives. Throughout the years, our house welcomed my father's brother Frank, my grandfather Pop, my Uncle BooBoo, my Great-aunt Al, and my father's first cousin Bill Sheen, all for extended stays.

Reflecting on this situation as a married woman, I have often wondered how my parents made it work: Where did my parents find the privacy—to talk, to argue, to hold and comfort each other, to enjoy an intimate relationship? They were always taking care of someone else in addition to their four children. They had no privacy and lots of unsolicited opinions and advice. I don't know how they did it, but they did, and to us kids it just seemed natural. It was home.

Each member of the Biden and Finnegan families who passed through our lives left their imprint on me. First there was Pop, our grandfather Finnegan. BooBoo would drive him down from Scranton for visits on the weekend, and he'd stay for at least a fortnight.

Pop was mentally acute but physically disabled. He had suffered a stroke that left him with a paralyzed right arm. He walked with a cane and dragged his leg behind him. He would sit in his chair in our living room all day and generally get up only to walk to the dining room table or up the short flight of steps to my bedroom, which became his during his visits.

Mom waited on him and took care of him with pure grace. She loved her dad full throttle, and never acted like he was a burden. We kids all watched and learned by example and osmosis how to care for an aged parent—one who had come to be so dependent. This was frustrating for Pop, a proud man who now needed to be helped, whose speech had even become slurred.

I was Pop's pet, the only girl. After we moved to Delaware, I used to go up to Scranton for the weekends to visit BooBoo and Pop. I was a little tidykins as a kid, and during the visit, I would clean the whole house. I must have gotten it all out of my system then, because none of that appeals to me now. Pop was a strong man, but the fire in his belly that had led him to school Joe about working-class Democratic politics over the kitchen table in Scranton had dwindled to embers.

The Pop I remember from my childhood was a kind man who had begun his retreat from the world.

Dad's Aunt Al, with whom he had spent many of his childhood summers in Baltimore, came for a weekend and stayed seventeen years. Although she didn't sleep over, she spent every day with us in the house. She had permed gray hair with a blue rinse and always wore heels and stockings. She never missed an opportunity to make a critical comment. She was a thorn in my mom's side. Every day, Aunt Al sat in judgment on the left side of the couch. She was always proper, but that didn't mean she was always kind.

But, God bless her, Mom held her tongue with Aunt Al. She remembered Aunt Al's kindness to Dad when he was a kid, and she understood that Aunt Al had been dealt a tough hand. Being married to Bill Sheen Sr. brought its ups and downs. She had gone from being a wife to a wealthy man to a mother who lost her young daughter to the Spanish flu, only then to lose her husband to alcoholism and her son to folly and eventual alcoholism. Her husband had lost and gained fortunes—then lost them again—and in the process, she'd been treated as a disposable commodity.

Once we settled in Delaware, things seemed to stabilize. By the 1960s, my dad was the general manager of a Chevrolet dealership. He worked all the time, but he still called home from the floor multiple times a day to check in on Mom and us kids. I don't think he ever really liked his job, but you never would have known it from hearing him—my dad just did not complain. Dad had a well-earned reputation as an honest man; he made a deal with a handshake, and he kept it.

If Arden was home during the last of my childhood, Mayfield was the beginning of the rest of my life. We moved to Mayfield the summer before I entered fifth grade at Saint Helena's school. The nuns were from the same order as those who taught us at Holy Rosary in Claymont, the Sisters of Saint Joseph, so there was some consistency. And just as in Arden, a yellow school bus would pick us up at the house every day and take us to school. Many Mondays I would board the bus, knowing I needed bus money—the $1.50 each student was required to give to Sister each week. The money had to be in a sealed envelope with our name on it. If a student didn't hand it in, Sister would call out her name, and that student would have to stand up and explain why she didn't have it. Well, that student was often me. My mother had taught me to say, when called on, "We'll get it in later." It was a humbling experience. I don't think Sister's intent was to be mean—I think she just needed to collect the money for bus service. But she could have figured out a better way to do it.

All the kids in our neighborhood belonged to Shell Crest, the new community swim club, except us. There was a sizable down payment just to join, and then an additional fee was required for each member of the family. Whatever the cost, Mom and Dad couldn't swing it. I was so disappointed. Mom tried to talk her way out of it by asking me why I wanted to be like everyone else. Say that to a preteen girl and see how far it gets you.

Dad tried to fix the situation by buying a large aboveground pool for our backyard, but that was nothing like the real deal. The water in the pool had to be dumped out and refilled every few days. The grass died underneath it, leaving a sickly yellow circle, and you still couldn't even swim in it because it was too small. It was okay for Jimmy and Frankie to play in, but for me, it was a poor substitute for the big pool at Shell Crest.

A pool club member could bring a friend as a guest, maybe three times a season, for a small fee. I went once, and that was enough for me. Girls' locker rooms are never big enough to house the haves and the have-nots, the in-crowd and the outsiders. I didn't know the drill—where to hang my bag or my towel—but that wasn't even the problem. It was knowing that my bag, my towel, and I myself were not welcome. As I stood there shivering in my one-piece suit, it was abundantly clear to me to which group I belonged.

I never again asked if we could join, which put an extra impetus on getting to the ocean. The ocean belonged to everyone. On Sundays after early Mass, Mom would pack a cooler of sodas and sandwiches for all of us, as well as deviled eggs for Dad, and off we would go to the beach. As day trippers, we were decidedly a cut below the permanent beach residents—"shoobees," they called us. All four of us would be packed in the back seat, Jimmy lying along the headrest, his face inches from the rear windshield. He looked like a cat basking in the sun. No one put on their seat belts back then.

On our way down we wore our bathing suits under our clothes, and on the way home, we stopped at the first gas station we could find to run into the bathroom and change out of our wet, sandy suits for the remainder of the trip. The drive was two hours there, and easily three on the way back, with traffic.

I loved everything about the ocean. So did Mom and Dad. Dad could float on his back for an eternity, and he was a great bodysurfer. Mom was scared to death of the water because she couldn't swim, but she loved being near it. She'd sit in her chair and watch, ever vigilant of her children's whereabouts, but with a look of happy calm on her face.

What matters most in life are simple ordinary acts of kindness—one person being considerate, thoughtful, or unselfish toward another.

I read an article by the journalist Ana Menéndez that stated the essence of that message in a more eloquent way. In writing about the demise of personal relationships, specifically her divorce from her husband, she said that "the stuff of life" comes not from grand epics but rather from small individual acts: "War without is nourished by the war within, and every great conflict begins as a collection of small, individual acts of cruelty."

I was struck by the profound wisdom in her words—and their inverse: Great loves don't just continue—they must be nurtured by small acts of grace.

We all know that a simple act of kindness performed by us or for us can change our day—and our lives are lived one day at a time.

4

LATE BLOOMER

In the fall of 1959, I entered high school at Ursuline Academy, a Catholic prep school for girls. I wanted to go to Ursuline because it was said to be the best Catholic school education. It was expensive, and a stretch for my parents, so my Uncle BooBoo helped with the tuition.

The night before I started, I was consumed by first-day jitters. What if I didn't like it? What if I didn't fit in? What if they didn't like me? Would it be like first grade all over again?

Mom tried to calm me down. "It will be a great adventure," she said. "I felt the same way my first day at Archmere," Joe chimed in. They wanted to make me feel better, but as I got into my school uniform the next morning, I wasn't so sure I had made the right choice.

Ursuline's uniform was a pleated green skirt, a short-sleeved white blouse with an open collar, and a charcoal-gray blazer with green piping and a front pocket embossed with our school motto: SERVIAM, "I will serve." So far, so good. But the shoes were terrible. They were clodhoppers, heavy cordovan lace-ups, and they looked like men's shoes. They were also indestructible. Oh, and who could forget the green bowler hat required for Mass every Thursday? That was just plain ugly. We were required to wear nylon stockings every day, and, since it was a pre-pantyhose era, a garter belt.

That year turned out to be a challenging one for me. Not academically—I was ready for that—but socially. You see, I was a late bloomer, getting left behind by all the cool girls in my class. On my first day entering high school, I was tiny not tall, straight not curvy, tomboyish not girly, cute not pretty, and smart but not savvy. At thirteen, I could have passed for ten years old. I was getting impatient.

As early as sixth grade, there would be a "secret" announcement in the girls' bathroom every month or so: Cousin Ruthie had arrived! Cousin Ruthie was the euphemism we used for the menstrual cycle. But Ruthie was also the gatekeeper to the imagined glories of womanhood. These supposed glories were defined slightly differently by each young girl, but to me her arrival definitely coincided with bustlines, bras, and boys—which, in turn, opened up the possibility of glamour, romance, and love. We all waited to see who would be selected next. It was never me. I waited and waited.

I dreaded gym class at Ursuline. It was only once a week, but that was enough to sear my soul and self-esteem. Each girl had her own locker where she kept her gym uniform, which she never took home to wash until the holidays—Thanksgiving, Christmas, and Easter. Needless to say, the place was smelly. We didn't take showers, because we didn't have shower stalls. I thanked God every week for that small mercy. It was enough that I had to try to hide my undershirt, but to be naked in front of my classmates—I would have died. Since I was the only girl in my family, I hadn't been naked in front of anyone since

I was three, let alone in front of a room full of girls who were all in various stages of development.

Cousin Ruthie finally arrived at my door in September of my sophomore year, just shy of my fifteenth birthday. I was excited when she finally showed up. So excited, in fact, that I fainted—dropped straight down to the floor, out cold. Fortunately, I was home getting ready for school, so no one knew but Mom, and I suppose she told Dad. I stayed home from school that day; I was exhausted. The wait was over. Now I willed my body to bloom.

Despite Cousin Ruthie's arrival, my bloom was still maddeningly late to the scene. I believed everyone in the world was dating except me, and having a popular, football-playing big brother didn't help—it only exacerbated my discomfort to know everybody was having fun without me. I had long since been ready to hand in my dungarees— the pair I had lived in at Claymont and Arden, rolling up one pant leg like the boys did so it wouldn't get caught in my bike chain.

I was ready for the Lilt permanent instead of the pin curls Mom occasionally put in my hair. I was ready for headbands, high heels, sheath dresses, and dances. . . . I was ready to get in the game.

I was ready, but no one was quite ready for me yet. It would be another year until the guys ever came up to me to ask a question other than "Is Joe around?" or whether one of my girlfriends was available that weekend.

Joe knew this, and he also knew that my time would come. So he made up a wonderful little white lie that I held on to, to tide me over.

One night after he came home from a date, I was awake and watching TV in the living room. I felt as though everyone in the whole world had been out, except me.

"Do you know what my friend Dave said to me today, Valerie?"

"No, what?"

"Dave said, 'Joe, in six months, you're going to have to build a twelve-foot fence around your house to keep all those boys away from Valerie.'"

"Yeah, sure, Joe." I knew it probably wasn't true, but that didn't change how badly I wanted to believe it.

"No, really, Val—I swear it's true. I'm going to have my work cut out for me. As a matter of fact, I might go get started on it right now."

It was a kind white lie, good for my spirit.

As a little kid, all I wanted was to be just like my brothers. Specifically, I wanted to be a boy. I settled for what felt like the next best option: a tomboy. At an age when a lot of other older brothers pretended they didn't even *know* their sister, Joey took me everywhere with him. When his friends would ask, "Why did you bring a girl?" he answered, "She's not a girl; she's my sister. If you want me around, she's going to be around, too."

There was a corollary to this: If I was going to be around, wanting to play baseball and football, I'd better pull my weight. I had to really learn how to play as well as the boys.

Like a drill sergeant, Joe would wake me up early in the morning to practice pitching and hitting. Above all, I had to learn not to "throw like a girl," in the day's parlance. He stayed with me on that one, and my arm got pretty good. But the minute I reverted to the old style, he was on me all over again.

"Catch the ball in front of your face, not down in front of your stomach," he repeated ad nauseam. When I was six, he gave me my own bat, which happened to be half of one that had broken when he hit a pitch too hard. The entire top half was splintered, leaving ragged, sawtooth edges, but it had the benefit of being the perfect size for me. I couldn't choke up on it too far, and when I swung the bat, it pushed against my forearm, leaving a sea of purple bruises. I wore those bruises as proudly as an Olympic gold medal. They were proof I could hang with the boys.

Joey looked out for me and protected me, whether it was on the baseball field or at a party. My best friend Mary McGee's sixth birthday party was held at her house, just across the street from my grandparents up in Scranton. The day of, I got dressed in my party clothes, and Mom watched me walk to Mary's front door.

When I went inside, I saw a group of girls I had never met before. They were all friends from Mary's school, and they were not interested in this "other girl" from across the street. The minutes slowly ticked by. Not one little girl spoke to me. After a while, I told Mrs. McGee that I wanted to go home. She pressed me to stay, and I started to cry, so she called my mom.

I told Mom I wanted Joey to come get me. So, Mom did what Mom did: she went up to Maloney Field and got Joey from his baseball game. He hurried up and changed from his baseball clothes into a clean shirt and checkered sport coat, and in what seemed in a matter of minutes, showed up at Mary's front door—not to take me home, but to stay with me at the party. "Hello, Mrs. McGee, I'm Joey Biden," he said when she opened the door.

"I know who you are, Joey, come in."

He was the only boy at the party, but that didn't deter him. He played musical chairs and pin the tail on the donkey with us, always standing close by me with quiet reassurance. When it was time to leave, he thanked Mrs. McGee and took my hand and walked me back home. When I thanked him for coming, he said, "Thanks for inviting me, Val—I had a really good time."

It might seem condescending to have a big brother "looking out" for a little sister, but that's not how it worked in our family: I had Joey's back as much as he had mine. He reminded me that I was strong and beautiful, and he gave me confidence—the same confidence I would return to him years later.

There were times when he got carried away, however, like the way he handled my first crush. The high school boy in question was tall, handsome, and the best basketball player in the state. Every girl in town was in love with him, unless they were already in love with my brother. Wilmington was just barely big enough for the two of them.

I was fifteen years old when I spotted him at the Charcoal Pit, the place everyone went for hamburgers and Cokes after their dates. I still wasn't ready for prime time, so I had to content myself with riding to the Pit with Joe and waiting in his car while he picked up takeout. Meanwhile, my head on a swivel, I spotted him.

As soon as Joe got back in the car, I pointed and asked: "Joey, who is that guy?"

Joey followed my finger and then fixed me with a look. "That's Pete McLaughlin," he said. "He's fast, and he's a smart-ass. Stay away from him."

Well. That was not a wise thing to say to a kid sister. It was like putting a match to a tiny flame, which I fanned from that night on. It took another year and a half for Pete to even notice me, but eventually, he did.

Pete was from "the Yard." Everyone knew that the Yard was the outdoor basketball court at Christ Our King Church. COK was a city school, in a neighborhood where all the parents knew each other and, in summer, sat on their porches each evening to watch their kids play under the lights until midnight.

Both Christ Our King and Saint Anne's were first- and second-generation Irish enclaves in downtown Wilmington, and I often wished our family belonged to one of them. There was such a strong sense of community, of instant belonging. The kids' values were shaped by parents inside the home, reinforced by the nuns at school, and watched over by the looming church spire when they played outside. Suburban Mayfield was less than half an hour's drive from downtown Wilmington, but for a kid without her license, that might as well have been across the Atlantic.

I had no idea, in other words, how Pete and I were ever going to cross paths. But then one of those "city kids" moved to a house in suburbia, half a mile from ours in Mayfield. Her name was Pat Donohue, and we became friends. She was one year ahead of me at Ursuline, she could drive, had her own car, and had connections to Pete. (Her boyfriend, Bob, and Pete were best friends.)

Through careful contrivances, Pete and I started running into each other. It took a minute for his head to turn, but finally he called to ask me out. Unfortunately, Joe answered the phone.

"Hi, this is Pete McLaughlin. Is Valerie home?"

"Nope, sorry," Joe said. "She's out." I was upstairs.

When Pete called again, Joe said I was away for the summer. I wasn't.

I wanted to stab Joe with a kitchen knife—instead, I told Mom.

She told Joe to stand down with the big brother routine. "If your sister likes him, there must be something good about him, and I'll like him until he proves to me that I shouldn't," she said. "I suggest you do the same."

Thankfully, Pete was persistent, and the next time he called, I answered. We started dating my junior year in high school.

After Joe went off to college, my little brother Jimmy, who had been my biggest tease, became my favorite companion. Just as Joe had taken me with him wherever he went, I took Jimmy with me on my adventures once I began to drive.

Pete's team was top ranked and played throughout the state, so Jimmy, who loved basketball, was happy to come along with me to watch his games. Jimmy sat next to me in the bleachers, alternating between cheering for Pete and booing the rival team. Jimmy is funny and irreverent—he could be a bridge builder or bridge burner. Either way, he was my brother and always on my side.

Things ended with Pete and me my sophomore year in college. I read an interview with him on the sports page—he continued to be a star player during his undergraduate years—in which the interviewer asked him if he had "a girl back home." He answered no.

I put down the paper and said out loud, "You're right. Now you don't." It took a while for us to untangle, but that was the beginning of the end.

There was much good about him, although Pete remained a smart-ass until the day he died. He and Joe became friends, and he was in Joe and Neilia's wedding party. My crush may have been short-lived, but our friendship lasted forever.

Joe might not have relished the idea of my dating Pete, but he wasn't completely opposed to my going out with a nice guy. When I was a freshman, I met my brother's version of the perfect guy for me. Joe's classmate Eddie Cartieri didn't have a date to their junior prom, so Joe suggested that Eddie take me, and we double-date.

I still remember the yellow dress I wore. In the pictures, I look as if I were en route to a seventh-grade cotillion instead of a junior prom. I was still in preteen sizes, and poor Eddie Cartieri barely spoke. He was shy, but I was thrilled. I was at the prom!

Joe and I learned a lot from each other. Joe has always said that the most successful men he knows—successful in terms of security and self-worth—are the ones who have strong women in their lives: a mom, a sister, a wife. I have always said that if you have a good brother, he will also be a good husband, and a good father. It is a natural flow.

When I look back on my college years, sometimes I think, Where was I?

Why wasn't I outraged, active, challenging the status quo?

Besides Vietnam, we had a war for Civil Rights at home.

The country was in turmoil and on the verge of transformation—Selma, Martin Luther King and the March on Washington, voting rights legislation, Gloria Steinem.

Where was I?

I was in my dorm, 200 Harrington D, and on the Dean's List.

I was sheltered, and I didn't even realize it at the time.

Years later, I would recognize the privilege in that.

5

INTO THE WORLD

During my senior year of high school, I announced to my family that I wanted to go to New York City. I wanted to be an actress, star of stage and screen. I had had two years of rave reviews from my Catholic school drama career, and won a best actress award at the University of Delaware's play festival. I felt certain that fame lay ahead—notwithstanding the fact that when Mother Superior announced the best actress award after the final night of our school play at Ursuline, it didn't go to me. Upon hearing this, Jimmy, who was seated with the rest of the family in the front row, jumped up from his seat, yelling, "Valerie was robbed!" He kept it up until my parents could muzzle him and get him out of there. I was mortified.

Meanwhile, my friend Pat, who had graduated from Ursuline the year before, insisted that no matter how good I was, if I went to New York, I would be compromised—she informed me that all young pretty girls had to sleep with the producer in order to succeed. I wondered exactly how she had come by her insider information as a freshman at Immaculata Junior College, but it didn't really matter. Honestly, if I couldn't cut it in Wilmington, I probably couldn't make it in the Big Apple.

Another aspiration of mine was brain research, despite not being proficient in math or science. Once, in a high school survey of possible careers, I marked down *Nurse,* then, after turning it in, regretted it. I hated blood. *God, I hope no one looks at that,* I thought.

My three close friends, Pat, Maureen, and Tina, went into three different professions after college—Pat with the airlines, Maureen as a dental hygienist, and Tina with Xerox—but none of those paths appealed to me. I knew what I didn't want: the law, medicine, the nunnery, or the military. But what I *did* want was proving trickier to figure out. All I knew for sure was I wanted a career and the independence that came with it. I was confident that the rest of it—meeting someone, having a family, finding a job I loved—would fall into place.

I wonder whether I would have had an easier time imagining different jobs for myself if I'd grown up in a later era. My parents raised me to believe I could be anything I wanted, but in the early '60s, so many sectors of the workforce were still largely reserved for men.

Decades later, the only rule I made for our children, especially my daughters, concerning their education was that they had to pursue a profession. It would be fine if they happened to meet someone and fall in love, if that's what they wanted, but they couldn't be financially dependent on a spouse. I knew financial dependency trapped too many women in marriages with unfaithful or unkind spouses for forty, fifty years, only because they felt as if they *couldn't* leave. I didn't want that for my kids; even as a very young girl, I had instinctively grasped the need for this kind of independence.

In other words, for me it was a given that I had to go to college. During my senior year, most of my Ursuline classmates were visiting colleges, intent on getting into one of the Catholic Ivy Leagues—Newton College of the Sacred Heart, Marymount, Dumbarton, Manhattanville, or Trinity. Most of them came from upper-middle-class families: their fathers were doctors, owned companies, or were partners at law firms.

My dad took great care of our family. Still, our financial plans looked different from those of the families whose daughters were bound for these private schools. They didn't need to work in the summer for their extra money; Joe and I did, and we wanted to.

But I'd had it with all-girls' schools anyway. Ursuline gave me what I needed—an excellent education. I had my sights set on the University of Delaware. That's where Joe was. Tuition was more affordable at UD for in-state students anyway. I applied; my grades were good, and I got in. I was elated. I couldn't wait to get out on my own.

And then, sometime around April of senior year, my dad pulled me aside. With Joe already a sophomore in college, money was tight. I could attend classes, but tuition plus room and board was just out of reach. "You could commute," Dad offered, and my heart sank.

Dad tried his best to soften the blow the only way he knew how: he brought me home a brand-new, hunter-green Chevy Corvair convertible—something he could afford because of his job at the dealership. "So you can drive the last two months of school to Ursuline," he told me, "and then you can commute to the University."

I gazed at the car with mixed feelings: pride and disappointment, gratitude and sadness. My father was a proud man, and I knew he was trying to make the situation okay with the limited resources he had. I didn't want to act like a spoiled child, but I also yearned for the college experience that I already felt slipping from my grasp. I gave him my biggest smile and hugged him as hard as I could. I knew how hard he was trying.

Joe, meanwhile, was driving around a clunker at the time, so my dad knew he had an imbalance to address. And thus he committed a fatal mistake. "Look, Joe," my dad said, unbeknownst to me. "I gave Val the car, but in the summertime when you're home, you can use it, too. She thinks it's hers, but it's both of yours." He was trying to make everyone happy, and it blew up in his face.

The first time Joe casually asked me for the keys to the car so he could hang out at the Charcoal Pit, I said sure without thinking too much of it. I said sure the second and third time, too. But his air of entitlement began bugging me—it was *my* car—and things inevitably came to a head. One night when he had asked for the keys again, I decided that instead of sitting at home that night, I had places of my own to go.

"No, I'm going to Pat's," I said. He couldn't just take the damn car whenever he felt like it. The car was a bribe, my consolation prize, and what good is a bribe if it isn't even yours?

Joe was miffed; he couldn't figure out what my problem was. Once we sorted it out—"Dad told you what?!"—the two of us respectfully went to talk to Dad. As gently as we could, we told him the car had to go back to the dealer. We understood how delicate the situation was. We just explained that the car wasn't worth the fighting between us.

"Look, Willie," my dad said, using his pet name for me, "I know you want to go to the University of Delaware, but I can't swing it. Why don't you go to Goldey-Beacom secretarial school?" I'd learn to type, I'd get a great job, he went on. He wasn't wrong: Delaware was the corporate capital of the United States; corporate clerical jobs abounded. It wasn't as if I were going to wind up at a Podunk office. "You're beautiful, you are smart, you are capable," he urged me. "You've got it. Some man is going to see you and grab you up, you're going to get married and have kids. The world is there for you. Joey has to be the breadwinner; you don't."

By today's standards, my father sounds like a male chauvinist. But standards change, and my father was a devoted, caring man who was being truthful about the options in front of us at the time. I was disappointed, but I started mentally reconciling with the idea of a different path. I would commute.

A few days after that, Joe went to Mom and Dad. He didn't tell me at all what he was planning to say, but asked me to go with him. Standing in the living room, Joe said, "Dad, we can't do this. Valerie is smarter than I am. She's a spectacular kid. She does everything right, and she deserves to go to college. She's earned it. So here is what I am proposing: I am not going to go back to the University of Delaware this year. I will work and save money and go back next year. But she's gotta go forward." I remember looking at Joe and feeling overwhelmed with love and gratitude, mixed with alarm. Was he really going to derail his own college life for me?

"Champ," my father said, his voice breaking, "we can't do that. You can't drop out." I still remember the anguish in my father's voice. That conversation must have been a turning point for him. I don't really know what he did, or how he managed it, but he got a loan—I suspect it was from a friend named Charlie at Farmers Bank. Whatever needed to be done, he did it for me. I never asked. And off I went, that fall, to the University of Delaware to join my brother and live on campus.

During those four years, my father never said, "Look what I've done for you." Mom and Dad never held it over my head or made me feel guilty about the burden they assumed. They expected me to have a good time and be a good student. And I loved every minute of college, in that fierce way you love something that life almost snatched from you.

Despite my dad's assurances, the loan seemed contingent and uncertain until August, which meant I was late applying for room and board. When I finally did, all the freshmen had already been paired off with roommates. I wound up rooming with an upperclassman, a sophomore whose first roommate had left. I wrote a letter introducing myself, telling her about my family and that I had graduated from Ursuline Academy in Wilmington, and waited. When I opened her response a couple of weeks later, it contained an unpleasant surprise. "I'm sorry," she wrote, but she couldn't room with me. Her parents wouldn't let her—I was a Catholic.

I was stunned. I had never experienced anything like this before. While I was still processing the sting of rejection, she wrote again shortly afterward. "I told my parents I'm rooming with you and I don't care whether they like it or not," she explained. Okay, so, a strong woman. I liked that.

Unfortunately, it turned out that she and I weren't destined to be best friends after all, through no fault of our own—we were just different. After the first year, she left for a different dorm, and I wound up with a new girl assigned to my room. There were no sororities at the University of Delaware, so if you weren't best friends with your roommate, or didn't come in knowing a bunch of kids from your high school, you were kind of out of luck.

As a result, I spent a lot of time wandering around solo or with my brother. On campus, he and I would spend hours sitting on the library steps. I often talked to him about nothing—nothing profound or particularly enlightened, but in talking about nothing, I was speaking about everything. He listened as much to what I didn't say as to what I did, trying to distinguish my cadence from my noise, my pauses from my obvious deletions, and my sighs from my real sorrows.

As luck would have it, we wound up sharing one class together during my first semester, despite being two years apart in school. Joe needed only three credits to complete his history and political science major, and the only course that fit in his schedule and satisfied those requirements was my entry-level course on European history.

As the first exam approached, I grew increasingly nervous. I had received a good education at Ursuline, but something about the fact of my first real college test filled me with anxiety.

"Look, Val, you've got this," Joe said. "It's not a big deal. You're going to be fine." This was back in the days when boys and girls couldn't share dorms, but I took my notes over to the common room in Joe's dorm, Harter Hall, and we studied together for hours.

Joe's gift, then as now, was to see the big picture and then break things down into manageable parts. He could help me connect the dots, grasp how the various eras flowed into one another. He helped me comprehend why various wars were fought and what caused different movements to sweep across the Continent. Meanwhile, I had all the names and dates down cold. That was always our divide: he saw the forest, while I watched the trees. I got a 96 on the exam, he got a 97, and I gained the confidence I needed for the rest of my college career.

During my four years at the University of Delaware, I was dorm advisor, freshman greeter, President of my dorm, and homecoming queen—all of it. But I was a bit of a loner, with no close friends. For example, I never had a regular dinner companion. If I missed the groups going en masse to the dining hall, I would walk over by myself, hurrying at the last minute as if I had been delayed by doing something terribly important. I would usually sit by myself, staring intently at whatever book I was pretending to read.

Often, I would look up from that book to a "Heya, Val," only to find one of the football players standing over me, coming in late from practice and holding a tray. Sometimes one or more of them would join me, and we would talk easily.

Maybe because I was raised with men, I always felt more comfortable around them, more at ease and able to be myself. I hadn't had lots of female friends in high school either, and that had been fine by me: I had my world at home, and I had my brothers.

So it was with a sense of patterns repeating themselves that I settled into college, saying hello to all the football players as they passed by. The freshman class had had to arrive a week before everyone else for orientation, and the only other students on campus had been the football players. When it was too hot to practice, they had lounged against a wall and scoped out the new girls, all of us wearing the required freshman beanies, as we walked past.

They had noticed me early in my days on campus because Joe had already alerted one of his football buddies and roommate, Don Brunner, to keep an eye on me and let him know if there was any "trouble." Joe reminded me that none of these guys had seen a woman for four weeks of football camp. Joe's warning created an interest in me from the start: *Who is this girl that we are supposed to stay away from?*

I liked them, and over time a handful of them became my friends—not my dates.

My friendship with the football players wound up paying other dividends. Because of them, I formed a lasting friendship with one of the girls on my dorm floor, a strikingly beautiful blonde named Priscilla. She looked exactly like the Wilmington girls who belonged to the country clubs that my brothers and I were not able to join. I was surprised when she spoke to me.

The catalyst was the alarm on my new clock radio. I had never used one before. I set it incorrectly and overslept on my first day of orientation classes. Priscilla noticed me scrambling and yelling at myself, and that evening she approached me and offered to knock on my door the next morning to make sure I was awake.

Years later, I asked her why she had extended herself like that—clearly, I wasn't her type at all. She smiled and said, "You certainly were my type. Every single football player said hello to you. I thought, 'I want to know this girl. She's got something special, and I want to be part of whatever that is.'"

My college years coincided with a gradual shift in societal mores. This was the mid-'60s, and the false good girl–bad girl dichotomy surrounding sexual activity and partying was starting to shift. But because I grew up around an alcoholic—my Uncle BooBoo, whom I adored—I was scared to drink. Drinking and drugs didn't seem remotely worth it to me. This decision wasn't motivated by righteousness or courage; it was simply fear that kept me from experimenting while the '60s raged on.

Instead, I found my own path. I loved to dance and have fun at the fraternity parties, even though I always drank Coca-Cola while everyone else had beers. I loved music—the Kit Kats, Chubby Checker, Dion and the Belmonts, the Supremes—and like any other girl growing up in the '60s, I danced the twist. My social life (and its limitations) still reflected my mom's sensibilities.

The last two weeks in March at the University of Delaware marked spring break—a vacation rite of passage for many students, including Joe. But not me. I was never allowed to join the crowds traveling to all points south. Mom said, "I don't care what all the other girls are doing—you're not going." Joe agreed. Meanwhile, he took the money from his tax returns and piled into a car with four of his guy friends, bound for Fort Lauderdale and then Nassau while I stayed home and moped.

In retrospect, it sounds patriarchal—and it was—but that's part of what being a good brother meant back then. Joe was protective; at times, he treated me as if he thought I was still the little girl riding on his handlebars. I was inexperienced, for sure, but I wasn't naïve. I didn't like it at all that I couldn't go to Florida for spring break. I didn't drink, I didn't smoke, I didn't do drugs, and I didn't sleep around; I just wanted to get a tan.

I was not very happy the Saturday afternoon Joe arrived back home. It was chilly and cloudy. I knew that on Monday, everyone would be back in school, tanned, robust, and full of themselves. I would return pale, tired from doing nothing, and sad. When I first heard the back door burst open, it was accompanied by a yell so loud it could have blown the door open by itself. "Valerie!" Joe hollered. "I met the girl I'm going to marry." Joe ran up the steps and hugged me hard. "You'll love her," he kept saying. "I can't wait for you to meet her."

Her name was Neilia Hunter, a beautiful young woman from Syracuse University who, unlike me, had been allowed to go on break with her girlfriend. Joe was going up to Syracuse the next weekend to meet her parents, and then she was to come home to meet us. "She's beautiful, smart, kind," Joe went on, explaining, "her eyes are green, and she calls me Joey."

Joe fell head over heels in love. When he left Nassau, he told Neilia that he was going to marry her, and she said, "I think so, too." He was talking a mile a minute, grinning his face off. I fought a tug of resentment. If I had gone, maybe I would have met someone, too.

I was as nice a girl as Neilia, I mused, and she evidently wasn't in harm's way in Nassau. Why would I have been? And besides, she'd met my brother—just about the nicest guy who ever lived. Clearly spring break couldn't be so terrible if people like Joe and Neilia could meet.

Nevertheless, I couldn't begrudge Joe his pure joy—he was over the moon. "Tell me more, Joey," I urged. And he did, throughout the night.

That same spring, the UD football coach told Joe there was a spot for him on the team. He just needed to commit. Joe was thrilled; he'd played all his life, starting with touch football in Mayfield when we were kids. I always tagged along, just as I had back in Scranton at Maloney Field. He taught me to throw a proper spiral and relegated me to the sidelines only when I got older and "touch football" with his guy friends got awkward. Years later, when he moved back to Wilmington, he organized a neighborhood game every Thanksgiving, and when he was a young lawyer, he even started a city league. He loved the New York Giants, just as Pop Finnegan had. Football was in his blood, a part of his life.

But then Neilia happened, and everything changed. The choice became clear: he could either drive five hours every weekend to Neilia's home on the Finger Lakes in Skaneateles, or he could follow his lifelong dream to play football and stay on the Delaware campus. He chose Neilia. It wasn't even a choice.

The first time I remember meeting Neilia was early June. All the couples in our friend circle—me and my high school boyfriend, Pete; Joe and Neilia; his friend Dave Walsh and his girlfriend; plus a few of Joe's other high school friends—drove to the beach in Rehoboth, Delaware. It turned out to be a raw day, gray and cool, so none of us was eager to take off our clothes and show our new bathing suits. On top of that, we were painfully aware that we had a knockout in our midst—Neilia was tall, slender, blond, and had a great figure. I'd seen pictures of the bikinis she was wearing while she and Joe romped around Nassau, and I was pretty sure that if she removed her clothes to reveal one of those, all six of the other girls would bury their heads in the sand.

Instead, she had chosen to wear a plain, simple one-piece bathing suit. The relief among the girls was palpable, as was the wave of silent gratitude they sent her. I thought to myself, *What a kind, smart girl.* She could have blown everyone's socks off, but she didn't want to alienate us. I think we all fell in love with her right then.

That was Neilia—she always had a larger goal in mind, something more important than the concerns of the moment. She wanted to be part of our family and wanted us all to be close. She went about it brilliantly. I was full of admiration for the skillful way she navigated our complex family dynamics. I took mental notes: this was how I wanted to treat my future sisters-in-law, whoever they may be—with grace, with strength, with love, and with understanding. She became my role model.

When Joe graduated from UD and started law school at Syracuse in 1965, I was in my junior year of college. Even though he had been gone only a few weeks, it was already the longest time either of us had been apart. I was eager to go visit him early that fall. He had invited me to come up the weekend of October 9, but there was one problem: Joe was insisting I go on a blind date with his law school buddy.

This was highly uncharacteristic of Joe. If history had shown me anything, it was that Joe held to an ironclad rule: I couldn't date anyone he *didn't* know, because he didn't know them, and I couldn't go out with anyone he knew, because he *did* know them. I couldn't imagine what kind of guy Joe would deem "suitable" for me, and I wasn't sure I wanted to find out.

I told Joe I had a boyfriend. "Just let me come up and see you and Neilia. Let's skip the date," I pleaded.

"You gotta go out with this guy, honestly," Joe said. "I've already told him you would, anyway."

I said, "Okay, I'll go, but just one date." He put Neilia on the phone. "Neilia, what's he doing? I don't want to go out with anybody—I think I'm in love," I said to her.

And then Neilia said something I will remember until the day I die. "Val, I promise you," she said—this was her expression—"if I could handpick any guy for you in the entire universe, I would pick Jack Owens." I mean, what do you say to that?—Yes. I was going up on a Friday night; that Saturday morning, I would go with Jack and four other law school couples to Syracuse's homecoming game and to dinner afterward. I was intrigued, in spite of myself.

Come Saturday's game at Syracuse, I dressed in my new red plaid skirt suit that I had worn for the homecoming parade the previous weekend. I was ready for the day. Joe, Neilia, and I went to the stadium, hopped out of the car, and waited for my blind date to materialize. And then, from around the corner, this guy came bustling toward us, and I instinctively grabbed Neilia's arm. "Oh my God," I said in disbelief. "Is that *him*?"

Plaid pants for men were a good two years away from hitting Delaware's fashion scene, but they'd reached Jack in Garden City, New York. He was wearing Black Watch plaid slacks and a camel hair blazer with a lining that matched his pants. He was a dandy, through and through, elegant and uptown. He was a cut above preppy; Jack looked like someone who could have waltzed off the cover of *Gentlemen's Quarterly*. I had *never* seen a man dress like that before. Unfortunately, he saw me grab Neilia and heard my reaction. His smile flickered and his gait slowed—he must have thought I was mocking him.

Joe missed my reaction, though, because he began introducing us with trademark overenthusiasm. "This is my sister, Val," he told Jack. "Isn't she great?" He kept extolling my virtues as Jack and I sized each other up. If Joe could have arranged for blazing trumpets to play behind me, he would have; Jack would joke years later that he was surprised there wasn't a picture of me in Joe's apartment with a vigil lamp underneath.

We said hello to each other coolly.

First impressions happen in a tenth of a second. Jack, intense and coiled, radiated energy. I thought all he needed was a match thrown in his direction to explode. I didn't like him, but I recognized he was a force to be reckoned with.

We went to find our seats. All the other couples were holding hands, but Jack and I kept apart. He marched purposefully up to our row, stood back to let me in, and then proceeded to let the next nine people in after me before sitting down himself. I was miffed. *Who the hell does this guy think he is?* I thought. No one had ever cold-shouldered me like that before. I had to get some of my pride back, so I turned and flirted with the guy next to me to pass the time.

Throughout the afternoon, Jack was dismissive if not outwardly hostile toward me. After the game, we went to a pub called the Brae Loch Inn. Jack pulled out my chair for me at dinner and then proceeded to sit himself at the *extreme* opposite end of the table. It was a deliberate statement, and I heard it loud and clear. When we went to

Neilia's parents' house to cap off the evening, Jack announced he had to leave early because he "had to study." Right—Saturday night, and he's leaving a party with his friends at eight o'clock to study?

Jack thanked me for a nice day, which we hadn't had. Then he said politely, "Maybe I'll see you again."

"Not if I see you first," I shot back, flipping my hair over my shoulder.

Jack walked out and Joe turned to me, furious. "What's the matter with you, Val?" he demanded. "Why were you such a jerk to my friend?" I replied that his *friend* was the jerk, and I never wanted to see or speak to him again. I didn't get my wish, and thank God for it. It would be a few years and several lifetimes later before I realized that I had met the love of my life.

By the time Neilia and Joe were married, in his second year of law school, she already felt like family. The pièce de résistance was when she asked me to be her maid of honor. It couldn't have been easy for her: she had girlfriends of her own, of course, and her niece, who lived next door, had been raised like her little sister. By all rights, the honor should have gone to her. But because I was Joey's sister, Neilia gave it to me.

The title and the status didn't mean much, but the feeling behind the gesture spoke volumes. This was a woman who had the same philosophy as we did: family above all. The only thing that mattered between us was that we both loved Joe, and that drew us closer and locked in our friendship.

Around that same time, I got "pinned" to a cool fraternity guy named Bruce Saunders. This was the term used to mean "going steady." I liked him. He was a little edgy for me, which made him intriguing—a public school boy from New Jersey, a pool shark who chewed on a toothpick when he was concentrating, and a horse-racing enthusiast who could handicap the trotters with the best of them. I loved that he was a great dancer, but equally important and endearing was that he didn't care who else I danced with. He knew he would always be the guy who walked me back to my dorm after the last dance.

We started dating late in our sophomore year. He was in ROTC (Reserve Officers' Training Corps), and when he graduated, he packed off to start basic training. A lot of our guy friends were being shipped over to Vietnam as soon as they graduated, but if you were married, stayed to teach, or went to graduate school, you were often deferred. Bruce decided to go.

We were a good college couple, but I wasn't about to get married and pregnant and then wave goodbye to him as he started his tour of Southeast Asia. When he left, he told me he was coming back for me, but he understood that he had no hold on me in the meantime. "Live your life," he said.

My junior year at Delaware also gave me my first inkling of my future career. I took a course in education taught by an older male professor. He stood out in my mind for two reasons: men in primary and secondary education were then still something of a novelty, and he was kind of a creep.

He would pass by my desk and pat my shoulder. Apparently, he flew airplanes, and once he invited me to go up with him. "No, thank you, Professor," I said. "I'm afraid of flying."

Teaching seemed like something I would be good at, so I kept going with it. I didn't want to be an elementary school teacher; I knew the limits of my patience. Elementary school is probably the most important part of education, the foundation of confidence and knowledge, but it took a better person than I to navigate that stage of life.

I gravitated toward the older kids, so, in my senior year, I spent my first semester as a student teacher assigned to Mount Pleasant Senior High, which my brother Jimmy was then attending. Many little brothers would be dismayed to find their big sister teaching at their school during their senior year, but not Jimmy. He drove me to school every morning, and during the day would often poke his head into my classroom full of sophomores with tongue-in-cheek advice: "Revolt! Don't take that from her." Mount Pleasant Senior High was about an hour from campus, but only five minutes from our house in Mayfield. So ironically, I *did* end up commuting to school for a while: I lived at home during the week, driving back to campus on the weekends for fraternity parties, dancing, and the feel of college life.

I walked into my first day as a student teacher to meet my mentor, Jody Ambrisano, who taught social studies. He was also the football coach. Mr. Ambrisano announced, "Listen up, this is Miss Biden. She's the student teacher—pretty cute, isn't she? Anyway, don't give her any trouble. I'll see you later." And off he went to the track to bet on the Thoroughbreds instead of teaching or supervising me. I was thrown into the deep end.

I discovered two things more or less immediately: I loved teaching, and I wasn't half bad at it. The girls in the class clocked me—what I was wearing, how I wore my hair, and so on—about as much as the boys did, but once the teaching started, everyone was engaged. I realized I had a knack for getting a roomful of kids on my side. I made a deal with them for when my supervisor from UD came to audit my class. "When I ask a question, everyone raise their hand," I told them. I wanted them to look like the world's most enthusiastic, participatory classroom. "If you don't know the answer, raise your left hand, but if you raise your right hand, I'll call on you and you can be a star." They played along, flashing conspiratorial smiles. They were in on the game with me, and they also learned a lot of history in the process.

Soon after graduating, I landed my first real job, teaching eighth-grade social studies in Prince George County, just outside Washington, DC. I was thrilled. I couldn't wait to get out of Wilmington, get my own apartment, and get a big paycheck with my name on it. I wound up talking to a classmate at Delaware named Marty at a fraternity party. She and I were acquaintances, not yet friends, which makes for good roommates, I find. Marty wanted to be a teacher, too, and we decided we would both head down to Washington together to look around. The city was unknown territory to me, and I was equally excited and nervous. Washington and New York—that's where you went. They were both enticing symbols of encroaching adulthood.

We chose a two-bedroom apartment in Hyattsville, Maryland, midway between both of our schools. We flipped a coin for the master bedroom with the private bathroom (I won), and we furnished it in true twentysomething style. We bought a secondhand couch; she took a wrought-iron garden table from her parents that we used for our dining room. I brought an old coffee table from Mom and Dad's house; Marty brought the stereo system. Marty was into all kinds of music, and she had more albums than I'd ever seen. My tastes ran more toward Ray Charles and Motown, but she introduced me to Nina Simone, Richard Harris, and gave me a crash course in the Beatles. (I knew and liked them, of course, but Marty's knowledge was next-level.) Our crowning touch was our living–dining room divider, a bookshelf made of stained oak boards and cinder blocks that we built ourselves. We were set to entertain.

This was my first time living on my own—no parents, no big brother, no dorm mother. Joe and Neilia had settled in Syracuse, and

Joe was in his last year of law school. He and Neilia drove down to check out my new place on a weekend that he had to be in DC for a law school event. He decided not to drive his Corvette convertible into the district; it was easier just to leave it in my parking lot.

Marty and I started school on the same day. We had double alarm clocks set for the morning and promised to awaken each other just in case one failed. That morning, I was out the door a few minutes earlier than Marty. I jumped into my Corvair and turned the keys to an ominous sputtering. It would not turn over, and it refused to budge in response to either my increasingly frantic prayers or my curses.

I ran upstairs, taking the steps two at a time in a panic, no easy feat while carrying a handbag and my teaching materials and wearing heels. Marty was still applying mascara.

"Marty," I blurted, startling her. "My car died. I'm going to be late for my first day. Can you drop me off?"

She paused and looked at me as though I were crazy. "No, Val," she said, as one would explain something very simple to a small child. "If I do that, then I'll be late for my first day of school."

Of course. Why hadn't I thought of that? Joe's Corvette whispered to me from the parking lot. I grabbed his keys and my belongings off the table and dashed out again. *Hope you don't mind, Joe,* I thought, smiling briefly as I remembered our car squabble from a few years before.

There was just one little problem: the Corvette was a stick shift. I had learned to drive stick at my father's insistence, but that didn't mean I was any good at it. I hadn't so much as touched one since getting my license at sixteen, so what commenced was the drive from hell. I lurched across the parking lot until I remembered to take off the emergency brake, and then I damn near stripped the gears riding in second the several miles to my school. I lumbered into the parking lot ten minutes late in a British racing-green Corvette and dashed to my classroom to find the Vice Principal waiting at my door, and a roomful of students staring at the empty space where their teacher was supposed to be. "I'm so sorry, Mr. Markey," I gasped. "My car wouldn't start." He nodded his head and walked away.

I walked in, face red from exertion and embarrassment, and tried to compose myself. I put down my stack of materials on my desk, took off the top folder, and then my face got a whole lot redder: underneath my lesson plan was an entire stack of *Playboy* magazines.

A boy in the front row saw them. I watched his eyes widen and heard the *ooh*s and giggles ripple throughout the room. As casually as I could, I replaced the lesson plan on top of Miss April 1967. When the bell rang, those kids could not hit the corridor fast enough—they had some juicy information to share. Thus began my career as an American history teacher.

Now, as anyone caught with a stack of girlie magazines immediately says, let me explain. They weren't mine! They weren't. They were on loan from a male teacher as a reading assignment. During teacher orientation, I overheard three or four of my male colleagues talking about reading materials. "The best articles are in *Playboy* magazine," one of them said.

"Don't give me that," I'd said, laughing. "That's a bunch of malarkey. It's okay if you like to look at beautiful women, but please, don't try to sell me on the articles."

He persisted. "Have you ever read any of the articles?"

"No."

"Then I am going to bring you some magazines. You'll see." And he came over one day and left a stack of *Playboy*s on the side table—the same side table that held my teaching materials and Joe's keys.

Without thinking I had grabbed everything as I raced to get out the door, intent on getting to school on time.

At lunchtime, I sat in the teachers' dining room, trying to live down the humiliation, when Mr. Markey walked up to me, wearing a peculiar smile. "I thought you would appreciate this," he said, setting down a plate of shredded lettuce. It took me a minute. . . . *Like the Playboy bunny.* Oh boy, it had spread everywhere. The cute young new teacher had shown up late on the first day in a miniskirt, driving a Corvette, and bearing a stack of *Playboys*. Talk about making a good first impression.

I never did read those articles.

Luckily, my infamy was short-lived. I wound up teaching there for the year and thoroughly enjoyed it. I had fallen into teaching as a profession, but I was learning that it fit me like a glove. I loved the immediacy of the classroom, the energy you get from a group of kids.

I still remember some of those early students. One was a sweet boy with a painful crush. At the end of the school year, he bashfully handed me an imitation gold watch, eyes downcast. "Thank you, Miss Biden," he murmured, his cheeks flushed. I thought immediately, *I can't take this.* But I also didn't want to embarrass him, so I thanked him graciously and beelined for the Vice Principal, who told me not to worry about it—it was a gesture of appreciation. I kept it for years afterward as a memento.

While I was at ease in the classroom, I wasn't so comfortable in DC. The culture around Washington at that time was young and carefree. The sexual revolution was in full swing, and at age twenty-two, I still had a ways to go. Everyone drank; I didn't. I dated a little, but I had no interest in the idea of casual sex.

There was a lot of silence about sex for women growing up in my era, particularly for Catholic schoolgirls. Thinking back, I can remember only two instances with the nuns where the implication of sex made its way into our classroom. One of them happened right before high school started.

Mother Agnes Constance was my eighth-grade teacher, right around the time everyone's hormones started raging. Not mine—I still looked like a fifth grader—but most of the other girls and boys were going nuts. Mother Agnes Constance told a story about a young teenage couple who went out on a date and got in a car crash on the way home. The boy was inconsolable, and when the authorities said, "It's not your fault," he answered, "Yes, it is, Officer. You see, I know she's going to hell, because she died in mortal sin."

Mother Agnes Constance didn't elaborate. In the silence that followed, we were meant to allow the dire implications to sink in. Maybe they French-kissed? All I could think was *How dare that boy tell on her! What a jerk.* I can't say it put much of the fear of God into me. It mostly seemed a lame attempt by Mother Agnes Constance to scare us into behaving.

The second instance was from Ursuline, junior year. We called the nun Mother Bug Eyes. Every Friday, Mother Bug Eyes, our biology teacher, would send us out the door, saying, "Goodbye, girls, and have a wonderful weekend. Get plenty of fresh air and horizontal bed rest." We elbowed one another and snickered. She had no idea how that sounded to us.

Nonetheless, I knew where I stood. I internalized early that my sexuality was a gift and a responsibility. For me, intercourse was not just a physical act; it was the physical manifestation of love. When I made love, it was going to be with my whole heart and soul, not just my body.

Throughout college, and even after, it was a confusing time to hold that belief. Occasionally, I would feel self-conscious, out of step.

Luckily, I had Marty as a roommate, who had similar beliefs, so I didn't always feel like the skunk at the garden party.

Once, just once, I considered going in a different direction. A handsome young Republican who worked on the Hill invited me to join him on a cruise to the Bahamas on his friend's yacht during spring break. Ah, spring break—some part of me still smarted from having to sit at my parents' house while other students bathed in the sun.

The man who asked me was a nice guy, attractive, with wavy blond hair. We'd gone out once or twice. I still hadn't made it to Fort Lauderdale, so the Bahamas sounded even more exotic and luxurious. I was tempted; I told him I would check my schedule. When I got home, butterflies in my stomach, I thought, *I'm going to do this.* This was what the cool sophisticated people did, right? I was going to step up to the plate. I knew full well that I wasn't going to sail around the Bahamas in a yacht for a week and just hold hands. As I said, I was inexperienced but not naïve.

As the time got closer, though, I got a sicker feeling in my stomach—not little butterflies, more like golf balls. I told him I couldn't make it because I couldn't take the time off from school. The second time he asked me, I told him I still hadn't cleared it with the Principal. Finally, he asked me: Do you just not want to be on a boat alone with me for a week? I admitted the truth, and he was gracious about it. I knew how the game was played, but try as I might, I couldn't play it.

Over Christmas vacation in 1967, Marty reconnected with a guy she knew from Delaware and fell in love. She decided she would go home at the end of our school year and save money so they could get married when he came back from Vietnam. Faced with the choice of being single and alone in DC—keeping the apartment and trying to make my way through an alien social scene—or heading back to Wilmington, I chose Wilmington.

Once again, I did not go on spring break. Instead, I went home for Easter, and during my visit, I ran into my former UD supervisor, Jim Smith, who had administered the student teaching program. He asked me what I was doing and I told him truthfully that I didn't know. I had decided to leave DC, but that was as far as I had gotten. He was the new Chair of the History Department at Wilmington Friends, a private Quaker school. It was a wonderful place, he told me. Would I like to join him there?

At first, the blue-collar chip on my shoulder surfaced: I told Jim there wasn't a chance in hell. "No way am I going to Wilmington Friends," I declared. "Someone else can teach those uptown kids." I'm not proud of that reaction, but my childhood aversion to the well-heeled country club kids whom I didn't like still reared its head sometimes. Old habits, old wounds, can have long shelf lives.

"Val," Jim said gently, "these are nice kids. Come visit us and give them a chance." He told me I could teach any grade I wanted. And since I didn't have anything else I could reasonably claim to be doing at that moment, I decided to take him up on it.

When I visited the school, I realized at once how stubborn and foolish I had been. It was a beautiful place. There was a young and idealistic group of teachers there, nourished in part by the new infusion of male teachers into the workforce. Even a few years before, the concept of a male first-grade teacher was unheard of, but thanks to Vietnam and the threat of the draft, an entire cohort of men in my generation became teachers. It was a way to get a deferment, and it was a boon for education nationwide.

The school building housed grades K–12, so when you walked down the halls, four-year-olds would lisp hello to you as high school seniors opened their lockers behind them. It was charming, and I immediately said yes.

One discordant note: when I started, my salary was $5,700, without benefits. The next year, I got a very small raise. I asked the Principal, a mild, decent man, why I wasn't paid more, the same as my male colleagues. I was a good teacher, maybe among the best at Friends. "Well," he explained, in the manner of someone outlining a simple diagram, "the other teacher has a family and two kids, so he needs more money than you do." I blinked it back, and simply said, "Oh."

Married male teachers were paid more than unmarried ones; I lived at home with my mom and dad, so I needed less money than the man with a wife and two children. That's how it worked back then. It was pay discrimination, pure and simple, even though I could track the logic, as skewed and patriarchal as it might have been.

I don't tell this story to vilify the Principal. I liked working with him. He thought nothing of what he was telling me. It seemed to him the most natural state of affairs in the world. I've seen "common sense" shift a lot in my life, and no matter what the current standards may be, it always seems clear as day to whoever's spouting it. Over time, I've become a bit wary of accepting anything chalked up to common sense alone.

Bruce returned from Vietnam in June of 1969, one year after I had started at Wilmington Friends. He'd been gone for over a year, and we had corresponded while he was away. Now he came to me with an ultimatum: we had to get married, now or never. He gave me until the end of the year to decide. I said yes, and set December 26 as our wedding date. I wanted one last Christmas Eve at home with my family. That instinct alone should have told me everything I needed to know.

I spent the next several months quietly spiraling. I developed colitis, lost eight pounds, and went into denial. The whole time, I kept asking myself: *What is the matter with me?* Bruce was kind and smart; he loved me. I wasn't a free-spirited '60s girl. I was traditional, committed to the institution of marriage, and I wanted a family. So what was my problem, exactly? Why couldn't I get my mind around marrying this man?

I expected Mom, Dad, or my brothers to weigh in any day. "Honey—are you sure you want to get married now?" But why would they? Heck, we were both old enough to make mature decisions, we knew each other well and had dated for years. But why didn't they pick up on the tremor in my voice, on what I didn't say? And why couldn't I speak up? Since they didn't come forward urging caution, I figured I must be making the right decision.

At my lowest moments, some of my more negative internal voices took center stage: I was pretty, young, and adored by three brothers. I turned down offers to date. I must be selfish, haughty, unrealistic—a spoiled princess. I was the last of my friends to wed. Here was this good man, right in front of me, and I was dragging my feet.

The night before the wedding, a blizzard raged outside. The storm hadn't let up by the following morning, and I carried that cold wind into the church with me. There were warning signs posted all the way up the aisle to the altar—snowbanks, black ice, road closures. I tried to ignore them. I walked tentatively, lest I slip and fall. I was frozen, and it would take years for me to thaw.

In the early '60s, Washington was the province of youthful, beautiful Democratic idealists. These were the years of Kennedy's Camelot, and everyone worth knowing was a Democrat. Republicans, back then, were seen as stodgy, old. The GOP was the party of Dwight Eisenhower, of the 1950s. The ensuing half decade turned that all upside down: JFK assassinated, MLK assassinated, RFK shot, LBJ not seeking reelection, the ascendance of Nixon. As the late 1960s edged into the early 1970s, *Democrat* became almost a dirty word.

To add to that, the Democratic Party in late-'60s Delaware, to the extent that it existed, was at its core a conservative party, especially in our two lower counties of Kent and Sussex. It was the well-heeled, tony Republican families, mostly in New Castle County, who were more socially liberal, and the young Republicans who were considered more socially chic. The waters were muddy on what being a Democrat even meant, both in the country and in the state, and it would take a few more years for the new generation of leaders to assert themselves.

Our family had always been rooted, first and foremost, in working-class Irish Catholicism. Those were the values that forged us more than any political identity. Pop Finnegan and Geraldine had been hard-core Democrats, yes, but my parents weren't so dyed-in-the-wool. My father was never in a union, because car dealerships weren't allowed to organize. I was not in the union because I worked in a private school that didn't have one. The Delaware Democrats of the day weren't fighting segregation either, which was hard for me to square with the Catholic doctrine of social justice.

Thus, when Joe returned from Syracuse with his law degree, he registered as an Independent. He knew he wasn't a Republican, but he knew he wasn't a conservative Delaware Democrat either. He began his career at a well-respected, prestigious law firm, which supported him during that summer while he studied for the bar. He passed on his first attempt, and ended up working on a case that let corporate polluters off the hook. His colleagues were celebrating, but Joe was wondering, *What the hell am I doing here? I'm on the wrong side.*

So he went over to the public defender's office, which could only afford part-time attorneys, to fight for what he believed was right.

He connected with a man named Sid Balick, a respected attorney who was on a mission to build out the new progressive wing of the Democratic Party. Joe joined his firm for a brief time before he started Biden & Walsh, but it was Balick who encouraged him to run for an open seat on the New Castle County Council in 1970. When he asked me to help run his campaign, my first reaction was "There's a County Council?"

My second response, when he told me he was running as a Democrat, was "Thanks a lot, Joe. You have now relegated me to a lifetime of dinners in fire halls eating off paper plates instead of fancy banquet halls with china." But he was right, as he always was when his conscience was speaking to him.

Joe, for his part, has always had my back, ever since I was a little girl. "Anything I can do, you can do better," he told me.

Obviously, that wasn't true. He was much older, stronger, and bigger— I knew that. But he had so much faith in me, I felt I owed it to him and to myself to try harder to be better.

Whether it was riding on the handlebars of his bike or stepping up to the plate with my baseball bat, Joey was always looking out for me. When I got my own bike, my little legs pumped to keep up with Joe and his friends.

My earliest memories are of my brother putting out his hand to grab mine: "Come on, Val, we have things to do, people to see." And our journey began.

6

THE CHILDREN'S CRUSADE

I hadn't run a campaign for Joe since he was elected Class President during his senior year at Archmere Academy. Running for County Council was a *little* different. There were 350,000 people in New Castle County; the Fourth District, where we were running, was heavily Republican. We weren't expected to win, but Joe and I figured that with hard work and old-fashioned person-to-person politicking, we had a chance. It would be tough but doable.

To say I was unprepared to tackle an operation of this size would be an understatement, but I dove in right away. First, I looked into voter records going back a few elections and drew up index cards for every block in every neighborhood, discovering pockets of Democratic support in working-class neighborhoods like Elsmere, Newport, and Stanton.

Pretty much immediately, we ran headfirst into a major problem: Joe and Neilia had recently bought and moved into a home in a development called North Star to accommodate their expanding family—

Beau, Hunter, and their two dogs, a German shepherd and a Great Dane. Turned out, their dream house was outside the district that Joe was campaigning to represent. Mom and Dad's house on Woods Road, however, was a different story. A slight hiccup, but nothing the Bidens couldn't solve.

Joe went to Mom and Dad to explain the situation. Would they consider swapping houses with him for a while? They'd really love the house he'd just bought on North Star Road, he assured them. It was perfect for them.

"My God, Joe, really?" Mom said.

"Aw, come on, Champ, this is a lot," grumbled Dad. But after initial misgivings, they agreed. If this was what Joe needed, they would do it.

Joe, Jimmy, and Frankie rented a U-Haul, conned a group of friends (who should have known better) by telling them how much fun it would be to move two houses in one afternoon, and drove to Mom and Dad's house to begin the switch.

When Dad came back that night to what had been his home that very morning, Joe realized that maybe he'd forgotten an important detail: he hadn't remembered to tell Mom and Dad the exact day they were moving. Thankfully, our parents had a sense of humor. Mom and Dad ended up living at North Star for the next few years.

We organized the campaign out of the basement of the house on Woods Road, and set to work. With no money in our coffers, we were going to have to rely heavily on volunteers—and I had a hunch some of my students at Friends School might be willing.

I invited the entire upper school, grades nine to twelve, to an assembly in the auditorium, which was relatively small and looked like an old movie theater with its red-cushioned, fold-down seats. There were 230 kids in the upper school, all of whom were required to attend assemblies. The senior couples were seated in the back, holding hands.

"This is my brother Joe," I said. "He's running for the job of New Castle County Councilman, and he needs your help." I told them that instead of learning social studies in a classroom, they could study it in real life and help the campaign. "But first," I explained, "listen to what Joe has to say, and you can decide for yourself."

Joe was his usual warm, optimistic self, and I could see the kids were immediately taken with him. He was passionate, enthusiastic, and above all, hopeful—he knew the future could be better than the present, which made him a resonant voice for those kids.

These were harsh and divided years in America, and many of the kids sitting in that auditorium were keenly aware of history unfolding around them. After Martin Luther King was assassinated on April 4, 1968, riots broke out throughout the country, and Wilmington was set aflame. The National Guard was called in by our Governor to establish order and keep the peace—a National Guardsman with a bayonet was stationed on every corner in Wilmington to enforce the curfew. Wilmington was occupied for nine months, making it the city with the longest guard deployment in the nation.

In early June when Joe received his diploma from Syracuse law school, Robert Kennedy was assassinated. The loss of two giants in such a short time period was a blow to hope and idealism. MLK, a man committed to social justice, and then Robert Kennedy, the political leader Joe most admired and viewed as representative of change and grace in America, were gone. He told the students that day that these events catalyzed him to run for public office. The world needed to change, and as always, young people were going to be the ones to drive it.

Many of the kids sitting there had older brothers and sisters who were away at college, marching for Civil Rights and against the Vietnam War. In 1970, my students weren't old enough to vote—

back then, you had to be twenty-one—but at eighteen they were old enough to be drafted. They saw working on Joe's campaign as a way to get involved, even in just a small way.

After he left, a line began forming at the back of the auditorium, with student after student adding their name to the sign-up sheet for volunteers. One of my eleventh graders tossed a few questions my way before he would put his name on the roster.

"Is Joe a Democrat?" he asked.

"Absolutely," I said.

"Do you think he has a chance of winning?"

"Are you kidding? He's going to be President someday!" This earned me an incredulous look. The last person from Delaware to be part of a presidential cabinet had retired nearly a century earlier, in the 1880s. Democrats were nowhere on the local political map. But optimism is contagious, and by the end of the morning, I had close to one hundred signatures from student volunteers. I took it as a good omen.

That spring, we launched the campaign and debuted our slogan: *For All Our Families, Joe Biden for County Council.* For the Bidens, it was considerably more than a slogan. While Joe, Neilia, and I were at the center of the team, Mom, Dad, Jimmy, and Frankie were all in as well. Mom was "the Coffee Chair," responsible for organizing neighborhood meet and greets in people's homes. Dad, while commonly mistaken for the candidate himself, was at the ready to shepherd us around, and Jimmy became our official campaign fundraiser. There weren't many people willing to donate at the start, but Jimmy did what he could to solicit contributions from local businesses and community members; no amount was too small. Frankie was a sophomore in high school, which left him perfectly placed to rally our student volunteers and help coordinate the distribution of Biden campaign literature.

We fanned out across the district, walking up to people in their neighborhoods as they watered their lawns or played ball in the streets. "I am Valerie Biden. My brother is running for County Council. Would you take a look at him and his positions?" I'd ask time and again. If no one was home, I'd tuck a piece of literature in the screen door along with a brief handwritten note: *I stopped by to tell you about my brother. Will you take a look at him?*

We won that race by two thousand votes, defeating a man named Larry Messick. Larry was a gentleman, and went on to become one of our biggest supporters. In fact, he and his wife, Blanche, were the first chairs of Republicans for Biden during our US Senate elections.

County Council met one night a week. It was tedious work, but Joe put his heart into it, using his position to contain the tide of unchecked development that was devouring green space in Delaware at the time. The state government seemed eager to make Delaware into one large, ten-lane superhighway, so big trucks from Pennsylvania and New Jersey could conveniently drive through. But the kicker was that they would have to pass through the blue-collar neighborhoods of New Castle County—never coming close to the wealthy areas. In just two years, Joe got a reputation for standing up to builders and corporations.

The 1970 election was a mess for Delaware Democrats: Joe was one of their only success stories, so they nurtured him. They invited him to take part in a blue-ribbon commission staffed by former Governors, Congressmen, Supreme Court Justices, and prominent Democrats. Together, they tried to strategize their way out of the hole the party had dug for itself.

From our perch in New Castle County, Delaware, we could see that the party was in the early stages of redefining itself, and Joe was central to that new identity. Neilia and I were right there with him. She and I organized dinners with party officials and cultivated the leadership.

Two years later, in 1972, the Fourth District was redistricted to become more Republican. We had a decision to make: run for reelection for New Castle County Council—or for the US Senate. Both were predicted to be equally solid wins for the Republican Party. It was a natural inflection point in Joe's political career—he was either going to move up or get out. Everyone assured us that we would lose either way.

That year was also full of uncertainty for Democrats nationwide. President Lyndon Johnson had announced he would not seek a second term, and George McGovern was slated to run for President against Richard Nixon in a matchup he, too, was widely expected to lose. The national pundits told Joe he was a hotshot with no shot. And looking back, it's easy to see why no one took us seriously. Our family had neither influence nor power in the party nor any financial connections to anyone who did. Moreover, Joe would be challenging J. Caleb Boggs, a former two-term Governor and three-term Congressman now running for his third term as US Senator. Boggs was universally known and admired in Delaware. While Joe was twenty-nine years old, Boggs had been *in political office* for twenty-nine years.

When Joe, undeterred, continued to express interest in running for the Senate, they also told him that if he *did* enter, he would need someone experienced, a true Washington veteran, to run his campaign.

Instead, he picked me again. I don't think it ever occurred to him not to pick me. We were a package deal.

I told Joe that I knew nothing about running a statewide campaign, and he said: "All campaigns are local and personal—some are just bigger than others. I need you because you won't take anything for granted. We'll figure it out."

A typical sister would likely have offered any number of reasonable objections: "You're not even old enough to be a US Senator! You have no money; in fact, you owe *me* money! You've got to be kidding me—you're going to take on the beloved Senator Boggs?" But I didn't say any of that. Instead, I said, "Let's do it."

There's an old expression describing the young and naïve: "You don't know what you don't know." In our case, that was a good thing. For me in particular, I wasn't as intimidated as I might otherwise have been. I had no inkling of the hostile environment for women in politics at the time. I didn't know that the prevailing sentiment was that women had no business running political campaigns. Back then, women in politics managed the office and answered the phones. But I didn't know, and thank God for that.

And luckily, Joe and I *did* know a few things. Although we didn't have any money, power, or influence, we had vision and courage; we had the best candidate, and a smart and tireless advocate in Neilia. She was all in, and so was I. I was not building a résumé, and I had no agenda other than Joe's. He didn't have to be in the campaign office motivating volunteers, answering the phones, or writing the brochures. He could just go be Joe. My team would take care of the rest.

Our partnership allowed him to do what he did best—meet voters, listen, share his vision, and explain how he would work to make the dream a reality. Joe's candidacy reminded me of a song by the Teddy Bears called "To Know Him Is to Love Him." I knew that if Joe got out in front of people, they would do just that.

A good campaign is about the voters—their aspirations, their hopes—not about the candidate. Joe knew this instinctively. In 1972, and in every subsequent race, Joe knew that he himself was not the main event, but a vehicle for helping people get where they wanted to be and live how they wanted to live.

We knew we could not afford to stumble out of the gate. We needed to look like winners, like we knew what we were doing (a tall order, given our inexperience). We decided to launch our bid with a grand gesture: we would announce Joe's run for US Senate on March 20, 1972, at the Hotel Du Pont—a Republican bastion in New Castle County, which was the seat of our business community and corporate Delaware. We wanted to be the candidate that Democrats, Independents, and Republicans could rally behind, and choosing the Hotel Du Pont as our launching pad seemed like the right message.

Now all we had to do was make sure we didn't announce to an empty room. I was left with the task of summoning a crowd to the hotel by half past seven on a workday, when nearly everybody had to report to work by nine in the morning. We asked everyone we knew to come to the hotel on the morning of March 20, and then asked *them* to invite everyone they knew. We sent invitations to all the Democrats in the voter registration files, which were a mess, and called all the county chairs to come and bring their organizations with them. For many, going to downtown Wilmington was a trek and a major inconvenience given its limited parking and the early-morning rush hour. It was a big ask, and it could have gone either way.

The morning of the press conference, I began to doubt the wisdom of our big gambit. I remember arriving at the hotel at six o'clock, thinking, *Lord, what have I done? What if no one comes?* We'd be finished before we started. My small group of volunteers had kicked into high gear, and I had gone into planning overdrive, but there were so many things I could not control: traffic, weather, disinterest . . . I steeled myself. *Oh well,* I thought. *No turning back now.*

We had reserved a medium-sized meeting room that was separated by a partition so that if the crowd was small, it wouldn't look like the place was completely empty. When I walked in that morning, it looked bigger than I remembered. I imagined the look on Joe's face if this went south. With my heart in my throat, I waited. One by one, people trickled in, and with each new arrival, my blood pressure went down a notch or two.

In the end, we had to open the partition to accommodate the over-flow crowd, and even then, it was standing room only. It was one of many thank-you-God moments that day alone.

My second challenge was to get Joe to the other two Delaware counties, Kent and Sussex. As a show of respect, we had decided to announce our candidacy there, too. No statewide candidate in Dela-ware had ever done this before. (Traditionally, Democrats announced at a fire hall, and only in one county.) Three announcements, three crowds, three press conferences. This was another part of our big "make a splash" strategy, and it was up to me again to make sure we didn't belly flop. I asked my friend Billy Meyers, a former navy pilot, to fly us down in a Piper Cub airplane, which he agreed to without blinking an eye. By the end of the night, the result was clear: somehow, by the grace of our organizing and total buy-in from every single volunteer, we'd pulled it off. Our announcement did exactly what we hoped it would—it turned heads. Whatever else people thought about Joe, he no longer looked like a total amateur. And little did we know at the time, we had set an announcement-day precedent for future Democratic candidates in Delaware.

With the announcement behind us, we focused on building momen-tum. Improvisation became one of the hallmarks of the campaign. Since we had limited resources (read: none), we had to get creative. No money to pay for glossy paper brochures? No problem. We printed ours on rag newspaper stock, just like the local tabloids. No stamps? We hand-delivered our paper each weekend to about 150,000 homes in the state. We couldn't afford a media consultant, so we used a big handheld tape recorder to interview ordinary voters: the mailman, the milkman, mall shoppers. A friend and old radio guy, Bob Cunningham, then quickly turned those interviews into sixty-second radio ads. The pros would have been horrified by our approach. Luckily, there weren't any on our staff to tell us how badly we were screwing up.

We turned the vacant space behind Joe's law office into our make-shift headquarters and furnished it with old, dented furniture we bought from the DuPont Company warehouse. We pinned a state map up on the wall and divided it into our representative districts. Then we methodically went street by street, checking to see if we knew some-one, even a friend of a friend, who lived there. When we came across someone we knew, we'd call and introduce ourselves and our campaign, asking if that person would consider becoming our point person in the neighborhood, our "block captain." We kept at it until we had a block captain on every street, or at least in every neighborhood in the state. They were our ears and eyes, and the foundation of our field operation.

As I focused on the field, Jimmy reprised his role as our fundraiser, saving our first major event from disaster. We had booked a fire hall and left the ticket sales to the local party chair, who insisted repeat-edly that he had it in hand. But hours before the fundraiser was due to start, I found out the truth: he'd sold just twenty tickets. Obviously, something had slipped between the cup and the lip.

I called Jimmy, and we went into high gear. We called everyone we knew, and even people we didn't. Jimmy even invited perfect strangers from off the street. "I don't care what your plans are," he said. "You're coming to dinner, and then you can go about your business. It's free!" In the end, we packed that hall, but the fundraiser wound up costing us a couple thousand dollars because we had to pay for all the food. Half of that night's dinner guests probably weren't even Democrats; God only knows if they even knew who Joe Biden was.

Even amid these white-knuckle near misses, we were cheerful. There's something exhilarating about being the underdog, and we embraced our freedom. Where big campaign machines lumbered, we were free to dart and swerve. According to conventional wisdom at the time, no one paid attention to elections until Labor Day, but we started going door-to-door in the spring, visiting the districts where we knew we had to get out the vote. We'd stand outside busy shopping centers on Saturday, and Joe would smile at everyone, saying: "I'm Joe Biden. I hope you'll give me a look." We went through the community newspapers, listened to our local radio stations, and spoke with our block captains daily to stay on top of the latest issues. If there was a street party in a neighborhood, a community arts festival, or a parade somewhere, we'd organize a "go day" and show up in full force. We prepped volunteers, stocked up on leaflets, and made sure someone in the family was there to represent Joe. It certainly helped that you could drive the entire length of Delaware in two hours, and the width in thirty minutes.

The campaign's real secret weapon came directly from my own classroom. The kids who had helped out in the County Council race were juniors now, and this was the first election in which eighteen-year-olds could vote. Vietnam (and the draft) still loomed, which meant that some of these kids had more skin in the game than others.

Frankie was a senior at Friends School that year, and a star football player. He had a magnetism about him. I was a young teacher, rocking go-go boots and closer in age to the seniors than I was to many of the kids' parents. Several of the boys in my class signed up to volunteer with the campaign immediately, and when they came along, so did all the girls. The campaign became the place to be, not just for the kids who followed politics but for the "cool" kids and the "sporty" kids, too. I would be fired for this today, but I told them that if they didn't work for my brother, I would flunk them. They weren't sure if I was kidding (neither was I), but they didn't want to test me.

Neilia, who taught eighth grade at Saint Catherine of Siena's grade school, took a similar approach to engaging her students. She was magical with those kids, and they convinced their parents to join the events. Unlike the high schoolers, who could carpool or drive themselves, these kids needed mom and dad to chaperone, and their parents got a firsthand look at what we were up to.

These kids were the backbone of the campaign; they did everything. One of my students, a sophomore named Wendy, created our logo—a square pin with a donkey on it. After sports practice let out, we would meet at headquarters and I would hand out poster board, paint, and pizza. Then we'd make our signs—by hand. While we did this because we couldn't afford to print them, our homemade signs communicated enthusiasm and exuded a genuine grassroots feel along the various parade routes where we placed them. It's one thing to stick a candidate's professionally printed sign in your front lawn. It's another thing entirely if that sign was handmade by a seventeen-year-old high school volunteer.

For their part, the kids weren't shy about asking their friends and neighbors to support their candidate: "Would you put a Biden sign in your window or on your porch?" On weekends, we'd pile groups of five or more kids into cars and drive to different neighborhoods, where the kids would fan out to distribute literature and ask voters to go to the polls for Joe on Election Day.

Oftentimes, our student volunteers signed up to the dismay of their parents, who couldn't understand why their child was working for a Democrat. Wilmington Friends School, where I'd been teaching, was private, wealthy, privileged, and Republican; most parents wouldn't have voted for the good Lord Himself if he were a Democrat. But even parents in sheltered suburban communities could see that new social boundaries were being tested every day. The country was fighting two

wars—abroad in Vietnam, and at home on Civil Rights. Political cor-
ruption, then most blatantly seen under the name "Watergate," was on
TV every night. Campus riots were breaking out; the Kent State massa-
cre, in which nine college students were shot and four died while protesting the war in Vietnam, occurred in 1970. The Pill was available,
recreational drug use was growing, the Equal Rights Amendment was
being debated, Earth Day had been created, and educational tools
like busing were being introduced in some states to deal with racial
segregation. Given all of this, I think these parents looked at their
children's commitment to peaceful political activity and decided that,
on balance, it was a plus. Better volunteering for some young Catholic
Democrat than throwing bricks through windows, some thought.

It was around this time that the press started calling us "the Children's
Crusade." Some people might have read it as derogatory, but I liked it;
it meant our approach was working. And the pundits didn't know how
true it was. At any given event, ten to twenty students would show up
with Biden signs and bumper stickers. They walked with Joe when we
went door-to-door, and marched beside him along parade routes. There
were no campaign selfies back then, so we snapped Polaroids of Joe with
local business owners. They would put them on their cash registers or
stick them on the wall, and when customers asked, they'd say, "Oh, well,
that's a nice young man, he came in here and he's running for the Senate." Most of our budget went to buying film for those pictures.

We kept our kids plied with pizzas and sodas, and engaged them
in whatever aspect of the campaign interested them. Since we had
no party bosses to answer to, we had no real hierarchies. The kids
could jump on whatever they wanted, whether it was door knocking,
answering the telephones, or manning headquarters. Because we
considered these newly eligible eighteen-year-old voters a serious
prospect, Joe went to high schools and answered their questions. At

every step, we engaged them, asking, "How are you going to change the world?"

Not all our volunteers were green and inexperienced. Joe knew one guy who had run a campaign before, and to my dismay, that guy turned out to be Jack Owens—the man with whom I'd had a disastrous blind date in college.

By then, Jack was something of a hotshot in his own right. After law school, he went to Pittsburgh to work as an attorney at Koppers Company. There, he also joined the mayoral campaign of a young upstart named Pete Flaherty. Flaherty upended the Democratic machine and scored the biggest upset in Pittsburgh, becoming part of political history. This victory earned Jack membership in a group of emerging political operatives called the Young Turks.

After Flaherty, Jack left Koppers and started his own law firm, flush with victory and the optimism of youth. Having also helped lead Milton Shapp's successful campaign for Governor in Pennsylvania, Jack had two big notches in his belt. "Call me when you want to run for President," Jack told Joe in a fit of swagger.

Well, we weren't running for President—not yet—but Jack still came to Delaware to help out. The second we laid eyes on each other, it was as if we were back at that football game, knives drawn. He knew one way to win the election—his way—and he didn't like that I wasn't enthusiastic about all his ideas.

I might have had little experience, but I was still running the show, and I was not eager for this presumptuous guy to come down from Pittsburgh to tell us how to do things. We took turns getting under each other's skin. When he walked into a meeting, I would turn to him, the big shot who had spearheaded two winning campaigns, who had been responsible for thirty-two counties in one gubernatorial election, and say loudly, "Hey, Jack, take a memo, would you?"

Things soon came to a boiling point. "I can't stand this guy," I told Joe, arguing, "we can't be in the same room together. I know I've never made you choose, but this time, you've got to choose; it's either him or me on this campaign."

Joe couldn't believe I had given him an ultimatum. He was about to make the call when Jack did it for him.

"Joe, I know blood is thicker than water, but I really can't deal with your sister," Jack said. "You can call me whenever I can help—but I'm not working through your sister." He and Joe still spoke directly and regularly, but he left the campaign. Everyone thought that was for the best.

When the Democratic nominating convention rolled around in June, we faced an all-too-familiar challenge: we needed to make an impression but didn't have much money or a big team. Once again, the campaign had to come up with something despite the low tremor of fear I battled constantly.

The convention landed late in June on the last week of school for our public school volunteers, so I asked kids from all over the state to show up for one final weekend before they went off on vacations or to summer jobs. I asked all the high school marching bands to see if we could put together our own Biden Band. On the day of the convention, we all met in the parking lot outside the convention center in Dover. When Joe's name was put into nomination that Saturday morning, we burst through the auditorium, drums beating, horns blazing, chanting "Go, Joe, Joe, Joe!" The band led us as we wove between the aisles and got the delegates out of their seats to join us in a snake dance. It turned into one big conga line. Finally, the gavel came down for the last time, and we left—to thunderous applause.

We adapted another winning tactic straight from the "John Kennedy for Senate" playbook. We organized coffee parties in suburban homes—one every hour from 9:00 a.m. to 9:00 p.m., four days a week—because we didn't have the staff or facilities to organize a rally or the money to appear on TV. This was a way to get Joe face-to-face with voters. It was labor intensive—up close and personal for the candidate and for the volunteers. Mom, Neilia, and I would take turns hosting while one of us ran up to the next house to prepare for the following gathering. Afterward, Neilia and I wrote thank-you notes to each voter by hand, trying to remember something personal to include about each one.

During that summer, some interns from the New Democratic Coalition in Washington, DC, came to work on the campaign. These young volunteers had a short training period—"Campaigns 101" in DC—and then were placed in various campaigns throughout the country. They were paid $50 a month. Our commitment was to find them room and board in supporters' homes. They slept in spare bedrooms, on couches, and on floors. Some made out better than others as to accommodations, but all realized after a short period that campaigns were a lot of plain hard work.

They also realized that you did more than labor on a campaign—you *lived* a campaign. It stayed with you. What they did not yet know was that campaign relationships last a lifetime, for better and for worse. I joked to anyone who wanted to join our staff that we issued adoption papers, not employment papers, and warned them that if they were currently involved in even a tentative romantic relationship, they could pretty much count on it being sorely tested at best, and ruined at worst.

Of all the tireless volunteers who joined our cause, a few stand out in my mind to this day. I called Terri Jaquet, Eileen Eisenman, and Diane

Butler "the Three Horsewomen." They walked into our headquarters to help one day and almost never left. They were there for whatever had to be done; they stayed late every night with me, helped get out the invitations, manned the phone banks, and built voter registration lists.

There was also Bobbie Greene, Neilia's roommate at Syracuse. Bobbie was an oral historian for the RFK Oral History Collection, and one of our only connections to anyone in Washington. She was book smart, well informed, and knew how politics, families, and "families and politics" worked. She joined the campaign with baby Davey on her hip, coming down every Sunday night and leaving Thursday to get back to Maryland.

I always said Bobbie knew the world on a first-name basis; everyone took her call. It was thanks to Bobbie that Wes Barthelmes, a seasoned Washington veteran, joined the campaign. Wes was key to the press corps and was invaluable, giving us some credibility on the national scene. Then there was Roger Harrison from Syracuse's Business School, Joe's multitasking friend who covered every base that needed covering.

Paula Levine and I met in 1970 on a beach in Florida and became fast friends. In July of 1972, her father died of a heart attack. She was devastated. I invited her to come see me, and she said, "If I came, all I would do is cry."

I said, "Come, and I'll cry with you."

She did. When she was in town, we talked about her moving to Delaware to work on the campaign full-time. She immediately said yes, and arrived two weeks later with a suitcase and no place to stay. No problem, we had plenty of places for campaign friends to hang their hats.

Paula proved to be strategic, savvy, and a gifted fundraiser, not to mention a dear friend. But at the time, her biggest asset was that she could cause anyone to stop dead in their tracks. She was a "looker," as we used to say, and a compelling campaigner. Paula and I would head to downtown Wilmington in the early-morning hours to catch the employees as they hustled into their offices at DuPont or one of the banks. We'd stand on opposite sides of the street and try to catch people's attention. No matter what—whatever the weather, whatever rush they were in—with Paula, men slowed their walks, widened their smiles, and took the literature. Meanwhile, on my side, it might as well have been a drive-through.

Not only had Paula come to Delaware to work on the campaign, she had also brought with her a colleague and a force of nature named Chazy Dowaliby. Chazy looked like Mama Cass, the singer of the Mamas and the Papas, complete with flowing muumuus that she wore to the office and false eyelashes that looked outrageously glamorous. She was a totally extravagant and brilliant character, and she became our press secretary. We all loved her.

Thanks in large part to the combined zeal of our volunteer army, reports on the campaign grew steadily more charitable. Joe Biden was still going to lose—and badly, pundits argued—but he was clearly a serious guy, a committed campaigner. The attitude of the delegates seemed to be the same as the press: "Nice kid, such energy. Too bad he can never win." Joe himself acknowledged the steep uphill battle in an interview, saying that if he were a bookie, "I'd give myself five-to-one odds."

From the point of view of Delaware politicians, Joe was a sacrificial lamb. The Republicans straight-up ignored us. They used what is called the Rose Garden strategy, which basically means "ignore your opponent"; if you already have the throne, why acknowledge that you have a contender? Truthfully, they had cause to be confident.

But we'd also heard talk that our opponent, Senator Boggs, didn't want to run again. He'd been in government for a long time, and had done a lot of good. His reputation, which had never dipped or wavered, was at an all-time high. Word was he was running again only

as a favor for Nixon, who choppered in to one of the biggest estates in
Delaware to personally knight him again. As the story goes, he said,
"Cale, we're counting on you." Nixon needed the Senate, and Boggs
seemed like a sure bet. There were even murmurs that Boggs would
run and win only to step down, so that someone younger and hungrier
could step in to replace him. "This is not a campaign," his advisors
told him. "You're running against a nobody."

That was the refrain across the state and across party lines: the
Honorable J. Caleb Boggs versus A Nobody. By and large, people
weren't rude or mean to us; they just dismissed us.

We knew that any possible margin of victory would be slim. We
were walking a tricky line, and we needed to build a coalition. Our
state was Republican, yes, but moderate. We were campaigning on
Civil Rights in a segregated state. We were one of the first campaigns
to focus on the environment, which was a growing concern, particularly in Delaware. The Delaware River was studded with oil refineries.
Thanks in large part to Shell Oil and DuPont, we were the chemical
capital of the world. The DuPonts were a huge name in the state, and
employed thousands of people, all of whom had an ironclad loyalty to
the company. On the national stage, McGovern was to our left, but
we could not disown our party's candidate, so we simply chose not
to embrace him. We thought we could crack the Independents, who
would be key, but we also needed to turn out our Democratic base—
who, by the way, weren't for McGovern. It was a delicate balance,
vulnerable to crosswinds.

As our fundraiser, Jimmy always had his back up against the wall.
He knew that Delaware was not a deep well, so he went about finding
money out of state—from Texas, California, and Alaska. Campaigns
are money furnaces, and without a broader base of donor support,
money was forever burning up on contact.

On Labor Day weekend, with the election just two months away, we had $7,000 to our name. A lot of potential donors liked Joe, but they didn't want to throw their money into a black hole. They needed to know how Joe could win. He had gained the strong support of Nordy Hoffman, Executive Director of the Democratic Senatorial Campaign Committee. Nordy recommended we hire John Marttila, a hot, young Boston political consultant, and Pat Caddell, an unknown young pollster. Caddell did a poll in late August and we got the results the week after Labor Day showing the horse race to be Boggs's at 47 percent, Biden at 19 percent, and undecided at 34 percent. In addition, the poll confirmed that Boggs had 24 percent of the Democratic Party vote. Boggs's favorable/unfavorable rating stood at 59/20, while Biden's favorable/unfavorable rating was 18/5. Moreover, three-quarters of all voters polled could not mention a single thing they disliked about Boggs. The poll concluded: "It is remarkable that a candidate for the United States Senate can be as unknown as Biden just two months before the general election."

We needed a Hail Mary pass, and we found one in our weekly "lit drops." We couldn't afford a single statewide mailing, which cost nearly $40,000. This is where those rag newspapers came in, full of campaign updates and statements from Joe on the issues. They were simple, bold, and direct. The logistics of distributing them were dizzying. First, we'd send the literature up to Boston to be printed in a union shop—it was dramatically less expensive to print there than at home. Then, the night before a lit drop, Bill Auth, a volunteer who later became a photographer for *National Geographic*, would fly to Boston to pick up the literature, rent a U-Haul, and drive to Delaware in the middle of the night to drop off the bundles at our various pickup locations across the state. Next, hundreds of our high school volunteers, along with our block captains who literally represented every community in the state, would meet at the pickup locations to retrieve the literature and begin their distribution.

That fall, when UD was back in session, Dennis Toner helped organize college volunteers for us. He didn't know it at the time, but his work on campus would lead to thirty-four years working with my brother in the US Senate. He was a Biden original, from the start.

We had to learn to move fast—literally, in some cases—because many of the dogs that saw us approaching during predawn hours took us for intruders.

By October, people would be waiting outside for us as we walked up. If it rained, there would be calls to the HQ: *Where is my newspaper?*

All of it was working; we could feel it. Buzz was building. The tabloids, the kids, the coffees, the door-to-doors were beginning to have a cumulative effect. Toward the end, we had even gotten the Boggs campaign's attention, and were braced for some late-breaking negative ads from their team. But if we kept on track and there were no major flare-ups—well, who knew what could happen. We could win this thing.

Said major flare-up arrived on cue, the weekend before the election. A young intern for the *Wilmington News Journal* who had volunteered for the campaign wrote a story alleging that Joe's support of Israel was opportunistic and politically motivated. The accusation that Joe was not supportive of the Jewish community or the State of Israel was patently false and designed to bring down his campaign by jeopardizing one of our most important constituencies at the worst possible moment. We knew we had to get the truth out immediately to staunch the bleeding. And to do that, we needed a credible leader in the Jewish community, someone who could vouch for Joe and quell concerns about where he stood on the issues.

Joe called Jack, who called Milton Shapp, the man he'd helped elect as the first Jewish Governor of Pennsylvania. Could Jack ask

Governor Shapp if he would come down and speak to local leaders in the Jewish community to help set the record straight?

"Jack, I don't really know this guy," Governor Shapp responded, "but if you know him, and you think he's the real deal, I trust you."

"I do know him, and he is," Jack answered, adding, "he needs you."

To give Governor Shapp a chance to get better acquainted with the candidate, Joe drove to pick him up ahead of the event we'd scheduled for that Sunday afternoon. It seemed like every major Jewish leader in the state, religious and political, came to the reception we held at the Hotel Du Pont. The place was jammed. Governor Shapp stood up in front of all of them and shared what Jack had told him about Joe: "Joe Biden is a fine young man, a man of honor, a man of integrity, a man who supports Jewish values, principles, faith, and the Jewish State of Israel. I don't know who this other guy is, but he's not telling the truth." As the event with the Governor was winding down, Jack learned that a large wedding reception for members of Delaware's Jewish community was being held at the same time as the Governor's visit. In order to maximize the impact of Governor Shapp's endorsement of Joe, Jack explained the situation to the Governor and asked if he might be willing to stop by that reception on his way out. The Governor generously agreed. The joyful reception he received from the surprised wedding revelers was an effective and wonderful cap for the day.

Afterward, the message spread throughout the Jewish community. Shapp had righted the ship. Even I had to admit that this Owens guy had really saved us.

Joe had decided he would give up his law firm if elected. There were no laws against maintaining it, but he felt it might present a conflict of interest. He carried through with his promise, and to my dismay, he asked Jack Owens to take his place in the firm. "Joe," I said, "of all the people in the country you could sell our law firm to, why Jack Owens?"

"Well, Val, the last time I looked, it was *my* law firm," Joe answered. "And the reason I'm selling it to Jack is because no one can put a patch on his ass in the courtroom."

This was the maddening thing about Jack: he was so damn *good* at everything he did. He had an Irish heart, which I would come to appreciate later, along with an ironclad grasp of Jesuit logic. It was a lethal combination for anyone on the opposite side of the courtroom, and if you were his client, he treated you like a blood brother. He was widely respected, and the world was basically his oyster for whatever he wanted to do.

He and I never did speak again during that campaign, by the way, except for one brief exchange the day before the election. The phone rang in my office that day. It was Jack. "Where are the election results going to be held? What's the lay of the land?"

"Why do you want to know?"

"Because I am going to come down for election night."

"Why?"

"Because he's my friend, that's why."

"Okay, I'll tell you, but let's make a deal. It's at the Hotel Du Pont, but just stay away from me."

"Great, because I don't want to see you either."

At headquarters on election night, I got my first inkling that things might break our way when the numbers came in from the Republican districts in Brandywine Hundred. We lost them, as expected, but by a lesser margin than I had anticipated. That's when I started doing the math in my head, and I said to myself, *Holy cripes, we might get this.* I hurried to get dressed and headed to the Hotel Du Pont, where the crowd was already gathering.

It was particularly rewarding to host our election night returns there because the hotel was traditionally where state Republicans held their victory parties. That was just de rigueur. However, the previous April, a few weeks after we announced, I went to the hotel and reserved the Gold Ballroom for election night. We took their prize, and they didn't even notice until they strolled through, in September, to claim what they viewed as their birthright. You could hear the roar throughout the city: Biden did *what?*

The coalition we stitched together in 1972 was pretty remarkable. First, our conventionality helped us in the conservative neighborhoods. We were fighting for the same things as those who were protesting with McGovern, but we gave out balloons, for God's sake.

Next, it was the *kids* who got the uninterested interested—by that, I mean their Republican parents. We like to think we teach our children—and we certainly do—but our children teach us more. In 1972, our young volunteers' parents looked at their children and said, "Good God, I couldn't get my teenagers to roll out of bed before noon. And now, they're up at five thirty to hand deliver campaign papers for Joe Biden?" I believe that convinced the parents to take a second look at Joe. *What was it about that guy, anyway?* They did, and despite voting overwhelmingly for Nixon that November, they also voted for Joe.

Then there was labor: while I was working with the campaign kids, Joe and Jimmy were working hand in hand with labor leaders. Though Boggs had enjoyed labor support in prior elections, it was different this time around. The Steelworkers, International Brotherhood of Electricians, and United Auto Workers and Laborers were the first unions to support Joe. Many others followed. Labor was more organized than the state party—and my brother has never forgotten.

Finally, the overwhelming support demonstrated by the Black community, especially in South Wilmington, was incredible. Joe's friends, many of whom he got to know while lifeguarding at the city pool at Prices Run, were a force. The pastors invited Joe to speak at their churches and our supporters brought Joe to their union halls. They hosted dinners and events, and organized volunteers to get out the vote on Election Day, leading to tremendous turnout among African American voters.

That night, when we were declared victors, Ted Kaufman turned to me and said, "I will no longer believe anything is impossible."

At the Hotel Du Pont, I stood next to Joe as he was looking in the mirror, fixing his tie. He caught my eye and grinned. "Hey, Joe," I said. "Take a good look. That's what a Senator looks like."

In the end, we won by 3,163 votes—less than 1.5 percent. It remains my most personal victory, and it's the one I savor more than all the others. With our kids, our volunteers, our hand-painted signs, our homemade spaghetti dinners, our one-on-one coffee dates, we had done it: we'd beaten a candidate personally anointed by Nixon. With nothing but creativity and gumption, we had shaken up the political world.

After it was all said and done, Wes Barthelmes presented me with a small gold charm with a simple engraving. "The Iron Butterfly," he said, smiling. "For running this campaign with grace and strength."

We all like to imagine we're in control.

But in growing older, we experience many reminders that we are not.

As much as we try, we cannot will life's outcomes to our specifications. Perhaps we can bend the arc of our journey, but we cannot forge it in steel.

In the dark of my night, in the dark of my sadness, I let go and take the plunge into faith's deep waters. Thy will be done.

To maintain my sanity, I choose to believe, against the odds as I know them, that I will be helped, I will survive. Some good will come.

7

SHATTERED

My most vivid memory of December 18, 1972, is just a sound: *clack, clack, clack*. Joe and I were alone, hurrying through the vacant marble hallway of the Capitol, our heels echoing into the emptiness. The Senate was in Christmas recess, so there was no one in sight. We'd been using Senator Byrd's empty office to interview prospective staff. The desk was piled high with résumés of people clamoring to work for my brother, the twenty-nine-year-old kid from Delaware who'd just landed himself a Senate seat out of nowhere. Minutes before, we had been on top of the world; now it felt as though we were alone in the universe.

Jimmy had called me just a few minutes earlier. "Come home," he said. I don't remember anything else he said during that call, just the feeling of ice that filled me. Neilia, Hunter, Beau, Amy—Joe's entire family. A tractor trailer. A massive collision. I hung up with the unbearable knowledge that Neilia and Amy, Joe's wife and baby daughter, were dead. My mind drifted, visualizing an intersection a few hundred miles away, somewhere back home, where ambulance lights flashed against a twisted-up Chevy station wagon. My mind recoiled from envisioning what was inside.

Joe turned to me, eyes stricken, voice choked. "She's dead, isn't she?" I remember his eyes. I wish I didn't. Staring into them at that moment was like staring straight into hell.

I answered with the only words that would come. "I don't know." I didn't have the strength in me to tell him the truth, but he knew me too well, so the words didn't matter. Joe and I had always known how to communicate without speaking, and while that gift had served us so well throughout our lives, I cursed it now. Joe spoke my language, so he knew the truth. *Yes, Joe,* I had said to him. *Yes, it's true. The worst thing you can imagine has already happened, and I don't have the strength to say it out loud.* I saw the truth settle into his bones, where I couldn't root it out if I tried.

When trauma hits, our minds decide what to remember forever, what to forget, and what to bury. In writing this chapter, I've had to piece together the details from interviewing my brothers. Memories of that night are buried deep within each of us, like pieces of shrapnel that stopped just shy of killing us but are impossible to extract. What I learned later was that Joe had gotten a call, too—from the state police or the EMTs, I never learned who had told him. Despite our desperate, hopeless efforts to shield him from the truth for as long as we could, he already knew.

Here are the events of that night, as best as I can reconstruct them.

Jimmy had gotten breakfast that morning with Neilia, the boys, and Amy. They were discussing some political issue, something related to Joe's staffing or the campaign. It's all lost to history now. After they parted ways, Jimmy went to the campaign office to do some more work while Neilia piled Amy and the boys into the car to take them to get a Christmas tree.

Every Christmas-celebrating family has its own traditions, and ours was sacrosanct: we waited until Christmas Eve to put up the tree. My father had a concoction of Ivory Snow detergent and water that he would layer on the branches to look like fresh-fallen snow. All of this—the tree going up, the lights, the foamy snow, the presents—happened on Christmas Eve while the children slept. The point was to produce the maximum possible sensory overload on Christmas morning when the kids came downstairs to see what Santa had done overnight.

Joe's election and the ensuing craziness had complicated this tradition a bit. For one, this would be the kids' last Christmas in their old house. In anticipation of their new lives, Joe and Neilia had bought a white colonial house in Chevy Chase, Maryland, only a short drive from the Capitol. It was going to be tricky to manage all the usual Christmas bells and whistles while gearing up for a big move and staffing Joe's Senate office. But Neilia and Joe thought it would do the whole family some good to celebrate the holidays together in familiar surroundings before the next big adventure.

As a result, Neilia was getting the tree a full week early, even if the important stuff—the decoration, the foamy snow peaks, the presents—would still be handled by Santa and his elves. They stopped at a Christmas tree farm, picked out a big one, strapped it to the car, and headed home.

They were about four miles away from home when it happened. Jimmy was the first one who was contacted. He got a call from a man named Mort Kimmel, who worked with the state police. "Neilia's been in an accident," Kimmel said, explaining, "they're taking her to Saint Francis Hospital, and someone needs to get down there right away."

Jimmy hung up and raced the ten minutes to downtown Wilmington. When he arrived at the ER, a sober-faced doctor sequestered him in another room to give him the details: Neilia had been broadsided by an eighteen-wheeler as she was crossing the two-lane highway. The truck was coming off a very steep hill, and it was a massive collision. Apparently, the car was in the air 150 feet, hit three trees, and flipped over. The boys were severely hurt. Hunter had some serious head injuries, and Beau had so many broken bones, he was put in traction. Amy and Neilia had both passed.

I still wonder about Jimmy, alone, learning all of this. Absorbing, calculating. Jimmy has always been the one we have leaned on during the most difficult times. He is courageous and has a strength of will that allows him to handle anything life, or his family, throws his way. Jimmy is the problem solver. You can't fix what's irrevocably shattered, but Jimmy tried his damnedest that night, doing what no one else could. First, he went to see Neilia and Amy. He identified the bodies. Then, he went about informing the Hunters and Mom and Dad. He didn't want either set of parents to be alone when they heard. So he sent a close friend of Mr. Hunter's, a doctor named Tony Leash, over to their house in Skaneateles. "Call me from their house the minute you get there," Jimmy instructed Dr. Leash. Leash did as he was told, telling the Hunters only that "something horrible happened," before calling up Jimmy and having him deliver the news.

He did the same with Mom and Dad. He had our family doctor drive to get them, bringing a mild sedative in case they needed it. The doctor escorted our parents to the hospital.

Jimmy also sent the state police to collect Frankie quietly from

Friends School, where he was a senior. He didn't want Frankie driving while upset.

Somewhere in there, he called me. Poor Jimmy, having to spread the news around like some airborne contagion. He arranged a private plane for Joe and me—a two-seater, a fragile thing buffeted by heavy winds. It kept dipping and rising as we flew to Wilmington. Neither of us spoke a word; we simply prayed. What point was there to words? I kept one hand on Joe's leg, maybe to comfort him, maybe to keep myself from feeling like I was going to fall off the face of the earth.

The next moment I remember clearly was under the harsh lights of Saint Francis Hospital. Beau and Hunt were in surgery—Beau's hip, arm, and leg were broken, while Hunt had a broken arm and head injuries. Someone must have authorized the operation—again, Jimmy. But the boys were alive. They were alive. They were alive.

An accident this tragic doesn't stay quiet for long, especially not in a close community. Once it became known that the family in the crash was Joe's, word spread like wildfire. This beautiful young couple, these magnificent little children, this young man who had so recently conquered the world—it was horrific, and it attracted crowds. There was an invasive outpouring of love, concern, morbid curiosity. Crowds outside the hospital, news trucks, microphones, the whole bit. Inside, calls were washing up on the switchboard like a tsunami. While we were in Saint Francis, at least, none of those curious, prying voices reached our family. For Jimmy, who somehow managed to shield us, it must have been like trying to hold back the ocean's waves with his hands.

The next few days passed in a blur. The sun went up and down, but it felt like opening and closing our eyes on the same never-ending day. After their surgeries, Hunter and Beau left the ICU and were moved to a room where we could stay with them. Joe went into his boys' hospital room to explain that Mommy and Caspy, the boys' nickname for

Amy, were gone. The nurses brought in a bed so that Joe could sleep in the room with his boys—and another cot so that Jimmy could sleep near Joe.

Jimmy became Joe's silent guardian, never leaving his side. If Joe woke up at 4:30 a.m., racked with anger or sobbing quietly, Jimmy wanted to be there, and he was. Joe would shake him awake and they would go out for a walk. Jimmy would follow Joe outside onto the streets of downtown Wilmington, Joe never saying a word. The understanding between them was unspoken but clear: Joe was looking for a fight. And Jimmy was there for whatever happened.

Joe's suffering and anger radiated outward from him like a heat signature. His rage was incandescent, horrible, and I could tell that he was nearly breaking under its weight. Joe was a kind man. Rage was unfamiliar to him. It seemed to bend his frame. He didn't want his boys to see the black thoughts that were consuming Daddy—for them he smiled, he was tender. He squared his shoulders and showed them Daddy would make things all right. Just beneath the surface, though, he was howling in pain.

There were people who told us it was God's will. *God's will.* Every time I heard that phrase, it burned inside me. I wanted to scream in all their faces: *God didn't want this!* If any of us had had a baseball bat, we would have smashed every window in that hospital, shattered the windshield of every car. I was so angry I wanted to crack the surface of the earth.

The awful irony of it all was that it was nearly Christmas. Hunter and Beau weren't going to be discharged from the hospital until after the New Year, so Christmas morning, whatever it looked like, would happen in their hospital room.

On December 23, Jimmy went out to Strawbridge & Clothier, Delaware's version of a Macy's, and pointed to the huge artificial Christmas tree in the display window, covered in ornaments and tinsel. "I want to buy that tree," he said. The clerk looked at him, aghast. "Sir, you can't buy that," he said. "It's our display tree."

Jimmy said, "I want that tree. And I'm buying the fucking tree."

Well, what Jimmy wanted, Jimmy usually got. So there he was, God love him, striding through the revolving doors of the hospital with the biggest, sparkliest fake tree you've ever seen, raining tinsel and glitter behind him. Some members of the hospital staff (understandably but unwisely) tried to intervene and stop him.

"You can't bring that into the hospital," someone said.

"Watch me," said Jimmy.

At that point, some of the nurses figured it out: this was for the little Biden boys, who had lost everything. They turned their heads. "I don't see a thing," one of them declared. And that is how Hunter and Beau wound up with a fully decorated, department store Christmas tree lighting up their hospital room. It was the only source of light at that time.

Neilia's funeral Mass and burial were private, just for the family. But first, Joe had to figure out where she would be buried. We were so young, still in our twenties, so none of us had a burial plot picked out. Neilia's parents had their own family plot in upstate New York. "We'll bring her home," Mr. Hunter said. "This is home," Joe said quietly. He wanted the boys to be able to visit their mother's grave. Once again, Jimmy shouldered the burden of figuring things out. He picked out a plot in a Catholic cemetery called All Saints. He ordered a headstone and Joe didn't even have time to figure out what he wanted engraved on it before the burial. Later, Joe chose an inscription that summed up the depth of his loss: DEATH LIES UPON HER LIKE AN EARLY FROST UPON THE SWEETEST FLOWER OF ALL THE FIELDS. A quote from *Romeo and Juliet*, commemorating another love lost too soon, a life cut cruelly short.

After our family Mass, we set the date for a public memorial, which would take place after Christmas. So many Senators and other elected officials, both Democrat and Republican, had called and sent prayers. Many wanted to come to Neilia's memorial, but Joe said no. Only one man refused to listen.

It was Jimmy who first spotted Senator Robert Byrd from West Virginia, standing in the rain outside the church along with all the others who had come to pay their respects. Jimmy brought Senator Byrd inside to meet Joe in the vestibule, and the two men shook hands. Joe disagreed with Senator Byrd on many things, but the look on Joe's face when he saw this old lion of the Senate, drenched through his clothes, was beyond politics.

As the boys recovered and Joe maintained his bedside vigil, it became clear that Joe would soon have to make a decision about what to do next. He was candid with any reporter who asked him about it: "Delaware can get another Senator, but the boys can't get another father," he told the *Wilmington News Journal*. The swearing-in ceremony took place in the hospital. Joe refused to leave the boys, so the Secretary of the Senate, Frank Valeo, came to Wilmington to administer the oath. The hospital staff set aside a room for us, and Beau and Hunt were rolled in on their hospital beds.

It was a mournful scene: Joe raising his right hand and taking the oath, standing over a makeshift lectern in a corner room of Saint

Francis Hospital; Hunter, up and moving, in his short pants; Beau still in traction. In his brief remarks after having been sworn in, Joe said he wasn't sure he would be more than a one-term Senator, or that he would even finish out his term. Watching him, I struggled with a confused, displaced sense of pride: my brother, the Senator, assuming his role amid ruins. The whole scene felt like a ghoulish parody of our dreams and ambitions.

Not long after, Joe told me it—Washington, DC, the Senate—wouldn't work. It would mean taking the boys away from their only remaining family. Either the boys could commute, or he could. The boys needed stability. The house in Chevy Chase that Joe and Neilia had purchased was no longer a viable option. He and Jimmy started to make other plans. They talked about moving to Vermont, and maybe Joe would start a law practice in a little village near Sugarbush Mountain. Joe told Jimmy to call the Governor to send a replacement for the Senate seat. That was it; the end.

One of the only reasons Joe Biden didn't become a small-town Vermont lawyer, then, is because of the kindness and persistence of his soon-to-be Senate colleagues. They wouldn't leave him alone. Senator Mike Mansfield of Montana and Senator Kennedy, in particular, reached out to him to dissuade him from resigning. "Just try it," they said. "Six months. See how it feels."

"Val, what do you think? Can I really take this job? What about the boys? How can I do this to them? I just don't know how we'll ever make it work."

I didn't second-guess my answer to him, which seemed to arrive out of some clear place inside me I wasn't aware of: "You have to try, Joe." Sometimes, the bigger the stakes, the clearer the choice.

For starters, I thought he owed it to the country. Maybe that sounds grandiose, but we had been raised with a strong sense of duty, and Joe had run—and won—on important issues: Stopping the war in Vietnam. Asserting Civil Rights. Preserving the environment, at a time in history when few even mentioned it. Voters had responded because they, too, believed. Those issues were just as pressing after the accident as they were the morning of December 18, when everything was right in our own little world.

Second, I thought Joe owed it to Neilia. We had just done the impossible, and Neilia gave everything she had to help him fight that battle and get him elected. I couldn't imagine what she would have thought if he had just walked away.

And finally, he needed a reason to get up in the morning. Joe Biden needed a cause, something to devote himself to that was bigger than him. That was part of his identity, was integral to who he was. If he disavowed that part of himself during his greatest moment of crisis, he might truly be left with nothing.

"Look," I said. "I can help with the boys. I'll move in. You have to do this, Joe."

There was no big discussion about my moving in, nothing that felt particularly heroic about it. I just said I was coming, and that I would stay until it was time to go. Joe's simple head nod settled it. Bruce and I moved in.

Hunter was released from the hospital first. Mom and Joe kept vigil in the hospital with Beau—together during the day, Joe presiding alone at night. Mom's presence allowed Joe to get out for a bit, walk around, clear his head. Jimmy, his sentinel, went with him. I brought Hunter back to "Aunt Val's place" until his brother was released and we could all be together as a family.

Little Hunter was quiet in the back seat that first night out of the hospital as I drove him home in my red Opal station wagon. I kept talking and talking, trying to fill the silence, trying to be fun and upbeat, hoping to hold back the darkness that seemed to be pressing in on us. But I knew I wasn't getting through. When I sneaked a look back at that sweet, nearly three-year-old child gazing out the window, I realized I hadn't the foggiest idea what was going on inside his mind. He was neither demanding nor sullen. He was simply quiet. Processing. There was nothing I knew how to say to make him feel secure. As we neared my apartment, I quelled my terror and helplessness, smiled wide, and brought him inside. He slept with me in the bed, the two of us curled around each other like little animals. The next day, I took him to Woods Road to be with Mom-Mom and Dada. I needed to clean out my apartment to get ready for the move.

It wasn't until late January that the doctor approved Beau's release. By then, we were all set up at Joe and Neilia's house, an old colonial on North Star Road. That's what we called the house—North Star. In the middle of the split-level staircase, there was a small sitting room that was going to be Aunt Val's room.

All of a sudden, I had a lot of time on my hands. Even during the madness of the 1972 campaign, I had kept my teaching job at Wilmington Friends, but now I resigned. Just like that, I went from a childless, working teacher and campaign manager to a full-time, stay-at-home almost-mom. Jimmy, for his part, dropped everything and started converting the room above the pool house on the North Star property into a little apartment. He wanted to stay as close as possible to Joe and to the boys. Mom and Dad were on hand to help every day, and the boys spent regular nights at Mom-Mom and Dada's house.

This was also around the time Jack Owens came back into my life in a profound way. When Neilia and Amy died, he dropped everything, too. He and Jimmy were a tag team, and in the process became best friends. No matter what Joe wanted to do, whether it was to catch a last-minute plane for a speaking engagement, or just sit through a midnight movie, Jack was there. Between the two of them, they made sure Joe was never alone with his thoughts. *I'm still not crazy about this guy,* I thought. *But he's got a good heart.* Shattered into many pieces, the Bidens began to pull together and assemble into a new shape.

A woman, as designed by nature, is a leader.

As a mother, she is the ultimate leader.

She is the first presence, the first consciousness; the first source of sustenance, the first source of inspiration, the first source of awareness, the first teacher.

8

BEAU AND HUNTER

I didn't grow up dreaming about having babies. It was an acquired taste. I guess I'd assumed I would get married someday, and children would just be a natural by-product of that union. When Neilia died, I was twenty-seven years old. I was no one's idea of a natural mom.

Suddenly, I was a temporary mother to my brother's boys. I was terrified of not doing right by them, but I had only one option. So I turned fear into determination. I swore a silent promise to Neilia: *I won't let you down. I will take good care of your boys and love them with all my heart.*

I had no maternal instincts to fall back on, and I had hardly even babysat growing up, so I learned on the fly. In my crash course on mothering, and being Aunt Val on a full-time basis, I had a few invaluable supporters. Chief among them was Maureen Greco, a close friend from high school. She and her husband lived half an hour's drive from North Star with her two boys, Matt and Jimmy, who were always ready to explore with Hunter and Beau. Maureen helped me navigate the challenges of raising two young boys who I knew were on lend-lease to me. She and I would map out adventures, as organized as a field trip to the site of the Battle of the Brandywine, or as easy as letting them run around the yard or the neighborhood. Later, when they were older, they would bike together to the swimming hole. Maureen has remained a constant in my life, even as she has migrated to the opposite end of the political spectrum and become a proud Republican. To me, she will always be a Biden.

I was uncertain about my future and where I was going, but I did my best not to show it, and the boys were incredibly kind and patient with me as I tried out my new role. I never wanted to take the place of Neilia, and I always hoped that Joe would find love again. I never aspired to be Mommy; I was Aunt Val, the master of ceremonies during our days together.

Early on during this new world of ours, Joe bought me a Jeep. I had never paid too much attention to cars, even though our childhood had been a procession of shiny new ones from the dealership, but I'd always liked Jeeps. I liked the shape, the zippy way they handled, and how high they sat. The Jeep became command central for the boys and me, the home base from which we launched a thousand expeditions. We were explorers and adventurers, with Davy Crockett raccoon-tailed hats, baseball bats, goggles, and roller skates at the ready in the Jeep's "way back." With our trusty Tang, the drink of astronauts, in our thermoses, we were ready for wherever the road took us.

Indeed, the Jeep took us many places over those years—especially back and forth to Woods Road (always our name for Mom-Mom and Dada's house). It took us on "doodlebug" picnics, to the public library, and to the zoo. It took us to Mass, to playdates, and to swimming lessons. It was a magic carpet. As we rode along, we would tell tales, share real secrets, and make wishes that we would bring to life.

From their perch in the Jeep, the boys had an ideal view into passing cars. They would notice something in a neighboring car, and we would be off, creating a story about its occupants and where they were going.

The radio was often on, playing the popular music of the day. They loved "American Pie," which was seemingly on the radio every ten minutes, and they bopped along to Jim Croce's "Bad, Bad Leroy Brown." The boys would belt out their version of the lyrics, which didn't always sync with the real ones. I would fish in my "pocket purse," as they called my handbag, for my hairbrush, which became their microphone.

During the summer of 1973, as Joe and I were taking the boys to five o'clock Mass at Saint Joseph's one evening, we saw a man cross the street in front of us as we waited at a stoplight. He probably looked older than his years, and he had a severe limp, dragging his leg behind him as he walked. I looked at my brother and grabbed his arm.

"Joe," I said, "I bet that man's mom and dad love him every bit as much as we love our boys. But you were able to afford the treatment they needed, and his parents probably couldn't. He'll struggle with that his entire life." (Beau had a pin put in his leg after the accident.) "That's not right," I said. "You have to do something about that, Joe."

My brother looked at me and replied, "I knew you were a Democrat."

Joe traveled a lot that first year. He did everything he could so he didn't have to walk back into his bedroom alone, without Neilia. I didn't change his bedsheets for weeks, so there was still some scent of her on them. We didn't discuss it until at some point Joe said, "You know, you can change the sheets now." I did.

When he started commuting to Washington, the first thing Joe did was buy a Cadillac. It was a huge, brown, preposterously fancy car, but Joe had good reasons for it. The back seat was spacious enough for him to spread out and do his work on the way to and from DC while still leaving room for Hunter and Beau on any day they wanted to join him. Hunter and Beau had a "get out of jail free" card; if they ever said, "Daddy could we come?," along they went.

This was also the era of early car phones, which, at the time, took up nearly the whole console. Joe kept one right by him in that Cadillac so the boys could call him whenever they felt like it. "Daddy, there's a rainbow outside," Beau would tell him. "Mom-Mom is going to take me on a pony ride today," Hunter might report.

"That's great, honey." No matter where he went, Joe made sure the boys knew they could always reach Daddy.

Soon, he began taking the train because it made the trip shorter, though it was still about two hours each way. Joe became Amtrak Joe, the young widower, single father, and Senator who commuted back and forth from Washington to his boys in Wilmington. The train delivered Daddy to work and then home, safe, where he could kiss his boys good night and read them a book, or be there for them in the morning to drop them off at school. A lot of politicians espouse family values, but Joe lived them—every night he was on the train home, the sun already setting.

The other Senators also took care of Joe; they treated him with the same kindness and care that we did. They didn't coddle him, of course, because he didn't want to be coddled. But Joe's new colleagues played their role in bringing him back into the world. They did everything they could to keep him engaged in the work. There was much more collegiality in those days than there is now. The rancor and the bile that characterize the Senate now was unknown—or at least un-common. Senator Hubert Humphrey called Joe every day for at least a year, often just to ask, "How you doing?"

Hunter and Beau became regulars in the Senate buildings. When-ever they went with Daddy to work, or needed to attend some formal event, I dressed them in short suits, knee socks, and saddle shoes. They hated those outfits and couldn't wait to get back into their OshKoshes and Timberlands, but they got to know those halls as well as they knew Mom-Mom and Dada's house.

Those were uncertain days, but we felt our way through. There was a vast wilderness in front of each of us—the children without Mommy and their sister, Joe without Neilia and Amy, and me, trying to figure out how best to nurture a pair of three- and four-year-old boys. None of us was quite sure what the future held. We knew that all we could do was "the next right thing." No one could predict what we'd be called upon to do, but we'd do our best.

You can say *I'll be there for you* all you want, but when the chips are down, it's what you do that defines you. We didn't waste time ask-ing Joe how he felt, because it was obvious. We just got down to the business of family, which is the business of giving someone you love exactly what they need without them having to ask.

The way it worked in our family was that whoever could do it at the time—whatever it was that needed to be done—did it. No drama, no heroics, no keeping score, no quid pro quo. Sometimes one of us carried a heavier load than the others, but it didn't matter; we trusted one another to give our best, and never second-guessed. The expres-sion we used was "You don't count the change."

Jimmy was always loaded down with toy trucks, airplanes, and candy. He would toss the boys into the air or into the pool, only to be met with gales of laughter and cries of "Uncle Jimmy . . . more, more!" Somehow, he always had more to give. Jimmy is among the most generous people in the world; he understands that if you have to ask, it's too late.

Frankie was fresh out of high school, still a kid himself. He often stopped by with his friends Stu and Wayne, and they would play football with the boys. The boys adored Frankie; he was charming, playful, and full of mischief, like so many youngest boys of the family are.

Frankie was just that much younger than Joe, Jim, and me (he was eight years my junior), which put him in a different generation—the Age of Aquarius, as opposed to the Age of Motown. What started out in his youth as edgy, bold, carefree indulgences grew steadily into controlling demons. He got caught in the snares of addiction.

Frankie has struggled much of his life with "the drink," as we Irish say, and sometimes he is more successful than others. But even so, he has a gift—he is like a pied piper of sorts. People always follow him and bathe in the warmth he reflects back. Just as with Hunter and Beau back then, and the kids he tries to help find their way into recovery now, Frankie is a source of light and a beacon of hope. Despite his own struggles, he never, ever gives up, nor will he allow those he loves to give up. He is the very definition of an optimist and a warrior in his own right, and I love him.

The shared understanding that there would be no bleeding hearts, no "look what I'm doing for you," and no martyrdom is what made things work at North Star. Everyone involved was receiving some healing from the arrangement, and that's exactly what we did. We began to heal—together.

At night, when Hunt and Beau had trouble sleeping, I would listen to the muffled pitter-patter of their footie pajamas as they made their way from their room, down the dark of the hallway, down the three steps to the landing, and up one step to my room. "Here comes Paddle Feet," I would whisper to myself. Silently, they would climb into bed, one of them lying across the top, the other at the bottom. I would lie awake for a minute, listening to the sound of their breathing, before slipping back to sleep.

One warm spring day in 1973, just months after the accident, the boys and I went to visit Roy Wentz, the finance chair for "Biden for Senate," and his daughter, Piper, who had been a student of mine at Friends (and remains a friend). Three seconds after getting out of our Jeep, Beau was on his belly in the driveway, calling for me to come over. "Look, Aunt Val, look," although in his baby pronunciation, it came out "Wook, Aunt Bal, wook." His nose was pressed on top of a fuzzy caterpillar making its way across the driveway.

I got down to look at it, too, the strange thing working across the expanse of the Wentz driveway on its own time. Seeing the wonder in Beau's face knocked something loose in me, readjusted my axis. I felt the world tilt back upright, if only for a minute. When that boy looked up at me, awe and trust in his eyes, everything became a little brighter. Tears surprised me, this time of thanksgiving. I got to be their Aunt Val. *Neilia, I know you are watching. I promise I won't disappoint you.*

That first year in North Star, as I settled in as Aunt Val, was also the last year for Bruce and me. Just as the campaign had been the glue that once held us together, it was our shared grief and commitment to the family that kept us intact for those final months. He was with me when I moved to North Star with Joe and the boys the January after the accident, but time had run out on us to make things right in our marriage. We put off doing anything about it for yet another day. There already was too much turmoil, and we didn't want to add to it.

Bruce was good to the boys, and amenable to the arrangement, but the distance between us grew wider every day. He opened a pizzeria in Newark called Red Fingers, and we barely saw each other.

I think we both knew, on some level, that we shouldn't have gotten married, but it had been "the next step" after dating throughout most of college. In those days, there was no "living together" for many of us who were raised Catholic. There were no tryouts—it was either the altar or the exit ramp. We tried for four years, but we just couldn't love each other the way we both needed. The fault was as much mine as his (if there was any fault to be found at all). From the start, I was not courageous enough to take charge, to listen to my inner voice about this marriage. I knew the answer all along, but I was just waiting for someone else—my brothers, Mom, Dad, sister-in-law, a friend— to step in and pull me out.

Troubled, Bruce and I went together to my priest, Father Szupper, for guidance. I'd known Father for years; he was the chaplain of the Saint Thomas More Oratory, the Catholic organization at the University of Delaware. He was a close confidant and exactly what a Catholic priest is supposed to be—not a pontificating hypocrite but a genuinely empathic and spiritual man who guided the troubled souls in his care with wisdom, humility, and wry humor. At those sessions, it became clear to both of us that we were leagues apart. The solution was equally clear, but I struggled in my heart with the thought of becoming a divorced Catholic.

It was Father Szupper who told me, to my surprise, that I *had* to get divorced. "If you do not get divorced, you will cease to exist," he said. "Valerie Biden as you know her will be dead, and you will not recognize her."

When I sputtered in surprise about the church's position on divorce, he said: "The Catholic Church survived the Renaissance Popes. It will certainly survive Valerie Biden getting a divorce."

When we finally separated, there was no bitterness between us, just emptiness—two good people who had made the wrong decision in the first place. Immediately after the Christmas of 1973, he moved out. My brothers gave me a round-trip ticket to Florida and arranged for me to stay for a week, alone, in a friend's apartment. The purpose of the trip was twofold: to get me some sun and strength, and to keep me from having to witness the actual departure.

I came home rested, but full of trepidation. I knew I had made the right decision, but it was still difficult. It was my first complete failure. I was embarrassed that I had made such a big mistake in the most important decision I'd ever made. I believed I had disgraced my family—they assured me I had not—but I did disappoint myself. At only twenty-eight, I was certain my life was over.

In walking through our collective darkness, all Joe and I had was one another's hands to hold. There was no guarantee that light would appear at any point, but imperceptibly at first, and then unmistakably—it dawned on all of us. The cure lay in what we gave to one another even when it seemed we had nothing left to give.

In the spring of 1974, Joe decided we should do some renovations at North Star—mostly to expand my small bedroom off the first landing to make room for a desk, TV, fireplace, and my own bathroom.

I was all for it. My king-sized bed currently took up just about the entire room, but with an extension coming, I needed more furniture. One spring Saturday morning, Joe, the boys, and I took a trip to the best furniture store in Wilmington, about an hour before they opened. Joe pulled out a stopwatch and said, game-show style, "Okay, Val— you have one hour to go through two showroom floors and pick any piece you want. Any price, but just one."

The boys and I raced, giggling, through the empty aisles, Hunter and Beau calling me eagerly: "Aunt Val, pick this one!" "Aunt Val, how about this?"

In the final minutes, I was stuck between a lemon-yellow upholstered Queen Anne chair on the one hand and a blue cushioned club chair on the other.

In the end, I chose the blue—and today, the chair lives in my daughter Casey's home. She adamantly refuses to replace the worn fabric or the sagging springs. To Casey, it's the chair of my own young motherhood, even though it was as a substitute mother. It's a family heirloom of sorts, and now that Casey is a new mom herself, she wants to keep the spirit close at hand. She sits in that chair with her own baby girls, holding memories of her mother close.

Pondering this period of my life, in which sorrow and joy were so closely entwined, death and life, I have trouble extracting the lesson. In my speeches, I work to distill whatever I've learned in my own life into something tidy, something that I can hand to listeners, like a flyer. But the hardest and most meaningful times in our lives resist this sort of moralizing, because they contain everything. Focus on the joy, and you will be lying about the pain; focus on the pain, and you will be telling half the truth.

What I do know is that these years highlight the vagaries of fate. Because if it weren't for the accident, and for the ensuing years I spent as Aunt Val, I never would have married Jack, the man with whom I've spent the last forty-six years of my life. I, too, was shattered in those days, and even though I hadn't wanted to draw any attention to myself, I am sure my pain and shame were obvious. So much of my own life had fallen away, so quickly. I didn't talk to Joe about what I was feeling, because I deemed that to be too self-centered. Joe was the one who was bleeding. *Grow up, Val,* I said to myself. *Your brother just lost his daughter and his wife, the love of his life, his essence, and you're moping because you made a mistake? Stop!*

For me to truly mend myself took time and a man I initially saw as an arrogant pain in the neck—albeit a handsome, green-eyed one. He grew to be my steady friend, a kind soul who, after a rocky start, went on to win my heart.

The world is truly more beautiful, more vibrant, more forgiving, with you in it.

Thank you, my Love.

9

JACK OWENS

A Love Story

Everyone understood Jack and I didn't get along, but after the accident, he became part of our team, and I accepted it. We treated each other like workers clocking in on opposite shifts. When he walked in, I walked out. Our focus was Joe and the boys, so we had quit bickering, and we quit making Joe choose.

One summer evening, Joe called me from the airport. "Look, Val, I hate to ask you this," he said, "but I don't know what else to do. I just got off the plane. Jimmy and Jack are here, and I know it's your house, too, but can I bring Jack home for dinner?"

I said, "Sure, Joe, don't be silly, of course you can invite him to dinner." I cringed a little, thinking that Joe should never have had to ask that kind of question anymore. I made one of my staples, boiled chicken breasts. I wasn't much of a cook then, and to this day, my dream house doesn't have a kitchen. Joe came in with Jimmy and Jack. We sat the two boys down, and we ate together.

After dinner, the phone in the library rang; it was for Joe. Jimmy had a girl he was seeing at the time, and he excused himself to go see her. The boys asked, "Aunt Val, can we go outside and catch lightning bugs?" They scurried out, leaving Jack and me alone at the kitchen table.

Jack cleared his throat. "Thank you very much, Val," he said. "The chicken was very good."

I laughed. "Jack, it was rubber chicken."

"Maybe I was just hungry, then," he said. A pause. "Thank you, anyway." Some more stupid banter, and then suddenly we both started laughing, the absurdity of my need to contradict him finally dawning on us. Over the next few weeks, we started talking, and it was like a balloon had popped. I hadn't realized how badly I needed someone to confide in. My marriage had failed, I was living alone with my brother's kids, I wasn't teaching, I had no idea what the future held—it all started pouring out of me. He sat and listened.

Soon, we talked whenever he came over and was waiting around for Joe to arrive. He sensed I was heartbroken, but he never said *poor thing*. He just made me feel comfortable.

These moments with Jack were the only time I allowed myself to let my guard down. Maybe it was because we had initially been so up front about disliking each other, maybe it was because I needed someone to talk to outside the family, or maybe it was because of his understanding and kindness, but I was vulnerable with Jack in a way I hadn't been with anybody. It wasn't until years later that it occurred to me: I talked to him the way I talked to Joe. He was warm, alert, and sensitive. He saved my life.

Sometimes love sneaks up on you. And that's how my love for Jack unfolded—it stole over me while I wasn't looking. I was so comfortable around him that I didn't even stop to ask myself how I looked. If I was interested in a man, I'd usually at least put on mascara, but with Jack, it never even occurred to me to run a comb through my hair when he was coming over. My guard was down; my truest self was exposed. That's who Jack fell in love with, and that's the part of me that fell in love with Jack. The deepest part of me.

Jack came to terms with it first. In early spring 1974, the boys were at Mom-Mom and Dada's, and Jack came over to meet Joe after he got back from DC. Joe's train was late, so Jack suggested that he and I run out to grab some pizza. When Jack helped me put on my coat, he brushed my shoulder. Years later, he would tell me that he felt as if an electric shock had gone through him when he did. He was in love with me, and he began planning how to capture my heart. He was careful with me and took it slowly—I was skittish, especially about him.

Still, I was so oblivious to my own feelings that it took someone else to point out the obvious. One morning, while I was dropping the kids off with her, Mom cornered me. "What's going on with you and Jack?"

"What do you mean what's going on? There's nothing."

"Valerie, you are dead in love with him."

"Mom, what are you talking about? You're crazy."

"I know my daughter. You are in love with him."

Tears sprang to my face, startling me. My body knew it; my heart knew it. It was true, even if I was too afraid to acknowledge it. Falling in love again hadn't been in my plans. When Joe got back on his feet, I was going to move to California with my friend Michele. Maybe I'd start teaching again; maybe I'd meet someone else out there, but I wasn't waiting around for it.

I laughed at myself through my tears. "I guess you're right, Mom," I said. "Now what do I do?" I was gun-shy, and didn't want to make another huge mistake, hurt someone else.

Once again, it was Mom who prodded me into action. "Get up,

Valerie," she said. "Take a chance. He's crazy about you. And you, you're in love with him."

We sidled up to each other carefully. Jack and I were both still raw from our prior relationships, hesitant. He had a young son, Jade, whom he was traveling to Pittsburgh to see. Needless to say, he didn't want to fall in love with me, either. Joe and Jimmy were his only friends in Delaware, and he didn't want to lose them if things didn't work out between us.

Eventually, we let love ruin our plans. I truly believe it was the only way we could have fallen for each other—over a kitchen table, my hair wild. If we had gotten dressed up in our finery, I don't think it would have worked. We would have been too guarded, too proud.

On August 8, 1974, the day Nixon resigned, I was legally divorced. Now I could finally look to the future. This time, I was old enough to know what kind of future I wanted: one with Jack.

Neither of us wanted a formal engagement; we just wanted to get married. That Christmas, we started talking about our wedding date. I suggested May, which was the Blessed Mother's month, and spring suggested new beginnings. He said sure. We sealed the deal with a kiss, and when he left North Star, I was happier than I'd ever been.

However, that Saturday night, I barely slept. May was just five months away. It was too much, too soon. I couldn't uproot our lives like that. As the night wore on, I thought I had been given a choice that was too difficult to make. If I married Jack, that would mean starting our own family. It would mean leaving the boys. How could I marry him and leave the boys without a mom for a second time? They'd been through so much. It just wasn't possible. By morning, I had worked myself into a frenzy.

When Jack came to get me for nine o'clock Mass, he found me standing at the top of the stairs, splotchy-faced and wearing my robe.

"Why aren't you ready?" he asked.

"I can't marry you," I said.

"What?"

"I can't marry you," I kept saying.

Jack, of course, was bewildered. "What the hell happened in the last nine hours?" What had happened was that I had come completely undone. I couldn't choose between living with the boys or living with him, I explained. Jack—my champion—walked up the steps and embraced me. "Is that all there is? Heck, that's no problem." I buried my head in his chest gratefully. "We will figure this out," he said. "We can all live together until it's time we don't. I will never ask you to choose—I choose you and the boys." And in choosing Jack, I also chose his son, Jade, who, although he lived with his mother and stepdad, would also become family to me.

In light of this, we decided that May was too soon—I needed more time. "We have the rest of our lives," Jack said. He made it easy. Jack was a strong Irishman who wanted his own house and his new wife to himself, but he truly loved the boys, and wanted them to be happy and well even more. He could wait, he told me.

One pretty summer day in June 1975, he asked me on a date. I said I didn't feel like it. I was tired, my hair was dirty, I'd had a full day with the boys. "No no," he insisted, "let's go." He had a reservation at a cute little place called the Lobster Pot. "Nothing fancy . . . let's just go out." I kept putting him off; I would have to take the boys over to Mom and Dad on Woods Road, and I just wanted to stay in for the night. "It's important to me," he finally said. I shrugged and said okay, and off we went.

I looked at him when we were finally seated at our table. I was still a little cranky. "Okay," I said, looking at him sardonically. "So what's so important about tonight?"

He reached over, took my hand, and said, "I want to make sure you're going to marry me." He handed me a box containing a stunning diamond ring. He'd worked it all out ahead of time: I learned later that he'd even gone to my father to formally ask for his approval the old-fashioned way. "What the hell took you so long?" was my dad's response.

In the fall of 1975, as our October wedding day approached, Jack and I were euphoric. It seemed impossible to both of us, a miracle beyond probability, that we could suddenly be this happy. One day, right before we got married, Jack in particular was so elated that I had to check him.

I remember him going on about everything that was going to happen for us—the children we were going to raise, the life we were going to build. We were in his green Chevy convertible, stopped at the corner of Weldon and Shipley; the sun was setting. Jack was positively beaming, looking like a man who had won the lottery. I shared his excitement, but deep in my stomach I also felt a tight knot of fear: How could I, or anyone, live up to these expectations?

"Jack, Jack, Jack, stop," I interrupted. "Look. I love you, I adore you, I would walk off the face of the earth for you. But slow down a minute." I could feel him putting me on a pedestal, and I knew that when you do that to someone, the only thing left for them to do is fall. I needed him to understand: I couldn't be his superwife, supermom, superchef. "Tell you what, here's the deal," I told him. "You pick *one* room in the house where you want me to be great, and I'll be great in there." He thought about that for a minute. In the end, he didn't pick the kitchen. If he dared complain about having the same thing for dinner again, I would tartly tell him, "You picked the wrong room, bud."

We were married on October 11, 1975, in the United Nations chapel in front of sixty-three people. We "ran away" from Delaware to New York so we wouldn't have to have a political wedding. We wanted something personal and small, with only close friends.

As I said to Jack in our vows, "I come to you filled with dreams and fears, triumphs and disappointments, variegated shades of light and darkness." But Jack's smile beat back the shadows. I had never felt a joy so pure.

We then immediately boarded a McAllister tugboat (Jack's sister had married a McAllister) for our reception. We cruised around New York Harbor so we could pass by the *QE2*, a cruise ship named for Queen Elizabeth.

The next morning my brothers and their dates came to see Jack and me off on the *QE2*. Jack had made all the honeymoon arrangements months before and asked if I wanted to sail to Paris. "Did you just say, 'Would you like to sail to Paris?'" I repeated back to Jack. "Are you kidding? Yes." But I did wonder where on the boat we would be sleeping, so that morning I asked him, "When we look out the windows, will I be able to see fish?" He said, "No, it's too dark under the water." That made me assume we were in the ship with the round windows belowdecks. As it turned out, Jack had reserved the penthouse, complete with our own private balcony. My brothers had sent flowers and champagne up to our room. I stood on the balcony, and they waved to me from below.

We returned from our honeymoon on Halloween night. Joe, with Beau and Hunter, who were dressed in their costumes, met us at the airport. When the boys saw us, they were hesitant—until I got down and held out my arms, and a pirate and a devil flew into them. Joe had bought a new home, and we all moved in together—Joe, Jack, me, Hunter, and Beau. A crowded house, you might think (that's why we ended up calling it "the Station," for all the comings and goings), but for us, it was second nature.

I remember my mom always saying that when something bad happened, something good would come out of it if you looked hard enough. Well, the most terrible thing imaginable had happened—and out of that tragedy, I, like Joe, grew unafraid to love once more.

Jack made me a believer—in myself. Old wives' tales say a woman marries her father. Not me: I married a combination of my mom and Jimmy Biden—passionate and compassionate; inscrutable and intense.

Bravery is a manifestation of courage.

Bravery is more than facing down the enemy; it is also facing up to ourselves. Courage is a personal measure—not a political statement—that lives in each one of us. It is sometimes fleeting, always vulnerable, and is as essential to life as breathing.

The quiet personal courage of just getting up and putting one foot in front of the other, like millions of us do each day, is no less heroic than the more public courage of affirming values not always embraced by the popular majority.

Whatever form it takes in each of us, it is indomitable.

10

NEW BEGINNINGS

J ack and I never lived together before we got married. So when we moved into the new house, "the Station" on Montchanin Road, as an unconventional family of five (me, Jack, Joe, and the boys), it was the first time we'd all shared a roof.

It was a grand old home that needed work, but it proved perfect for us. It had two separate bedroom wings that connected on the second floor and a common first floor. I don't know how we managed it, with two lions in one house—Joe and Jack—but somehow we never bickered. It wasn't because we were milquetoasts or saints; we were just committed to the concept of family. As when we were kids, if there were any misunderstandings, they were cleared up quickly.

Jack and I decided that while we lived with Joe, our first home purchase would be a beach house—an investment property we would rent out during summer and use ourselves in the spring and fall. Jack was an ocean boy—his summers had been spent in his parents' home on the beach in Westhampton. I had always loved the ocean, too, and some of my most peaceful moments in life have come from staring out at the waves. The immensity of the ocean, the constancy of the waves—something in the rhythm and vastness of it all encourages me to relinquish my grip.

Jack and I found a duplex in Beach Haven, New Jersey, which we furnished with refurbished tables and reupholstered couches we'd scored from secondhand stores. We rented the bottom floor year-round to a young couple, but kept the top apartment for ourselves. Beach Haven was completely new to both of us, a place to make new memories. Hunter and Beau had their own little toolboxes and paint-brushes, and we spent almost every weekend that spring getting it ready for our first rental season.

It took no time for Jack and the boys to grow even closer. He was already a familiar face, someone they'd seen in their kitchen countless times before with their dad and Uncle Jimmy. Now he was a constant, and all the better for it. Just as I was Aunt Val, he became Uncle Jack. The four of us set off on great adventures together.

One day we went to the natural history museum in Philadelphia. It was a Sunday morning, and we sat in the front row of a tiny room, with Beau on my lap, Hunter on Jack's. A man walked in with a boa constrictor wrapped around his entire body, and I felt Beau cling to me in fear. Beau looked up at me: Was that thing called a *Beau-a constrictor*? I nodded yes. "From now on, Aunt Val," he whispered, wide-eyed, "call me Joseph."

Meanwhile, Joe was still picking himself back up from losing Neilia. Between mourning her and getting accustomed to his new life in the Senate, his dating life was put on the back burner. He dated a few nice women—but never found "the one." So there is some sweet symmetry in the fact that while Jack and I were just starting to plan our wedding in the summer of 1975, Joe got off an airplane at the

New Castle County Airport and looked up to see Jill Jacobs. That first time he saw her, she was, quite literally, larger than life: Jill smiled down at him from a poster advertising New Castle County Parks. Joe was smitten. Who was the girl in the photograph?

Around the same time, our brother Frankie had been urging Joe to call an acquaintance of his. "You'll like her, Joe," he joked. "She has no interest in politics." Imagine Joe's surprise when he went reluctantly to meet Frankie's friend—only to be greeted by the smiling face from the New Castle County Parks poster.

I don't quite remember the first time Joe told me about dating Jill, mostly because when Joe falls in love with someone, he never shuts up about them. What I remember most about her introduction into his life was that he started smiling again. Really smiling. The difference was written all over him. He stood taller, and it seemed as if the little pool of sadness that sat in the center of his heart had begun to shrink. He was in love again. For that alone, I loved this woman before I ever laid eyes on her.

Laying eyes on her actually took awhile. Jill had been married before, and she was cautious, as I had been with Jack, about moving too quickly into something she might regret. The stakes were that much higher with Joe; he had two boys who had already lost a mother. Plus, there were a lot of potential deal-breakers on the table for anyone looking to become a part of Joe's life. What if the boys didn't like her? That would be the end. What if I didn't? Ditto. Not to mention Mom-Mom.

I understood all of this, even as I wished I could make her understand how much her presence in Joe's life had already meant to me. I was prepared to love her.

I could tell Joe was worried about what Jack and I might think the first time she stood us up on a double date. He felt that he had to explain her reasons, to make sure we knew she wasn't cold-shouldering us. Ultimately, we ended up having to reschedule that first date three or four times. But despite Joe's worries, I thought I understood where she was coming from, and I respected it.

It seemed pretty clear to me that this Jill Jacobs was not flaky. She was careful. When she did show up, she wanted us to know she was genuine and committed to doing the right thing. A lot of women in her position might have bum-rushed the family with a charm offensive—bought things for the boys, tried to compensate. Jill was wiser than that. She felt the gravity of the decision she would be making. In her reticence, I detected sincerity.

As I said before, when Joe loves someone, he makes you awfully sick of hearing about them, awfully fast. I'm pretty sure his nonstop hard sell of my unimpeachable virtues as the world's greatest sister had a lot to do with Jack's sour mood on that first blind date. And I'm willing to bet that Jill was getting as tired of hearing about *me* as I was about *her*. It comes from the best place inside his heart, but Joe's enthusiasm for his loved ones can make you want to reach for the fly swatter. Enough already, Joe.

So it was almost in spite of Joe that Jill and I finally met on our own terms. She came over to see me at the house. She was young and beautiful in bell-bottoms and a sweater, with long blond hair falling down her back. She had a quiet reserve about her. Given the long buildup to our meeting, I felt like we needed a joke to break the tension. I had made tuna fish salad, and I gestured toward it, calling to her as if she were a scared cat I was trying to coax into the house. She belly laughed, and that was the beginning.

Jill and Joe were married June 17, 1977, at the UN chapel, where Jack and I had wed. During the wedding ceremony, Hunter and Beau, seven and eight, stood up from the pews and took their place next to the two of them. None of them had discussed it, but the boys seemed to be silently declaring something—love, fealty. Jill was marrying all of them, and she was also marrying all of us. She became a Biden. Joe had a new love, I had a new sister-in-law, and the boys had a new mother in their lives. Watching the four of them from the pews, I was filled with joy—and a touch of pain.

Jill and I came from different worlds. She was younger than I, from Hammonton, New Jersey, and she had four younger sisters to my three brothers. As I told her once, "Jill, you speak girl and I speak boy." I am more direct, sometimes to a fault; Jill had learned to speak in a circuitous way that I sometimes had to decode.

I remember one moment when we started learning to speak each other's language. It was early on in their marriage, and we were preparing for some family get-together. She called me and asked, "Would you like to bring the potato salad?"

I paused. Because I grew up around men, this seemed almost like a trick question. Would I *like* to bring potato salad? Well, no. As I've always said, I'm not a cook, and my dream house doesn't have a kitchen. I was certain that I wouldn't like bringing potato salad in the slightest. But that didn't matter. Would I do it? Of course. I tried to explain myself to Jill.

"Oh," she said slowly, processing. "That's something I would say to my sisters." Then she laughed and said, "Val, you're bringing the potato salad. See you Sunday."

Over the years, we've become close friends and confidantes in addition to sisters-in-law. We are bound together by a rod of steel—commitment to Joe, the children, and the rigors of campaigning. Equally important, we are held together by ribbons—laughter, shared secrets, runaway trips to the beach with wine at the ocean's edge at dusk, makeup sessions at the Macy's counter, marathon shopping to find the perfect dress. Some of the ribbons that bind us are made of satin, some of twine, which could cause brush burns, but we made a commitment to always be honest. We made a deal at the beginning of our friendship: If we had a problem with each other, we would spit it out, not let it fester. We would fix it. She and I understand that above all other considerations—pride, hurt feelings—there is family. The whole is always greater than the individual parts. We are women of our word.

In September of 1976, our first daughter was born. Her full name is Valerie James Owens, but from the beginning, she was Missy, my bicentennial baby. Jack named her after his two best friends, me and Jimmy. I wanted Catherine Blythe, but once again, I lost naming rights. But this time, at least Jack bought me off with a present: he got the name; I got a new pair of shoes.

She was the perfect child—beautiful, like a baby doll that you would buy in a store—joyful, giving. I was in awe of her, with her big blue eyes and generous good nature. Hunter and Beau were enthralled by her. They would go near her and she would grab their fingers tightly and smile. They were convinced it was a secret message for them.

Beau was six years old when Missy was born, Hunter five. That one year's difference made Beau a little more introspective. His conscience, forever near the surface, constantly troubled him. One evening, I found him particularly upset. He was crying, and I held him close to soothe him. "What's the matter, honey? What's the matter with my big boy?"

"Aunt Val," he said, "Missy is the most beautiful baby in the world.

But Amy is my sister, and I'm supposed to love her best. Aunt Val, I feel so *awful*."

That was Beau at six, and that was Beau for the rest of his life—caring, tender, loving, and kind, duty-bound, always holding himself to a higher standard.

"Beauie," I said, "Amy sent you Missy to love and raise as your sister. She is your cousin, but she will always be an extraordinary gift that she and Mommy sent to you and Hunter. Keep loving Missy with all your heart, because you will be loving Amy then, too."

"Really, Aunt Val? Really?"

"Yes, Beau, really."

My first year of motherhood wasn't without bumps. Shortly after Missy's birth, I developed a condition that involved an imbalance in the way I processed sugar, resulting in extreme bouts of fatigue and debilitating headaches. I would wake up to my beautiful, joyful baby girl, kiss Jack goodbye as he left for work—and then crash. Not something you want to do with a five-month-old.

Because I was exhausted even after a full night's sleep, I was afraid I would pass out, stumble, or make a careless mistake that would harm the baby. So I would hurry to dress Missy, strap her in her car seat, and take her straight to Mom and Dad's home—a ten-minute drive. The moment I got there, I would literally push her into Mom's arms and proceed to fall asleep before my head even hit the pillow.

To add to the drama of the situation, doctors had trouble diagnosing my condition, which was concerning in itself. After many tests, they came up with hypoglycemia. It was kind of a catch-all diagnosis at the time: If you had any kind of unexplainable symptoms surrounding fatigue or headache, you usually were told you had hypoglycemia. In my case, though, it turned out to be accurate. My body was thrown off by my pregnancy and delivery—I was all of 104 pounds, and I'd just delivered a 10½-pound baby by cesarean after a long labor. Everything in my system was misfiring, and I needed a hard reset.

The treatment was diet, rest, and patience. My new, restricted diet cut out sugar—I would have sooner lived without water. If Jack is a gourmet diner, then I'm an ordinary eater: food has always been just fuel to me. In those years, I could live on pasta and red sauce, Tastykakes and Coke, ice cream and bread—and I often did. When I was pregnant and nursing, I was diligent about eating only nutrient-rich, healthy foods, but as soon as Missy was weaned, I went back to my evil ways. My girlfriends always wanted to kill me, because I could devour that black-and-white milkshake without fear of putting on weight, while they only had to look at it to gain a pound. Well, now the joke was on me: I could barely hold my head up. It took me months to readjust and establish a natural rhythm again.

These were my childbearing and child-rearing years, bursting at the seams with love and laughter, confusion and ambition, hope and heartbreak. Like many women at this stage of their lives, I found myself handed a proliferation of new roles. In the first third of my life, I had grown used to daughter, sister, Aunt Val, wife, and friend. During my middle years, I would also become mother, political advocate, business leader, and career educator.

Soon after Joe and Jill married, Jack and I started looking for a place of our own close by; it was time to move out of our shared home and let Joe, Jill, and the boys set up their own routine without Aunt Val, Uncle Jack, and Missy. Joe, always a prospector of properties, joined in, checking out homes on his own time. It's a wonder he wasn't arrested the night he found the Barn. Right up the street from where we all lived, there was a home that belonged to a widow named

Cookie Strange. Behind her home was a barn that she'd renovated with plans to rent. An enclosed brick courtyard opened onto the all-brick first floor. It was beautiful—three floors, with one side covered in windows. It was private, yet not isolated. I don't know how Joe found out about it, but he went to investigate the empty property one night on his way home from DC, thinking it might be perfect for us.

As a matter of fact, his investigation consisted of opening a window and letting himself in for a quick tour. While he was letting himself out, he bumped into Cookie, who had gone to see who her uninvited guest was. Oh, it was just her US Senator, for whom she had not voted, breaking into her barn.

Joe quickly introduced himself, although she already recognized him, and explained that he was looking for a place close to his home for his sister, Val, and brother-in-law, Jack, to live. He told her that her place was perfect. Would it be okay if he went to get Val right then so she could see the property? She had to think about it.

I was putting Missy down for the night when Joe came in and told me about the Barn, and that he had arranged for us to look at it the next day. The minute Jack and I saw it, we were all in. The boys loved it, too; their bus dropped them off there after school on the days that Jill was taking night classes. The boys now had three homes—their house, Mom-Mom and Dada's on Woods Road, and the Barn.

Transitioning from my full-time parenting role so that Jill could take over was hard—a fine line between easing the grip and dropping the reins altogether. It took deft hands for the handoff to work, but we did it.

I had to step back to let Jill fill the space. When the boys left for school in the morning, she was the one who handed them their lunch boxes. When they went to bed, she was the last one to kiss them good night. When they cried, she was the first one to hold them. That was

e was four and I was one when we visited our other's father, Pop Finnegan, at his office in the wspaper "morgue" at the *Scranton Tribune*.

Joe's hand on my shoulder—he was always close by—as we visited our Finnegan cousins in Scranton.

ad holding Jimmy, with Joe and me on the left, visiting some of our Scranton cousins in 1949.

Joe, around seven years old, when we lived in Scranton.

I was seven years old, wearing my first communion dress, with Joe and Jimmy in Delaware.

Dressed for the May proce sion at Holy Rosary School Claymont, Delaware, in thi grade.

A campaign postcard handed out to Delaware voters during the 1972 race: Joe and Neilia with Hunte Naomi ("Amy"), and Beau in the living room of their home. There was a recipe for Neilia's chicke casserole on the back of the card.

Beau, Hunter, and me in the fall of 1973, playing in the backyard of our home at North Star.

his family portrait was taken as an anniversary gift
or our parents in May 1974. *Left to right:* Joe, Jimmy,
rankie, and me with Hunter and Beau.

Frankie and me on October 10, 1975, the
night before Jack and I were married.

Jack and me on our honeymoon cruise to Paris on October 12, 1975.

Beau and Hunter with my daughter Miss at our new home, "The Barn," in 1977.

Addressing the victory celebration in Delaware on election night 1978, when Joe was reelected to th Senate.

Jack, Joe, and me at a campaign rally in Delaware in 1978.

Jack with Joe in his Senate office in the 1980s.

On June 9, 1987, we announced Joe was running for President at three separate events This one was in Washington, DC. (Photograph by Jim Harrison)

Holding four-year-old Casey while talking to a reporter in New Hampshire in August 1987.

Cuffe and Casey putting in a hard day's work making campaign posters at Biden for President headquarters in Wilmington in 1987.

Jimmy and me on the campaign trail for Joe in 1987. (Photograph by Jim Harrison)

Mom and Dad at our beach house in Fenwick Island in 1992.

Mom and Dad with Joe, Jimmy, me, and Frankie in 1990, in a family picture taken at Joe's house. (Photograph by Brad Glazier)

Jack and me whitewater rafting with Jimmy and Sara in Virginia in 1996.

Meeting Cuffe on the field after a football game in 1996 at Tower Hill High School in Wilmington.

the way it had to be for their family to grow. The first few weeks I woke up in the Barn and didn't hear those little voices calling "Aunt Val? Where are you?" were hard, for sure. But Jill and I were gentle with each other.

By the time Joe's reelection campaign rolled around in 1978, I was ready to jump back in. Joe never actually asked me if I was going to run his campaign. He just assumed I was on board, and he was right. The landscape was completely different in '78 than it had been in '72—you can really only shock the world once, and we'd already done that. "In 1970, you guys were Mickey Rooney and Judy Garland, putting on a show," a friend of mine said. "After the 1972 election, you were Giant Killers."

As a result, all the big shots who swatted us away in '72 suddenly demonstrated keen interest in helping Joe get reelected. Democrats from DC wanted a say in how we ran things and insisted that we needed a top-tier PR firm this time. We hired our first-ever media consultants on their recommendation and a Washington operative affectionately called Goose to "oversee" things. Goose was a good guy, a seasoned politician, but he must have discerned pretty quickly that things were going well without him, because I don't remember seeing him around very often. When he showed up, he would airily dish out directives, his feet up on the desk, without seeming to fuss much over whether those directives were carried out or not.

With Joe now running as an incumbent, I could sense some condescension coming from some of these professional politicos. Now the big guys were in town. Was his *sister* still really going to run the show?

Some of the men who came to work on the campaign—and they were almost always men—tried to treat me like a volunteer coordinator who had accidentally wandered into the wrong room. I remember a senior media advisor who patted me on the knee and said: "Don't you worry your pretty little head 'bout those radio buys—how 'bout you just concentrate on the volunteers." Never mind that I was the campaign manager.

At any rate, Joe set all these men straight more or less immediately. "Nothing gets sent out, not a single word, until Val okays it," he said firmly. "If she says no, assume it's me talking." If someone didn't understand that I was something more than Joe's tagalong younger sister, they either figured it out or didn't last long.

Joe won easily, with 58 percent of the vote, but he remembers it differently: he's said that winning that election felt more like an "escape" than a victory. It was a divisive year, and that particular campaign was a bracing education in the culture wars, which were then in their opening salvos. Conservatives were beginning to rally around a series of wedge issues, and 1978 offered a parade of them. One such issue was school prayer, and I remember an event in downstate Delaware at which someone raised it. Joe explained that he was against school-imposed prayer, outlining alternatives like silent prayer. To drive his point home, he went on to recite the entire Hail Mary. When he was finished, everyone in the audience was dumbfounded. Then Joe said, "That's what we say in my church. That's what a Catholic teacher says in his or her classroom. I know a lot of you aren't Catholic—you come from a variety of religious backgrounds. And that's exactly why we can't have teachers or school boards formulate one prayer for all students."

It was an example of Joe's genius for bringing an issue right down to people's fingertips, where they could touch and feel it. No one needed any further explanation as to why prayer in school might not be the best idea, and he did it by sharing a piece of himself.

Whenever the issue of school prayer came up in the years afterward, Joe would recite the Hail Mary prayer, and every time, you could hear a pin drop.

Another hot-button issue that cycle was court-ordered desegregation. Busing was scheduled to begin in Wilmington on September 9, two days after the primary, and was a topic of intense conversations.

To Joe, busing seemed like a classic example of good intentions running afoul of simple common sense. As was often the case, Joe felt conflicted, unable to find a home for his moral calculus on either side of the aisle. On the one hand, he detested segregation. He understood that the Black community had watched as Civil Rights gains were steadily stripped away, which left busing as that most difficult and loaded of political problems. Come out against it, in any form, and you risked telegraphing to Black voters that the dial was about to roll back on the very fragile progress that had been made in the name of Civil Rights.

At the same time, busing seemed to be breeding widespread dissatisfaction across racial lines. Busing was tearing at the bonds of community: when your school was an hour's ride on the bus from your home, people on your block and in your classroom were as good as strangers. It was an example of a terrible problem being addressed with a poor solution, and it was an issue about which no one wanted to back down.

During election season, the temperature on the issue was boiling hot. Joe's opponent, James H. Baxter Jr., was relentless in his demagoguery. But of the two Republican candidates in the primary, he was actually the more genteel; James Venema, who was to Baxter's right and lost the nomination, went after Joe and distorted his record even after the election.

Then as now, Joe never fell for the wedge issues of the day. He knew that social wedges were just that—tools, foreign objects meant only to pry something apart. In campaign literature and speeches, we focused, as ever, on common ground as opposed to division. When Joe won, it affirmed that we didn't need to hurl ourselves into the scrum, throwing elbows, to keep winning. We just had to keep being who we were.

Joe was back in the Senate, and now he considered it his home. We had two wins under our belt. After the unreality of the previous six years—our upset in '72, the shock of the crash, the reconfiguring of our lives, my marriage to Jack, Joe's to Jill, the birth of their daughter, Ashley—our new lives seemed solid to us in a new way. Joe was really a US Senator. And I was not just his sister, helping out: I was his career campaign manager.

There was a rhythm to those days, months, years. The work came in waves, then subsided. I found that I enjoyed the steady alternation of campaign season with long stretches at home. In between campaigns, I had Missy in 1976, Cuffe in 1979, and Casey in 1983.

I had the best of all worlds, I thought. Joe came up for reelection only every six years; we'd start to get ready a year and a half out, but we'd really be running the campaign full-time only from April to November. Then, the day after the election, Jack and I were on the first nonstop flight to anywhere warm, leaving the kids with Mom and Dad. And then, for the following four years, I'd have another baby and be home for them for a few years. Babies, Little League baseball games, dinners at Woods Road—I could step out of the political vortex and live a normal life.

The glue that held it all together was Mom and Dad. Woods Road was my children's second home during these middle years. Mom and Dad were warm, never intrusive, always at the ready. When the 1978 Senate election kicked into gear, claiming more and more of my time,

Missy spent more time there. Mom-Mom's imprint on her is indelible to this day. Later on, Cuffe and Casey had similar experiences. Just as they had with their children, Mom and Dad built their grandchildren's character, layer by layer, nurturing them from youth into adolescence and beyond.

I never pray for an outcome.
I pray for strength.

11

PRESIDENTIAL RUMBLINGS

In October 1979, I was watching the news while on bedrest in the last month of a tenuous pregnancy with my son, Cuffe. The nightly broadcast reported that President Jimmy Carter had invited the Holy Father Pope John Paul II to visit the White House during his trip to the United States, and I nearly jumped out of bed to call Joe in DC. I was worried about my baby, and in need of a good sign. I never ask for political favors from my brother, but that day, I made an exception.

"Joe, the Pope is coming to the White House and I have to see him," I said immediately.

"Let me see what I can arrange," he said. Shortly after, he called me back with bad news: the invitation from the White House extended only to Catholic Senators and their spouses. "Pick anyone else you want to meet and I can swing it, Val, any President or Prime Minister," he said. "But I don't have the clout to deliver the Pope." It crushed me, and Joe knew it, because he called me again that day:

Jill said I could take her place. "She knows how much this means to you," Joe said. Overjoyed, I called my doctor, who crushed me again: No way was I traveling two hours to DC. There was too much risk involved.

Thankfully, Joe came to the rescue again. He learned that after visiting DC, the Holy Father was visiting Saint Charles Seminary, only a forty-five-minute drive from our home in Delaware. My doctor okayed that trip, so Joe and I made our plan. We got to Saint Charles just as the big iron gates were creaking shut. "Hurry up and get inside," the guard advised. "Because the Pope's right behind you."

The chapel itself was tiny, meant only for seminarians and invited guests, and it was jammed. Instead of church pews, there were bleachers, and our docent, a kindly older woman, pointed us to our seats, which, to my dismay, were at the very top. We dutifully climbed up.

A man down in the center aisle ran up the steps to us: "Excuse me, are you Senator Biden?" Joe nodded. "You don't belong up here, this isn't right," the man said. "You belong down in front with the VIPs."

Joe has never been the type to pull rank. "Thank you, but this is fine," he said. I took my elbow and dug it into his side as hard as I could. He looked over at me. "On second thought," he said, suppressing a smile, "why don't you lead us down to the front?" We were squeezed into a front row.

Seconds later, the Pope walked in. After he delivered his remarks, he made his way back down the aisle, taking people's hands and giving blessings. Right before he reached me, I saw the priest who was accompanying him touch his elbow and whisper. I knew what was happening: The Pope was running late, and they were ready to leave. I was about to miss my chance. Now, I would sooner cut off my hand than reach for the hem of some rock star's garment. I had too much pride; no one was worth that. But the Holy Father—he was a different story. I was seized by a longing so profound that it propelled me right out of my seat. Bending over the low railing, I reached out to the Holy Father. I reached out for comfort; I reached out for courage. "Holy Father," I called out, sticking out my hand.

I caught his eye, and he paused. He came over to me. "Bless you, my dear," he said. And then he looked at my belly and said, "And bless your child." Then he turned with a smile, waved, and went away.

I sat down, overwhelmed, and cried. I didn't believe the Holy Father had the power to wave troubles away. But I believed that I had just been given his blessing, and thus I would find the grace and strength I needed to face whatever came.

I looked up at my brother. "Joe," I said, my eyes still watery. "You never need to do anything for me again in your life."

A few weeks later, on November 13, my healthy baby boy, Cuffe, was born. It was my dad's birthday. Joe came late that night to see us in the hospital. I was groggy, still recovering from my second cesarean, and Jack was at my side. "What's the baby's name?" Joe asked me.

"Cuffe Biden Owens," I murmured.

I'll never forget the look on Joe's face. I watched him swallow hard, his Adam's apple bobbing, as he took that in. "Cuffe," he said tentatively. "Did you say Cuffe?" I confirmed. His smile froze a little, but he rallied, brightening immediately. "That's . . . that's a *beautiful* name, Val! I love that name. Cuffe, what a great name."

It was an unusual one, for sure, an Irish surname from Jack's family. But it wound up suiting the Renaissance man that Cuffe grew to be. A gifted writer, artist, and intellect, Cuffe has always marched to the beat of his own drum, with a serene disregard for what others may think. It's a leader's quality; it's confidence.

Three years later, on May 12, 1983, our youngest, Catherine "Casey" Eugenia Owens, named after my mother, was born. For the first four years of her life, Casey pretty much had me all to herself because her older brother and sister were in school and Jack had his own law firm downtown. But that changed when I began to campaign away from home more than before. Casey hit the road with me whenever possible—I referred to her as my third leg. Work, family—in our lives, it all rolled together. You couldn't separate one from the other if you tried, so we didn't try. Public service had become a family calling.

Even now that Joe was in elected office, we never felt part of the political establishment—and that wasn't necessarily something to which we aspired. We worked to win people's hearts individually, over and over again. And that meant Joe's campaign staff and immediate family, who served as surrogates, pounded the pavement a lot.

Almost from the outset, the media liked to compare us to the Kennedys. It was low-hanging fruit: we were young, Catholic, liberal-minded, and Joe deeply admired Jack and Bobby Kennedy. But in terms of finances and political clout, we were pretty far from Camelot. My mom also liked the Kennedys, but she bristled at the comparison: "Damn it, we were Bidens before we ever heard of the Kennedys," she declared.

What the Kennedy comparison got right, though, was that politics grew into a shared sense of purpose for our family. And as closely as Joe and I worked, the tension of the job never really boiled over into our relationship. But sometimes it got pretty close. As a newly elected Senator in 1972, for example, Joe had to staff his entire Senate office, both in DC and in Delaware. He chose Wes Barthelmes for his DC Chief of Staff, whom I heartily endorsed, and he chose— let's call him Rob—whom I was not enthusiastic about, to be the State Director.

I couldn't believe Joe was considering him, and I told him so. "You can't pick him," I said.

Joe paused. He didn't like my tone, and he didn't like to be directly contradicted. Rob worked his tail off for us, he reminded me. He knew Delaware politics; he was a friend.

"Okay, Joe, fine," I said. "But he's an old-school, machine politician. You're supposed to represent youth, new blood, enthusiasm. Trust me, if you hire him, he will let you down."

I could almost see Joe's temple veins throbbing. He pushed his chair back and walked into the living room, trying to calm down. We had a firm family rule about not saying words you can't take back, and I could tell there were several choice ones for me on the tip of his tongue. He paced around the room for a minute, before he came back and sat down.

"Okay, Val," he said, a hint of edge in his voice. "You've obviously thought about this. Who do *you* think should be State Director?"

"Ted Kaufman."

"Ted Kaufman?" Joe echoed in disbelief. "Who the hell is Ted Kaufman?"

"One of the smartest people I've ever met," I answered.

Largely unbeknownst to Joe, Ted had come into our Senate campaign headquarters in mid-August 1972, and said he wanted to help even though he believed Joe didn't have a prayer. He admired Joe and what he stood for, and he was convinced that Joe's vision was the future of the Democratic Party. He was in upper management at the DuPont Company, and while he said he didn't have a lot of time, he sure made a lot of time for us.

"Do you have this Ted's number?" Joe asked.

I did.

"Hello, this is Joe Biden," Joe said when Ted answered. "Ted, I'm calling to see if you want to be State Director in my Delaware office."

"Thank you, Senator," Ted replied. "I'm flattered by your offer, but don't you think we should talk first?"

"We don't have to. My sister said you were the right person for the job, and I believe her. We'll talk specifics later."

As it turned out, Joe has long since said that Ted Kaufman is the wisest man he's ever known. Ted is his true north, and Joe calls hiring Ted the best political decision he ever made.

It's moments like that—my insistence on Ted—that led Joe to say I have the best political gut of anyone he knows; but I'm not sure about that. I'm not a political scientist, nor am I a policy wonk. However, I am an expert on Joe Biden. I can sense, like bad weather coming, how things could go awry, when he's getting bad advice, what might make him edgy, who has an agenda of their own that conflicts with Joe's. Joe knows that whatever the policy particulars, he and I share the same moral compass, and he looks to me to reaffirm for him what he already suspects to be true. We are both Bidens, and no one else in a roomful of experts knows what Mom would have thought or what Dad might have done; none of them can verbally articulate what we feel in our bones to be true, and why. It is from that deep well of shared experience and upbringing that I call my brother's attention to what I think will be effective, serve as his sounding board or gut check, and speak as a truth-teller.

My brother has always been a passionate speaker. Maybe it dates back to the time he spent conquering his childhood stutter, or maybe it's the Irish poet in his soul. From the minute he was elected to the Senate, he was in demand on the speaking circuit. Particularly during his

first term, he found traveling helped to take his mind off his grief. So
if an opportunity came up to speak to the Young Democrats of Somewhere, he took it. Pundits assumed he was building a base for a presidential run, but at the time I don't think anything could have been
further from his mind. Joe had found strength and clarity from public
speaking since his days as a lawyer, and he needed all the strength and
clarity he could get back then.

His success on the speech circuit arose from a murky alchemy.
He was a great speaker, yes, but it wasn't just his speeches people
were attracted to. He was "the Youngest Senator in American History" (never mind that in actual fact he was the sixth youngest), and
he'd suffered a devastating loss. People have a fascination with tragedy. I believe this fascination is rooted in empathy—by engaging
with someone who has endured the unimaginable, you can safely
envision what your life would be like if such a fate were to befall you.
It's normal, and it's natural. But, it wasn't just the tragedy that made
Joe magnetic, or his age, or his natural eloquence—it was *all* those
things, dovetailing together.

Joe stuck to the script at these events (mostly), speaking on behalf
of the candidates and the key issues. He was charismatic, unafraid of
crowds that were skeptical of him, and passionate. As he kept at the
speaking circuit, a steady, low-level buzz began building.

By 1980, Joe wasn't yet forty, and already his résumé was impressive. He'd been the first Senator to endorse Jimmy Carter for President in 1976, and he was the chairman of Carter's National Strategy
Committee before the Wisconsin primary. When Walter Mondale
was chosen as Carter's Vice President, Mondale sat down with Joe for
hours to get a sense of what made Carter tick, Joe was considered by
many to be a rising Democratic star, well known by experts in foreign
policy, by the press, and among power players.

All this attention came to a head startlingly early for us, during the presidential election of 1980. Jimmy Carter was the incumbent, and Ted Kennedy had launched a primary challenge, capitalizing on Carter's dismally low approval ratings.

Around this time, a handful of Democratic political operatives were making quiet overtures to Joe. A Carter and Kennedy primary was likely to be ugly and protracted, they said. In a bloodbath between Kennedy and Carter, Joe might emerge victorious. They wanted Joe to get in the ring. Joe listened—it's hard not to listen when a bunch of party operatives descend and enthusiastically tell you that you could be President—but he didn't bite. He didn't feel right primarying President Carter, whom he believed to be a man of real integrity and honor. But above all, it was all happening too fast. "It's too soon, Val," he said. "What would I even be running for?"

As it turned out, the inability to answer that very same question wound up dooming Ted Kennedy's own primary challenge. In 1979, he had the famous CBS interview with the journalist Roger Mudd that was meant to launch his campaign. He sat down prepared for a series of softball questions, and Mudd obliged.

In the course of the interview, Mudd asked the simplest question: "Well, Senator, why do you want to be President?"

Ted Kennedy stammered. He stared off into space. He rambled for a few minutes, trailing off with nothing to say. It was abundantly clear to Mudd, to viewers, and possibly even to Kennedy himself that he had never asked himself this question. In his mind, it was his turn. The interview was supposed to anoint him, but it severely wounded his candidacy.

Meanwhile, Joe's Senate reelection beckoned in 1984. His challenger was John Burris. Years later, Burris would tell me, laughing, that their campaign had two strategies: the first was to make Joe mad and lose his temper; the second was to make me lose mine. "You could stick a nail in Joe, and he would keep it together," John said. "But if we stuck a pin in you, you would lose your mind." He was kidding me, but he was right: Joe was and has always been better about brushing off personal attacks against him. I've always taken them personally.

In the early 1980s, Democrats were suffering an identity crisis. The pendulum swing away from "big government" was severe. In 1984, Senator Mondale was running against Reagan, and everyone was fearfully anticipating that he would get steamrolled. And that's exactly what happened. It was a bleak echo of McGovern's resounding defeat twelve years earlier. Both were good, honorable men, but we clearly needed another message if we were going to counter the Republican machine.

The reigning orthodoxy now was that big government was bad. The safety net was a trap, ensnaring all who fell into it. In response, those nets were being cut away with breathtaking speed. Republicans framed it as freedom to rise, but we saw it as the freedom to fall. Having discovered how well wedge issues worked for them in splintering off disgruntled voters, Republicans went into overdrive: the discourse became about so-called welfare cheats and racist scaremongering.

To counter the wave of conservatism that threatened to wash them away, Democrats felt as though they needed a new kind of candidate. Joe seemed to fit the bill. Joe could always break down real problems and abstract ideas into manageable, understandable parts. He never dumbed down, but spoke in ordinary language with metaphors or comparisons everyone could understand—just as he does today.

Once, his press secretary handed him a speech with the phrase *cadre of concerned citizens*. He circled it and wrote in the margin: BUNCH OF PEOPLE. He's always on the lookout for ways to communicate more directly and cut to the heart of the matter. He makes sense of things.

When party operatives came back for us in 1984, we heard them out. He was interested but ambivalent. When you run for office, you more or less make a promise to your family that they will see much, much less of you. It keeps you away for nights, weekends, days at a stretch. He and Jill were just getting settled; their daughter, Ashley, was almost three. While we talked about it more seriously this time, it still didn't feel right. Before flying off to Puerto Rico for a vacation, Joe signed the filing papers and left them with me, with the instructions to let no one else touch them.

After a few days, Joe called me. "We're not doing this," he said. He needed to focus on his family. The papers stayed in my drawer.

The year 1987 started out in fine shape. Joe was a veteran by then. He was a leader on foreign policy; he was Chair of the Judiciary Committee. From his years on the speaking circuit, he had developed a good potential base. This time, we were ready to take a chance on a run for President. We were testing the waters, we said. Couldn't hurt, right?

In testing the waters, we got in over our heads. When I think back on our failed presidential bid in 1988, the overwhelming impression I have is of a machine running so fast it got out from underneath us. We had a reluctant candidate, and the campaign staff was a stable full of bright, ambitious men who weren't yet ready for prime time. Individually, each was a star, but together, they could not work out and execute a plan. Our generals were many; our infantry, few.

In January 1987, in my role as Chair of the nascent "Biden for President" campaign, I headed to Iowa. With me was Bert Di-Clemente, Joe's Delaware Director, who would accompany me on his off days. We thought it prudent to take the pulse in Iowa, to gather information so Joe could make a decision about whether to run, so I hit the road. John Marttila, Tim Ridley, David Doak, Mike Donilon, Larry Rasky, Pat Baskette, David Wilhelm, and Pat Caddell, among many others, were all queuing up in various capacities to get the structure in place—especially in Iowa, New Hampshire, and a handful of southern states. Back in DC, Ted Kaufman was the Chief of Staff, handling all Senate matters.

My first trip was trial by fire—or more aptly, trial by ice, since I landed in a snowstorm. I had not been on the campaign trail since 1984; I felt rusty and had trepidations about this trip. When I landed, I was given a large briefing book of the top issues likely to be raised, and a list of key local leaders with whom I should meet.

Two hours later, I headed down to the conference room of my hotel—the Savery, where all the politicians stayed when they traveled to Des Moines. It was already dark and a snowstorm was raging, but the room was still packed with what looked like the yuppies of Iowa: progressive, young leaders who definitely had a point of view and wanted to be heard.

Beer was flowing and the questions came loud and fast: What does the Senator think about abortion? Busing? How does he expect to solve the farm crisis? While the issues were valid and important, the tone was argumentative from the start. I thought I was there for a discussion, to listen and learn. Instead, I felt as if I were at my own inquisition. *Oh God, get me out of here,* I thought. *This is not what I signed up for.*

When the meeting was finally over, seemingly hours later, my team—Bert DiClemente, David Doak, and Bruce Koeppl—and I headed for the elevator. As soon as the doors closed, I let them have it. "Don't you ever hang me out to dry like that again," I snapped. It wasn't my job to know the intricacies of the farm crisis, let alone the Middle East peace process. "Why didn't you guys speak up? I should never have been in front of a crowd like that."

Fair enough, my team said, but they had their own criticisms of me: "You either come on too hot or too strong, Valerie." I wasn't conciliatory enough, not persuasive. I needed to get better; they were not sympathetic to my discomfort. They weren't wrong.

My worst night on that trip was in Sioux City. One of the party chairs was hosting a dinner for the candidates and their surrogates, who were all seated at the head table. People came up to us and commented on and questioned everything. My team was out on the floor socializing, and I needed backup. I was drowning. Finally, I excused myself from the center head of the table and went to find Bert, who was seated at the other end. I pretended that I needed to get a Kleenex out of my purse, which I said I couldn't find. "Bert, will you help me find my purse?" I asked. God bless him, he jumped up and went to look for it for the next fifteen minutes—he missed my secret cry for help. I was on my own again. When it was my turn to speak, I told stories about growing up with Joe—not policy. I faked my confidence.

The reason I was filling in for Joe so much was that he had a killer schedule as Chair of the Judiciary Committee, and it was anticipated that at some point soon, Reagan was going to nominate a new Supreme Court Justice. Joe also sat on the Foreign Relations and Intelligence Committees, which meant he was either preparing for hearings or running to catch a plane to give a (still unwritten) speech to either future caucusgoers in Iowa or primary voters in New Hampshire—not to mention introducing himself to

Texas and Florida. Everyone wanted a piece of him, the price of running for President. In many instances, I was as close to Joe as they could get.

Years later, when I taught a seminar called "Politics: Up Close and Personal" at the Institute of Politics at Harvard's Kennedy School, I would tell the students that you have to get your personal life in order before you run for public office. In retrospect, Joe wasn't all in. Jill gave him her blessing, but her heart wasn't in it either. The campaign pros were frustrated by his commitment to family time.

Joe didn't want to announce his candidacy for President when they did because it was Ashley's birthday. The big guys threw up their hands. "You're not going to go to this state dinner because it's your wedding anniversary? You won't announce on your daughter's birthday? How badly do you want this? What is wrong with you?"

For Joe, there was no decision to make at all. Family came first, and not just his own—if Ted Kaufman's daughter, or any other staffer's daughter, had a birthday fall on the same day as a big event, Joe would say, "You do the birthday. We'll figure it out." To this day, he insists that his staff make time for their own families. Shortly after he was elected President, an old memo he'd sent out to his staff as Vice President resurfaced online, testifying to this belief: "If I find out that you are working with me while missing important family responsibilities, it will disappoint me greatly," he wrote. For Joe, it's an article of faith, but for the people trying to advise us on our 1988 run, it was just an eccentricity.

Worse, something new had begun to enter the picture: pain. For a man who never had headaches, who never took an aspirin, he was besieged by it. Physical pain attacked him with a furor. Tylenol and Excedrin were constants, sometimes swallowed without water. At a speech in March of '87, he wobbled and nearly fainted at the podium.

He saw a doctor, who chalked it up to the flu, so Joe kept pushing ahead.

In late May of '87, I was in Western Pennsylvania trying to convince the party chairs—who were not particularly warm toward Joe—to back him, when Joe called me, saying, "I don't know if I want to do this."

I said, "Joe, don't do anything, don't say anything. I'll be home tonight."

Jack picked me up from the airport, and we went right to Joe's house, and we talked it over with Jill, the boys, Ted, Jimmy, and more of the team. By that time, countless other people had already thrown their hats into the ring, and a whole lot of people had devoted large chunks of their time, energy, and politics to the idea of Joe running. We were too far at that point *not* to.

A week before the scheduled official announcement for President on June 9, Jack casually asked me what I planned to wear. "I'll find something in my closet—I don't have time to shop." I had run around to the downtown Wilmington stores, but didn't find anything. Jack kept at it: "You're announcing your brother's run for President of the United States, Val. Get yourself something you'll feel good in." It's not that I disagreed, but I was too busy to worry about it.

As the day of the announcement ticked closer, my tension reached its peak. The Friday night before, Jack came to me with a serious look on his face. "Valerie, you know I don't normally ask you this," he began, "but I have some very important clients coming in tomorrow morning. I really need you there with me to meet them. It won't take your whole day; just from about eight a.m. to one. Then you're done."

I hit the roof. "I don't understand how you could even be asking me this, Jack! It's three days before the announcement," I said. Besides being furious, I was baffled. I truly couldn't fathom what in God's name he could be thinking. He kept insisting, no matter how mad I got—and, boy, I got really, really mad. I went to bed not speaking to him. How could he have swung and missed this badly? The next morning, I got up early to get myself ready for his appointment. When Jack came downstairs, he probably felt the temperature in the kitchen drop about five degrees. He was serene, though, which enraged me even further. Any decent husband in his shoes would at least have had the common sense to look somewhat abashed, but he just was content to sip his coffee. My stare could have burned holes in his head.

Well, around eight o'clock, a limousine pulled up in the drive. I looked out at the limo, uncomprehending, then back at Jack, who had a cat-ate-the-canary grin. "What's your favorite store?" he asked. He knew the answer: It was Barney's on Fifth Avenue in New York City. "I'm taking you there now. You're going to pick out whatever you want, and then we'll come back home. You'll be back by one." This is not something I can say very often, but I was truly speechless.

As the limousine pulled out, I saw Casey's distressed little face pressing the window. "Mommy!" she pleaded. "Don't leave me!"

We weren't even out of the driveway. Jack looked at me. "What do you think?"

I nodded. We pulled back around, opened the door, and Casey hopped in joyfully to join our unexpected shopping trip.

At noon on Tuesday, June 9, at the Wilmington train station, my brother would announce his candidacy for President of the United States. My role was to introduce Joe. That morning, I tried to suppress the butterflies in my stomach. This was going to be the biggest crowd I'd ever been in front of by a factor of ten—maybe seven thousand people filled the surrounding roads and the park across the street. I wore my new white skirt, double-breasted navy blazer with white buttons, and a cream-colored blouse, all from Barney's. The size of the crowd overwhelmed me, but not in the way I might have thought; I was immensely moved to see all these people here, all in support of Joe. I prayed that I would not become too emotional when I introduced him. On the podium behind me sat Mom and Dad, Jack and the kids, Jimmy and Frank and their families, Jill's family, and our family members by extension.

Over the next three days, Jack, Jimmy, some campaign staff, and I traveled with Joe and Jill to DC, to Iowa, and to New Hampshire. Joe's speech was beautiful and resounding: "Today, on the surface, America seems to be a tranquil and prosperous nation. But though it is barely discernible to the naked eye, America is a nation at risk. And the greatest risk is not to ourselves, but rather to the next generation, to our children." He laid out a stark choice, the "quick and false prosperity consuming our children's future," in which we "devour[ed] the seed corn of our nation's children," delivering them "a lesser America," or a "more difficult" path, in which we built for a longer-lasting future. He railed against the me-first dictates of Reaganism: "In Ronald Reagan's America, we have honored not the valiant but the victors, not the worthy but the winners." It was a soul-stirring speech.

Our poll numbers, which started out pretty dismal, began climbing slowly. "You've started pulling away from everybody!" John Marttila, one of our top advisors, told us excitedly. We were on a crowded ticket that included Civil Rights leader Jesse Jackson, Missouri Representative Dick Gephardt, Tennessee Senator Al Gore, Massachusetts Governor Michael Dukakis, Illinois Senator Paul Simon, Arizona Governor Bruce Babbitt, and Joe. The press dubbed the crowded pool of Democratic candidates "the Seven Dwarfs"—cute—and by August, Dukakis and Joe were the two lead dwarfs.

I continued in my role filling in for Joe on the campaign trail whenever one of his many obligations claimed his time. On many trips, I was often the only surrogate. Some of the candidates I was happy to follow, but I knew that if I followed Jesse Jackson, I needed to step it up because he was so good at igniting the crowd.

I wasn't always at my best in those first months. Early in the campaign, we brought together our most important donors to keep them up to date on our journey. I opened our morning session, and among the crowd of supporters was a stone-faced, middle-aged woman who kept staring at me with a mix of disgust and intrigue, as if a button on my blouse were open or I had food in my teeth. Afterward, intent on winning over everyone in the room, I went to introduce myself. "Hi, I'm Valerie Biden Owens, Joe's sister," I said, putting out my hand.

I was rewarded with a dead-fish handshake and a cold stare: "I know who you are," she said flatly. Out of nowhere, she sneered: "How old are you?"

Without thinking, I shot back: "I'll tell you how old I am if you tell me how much you weigh." There was a frozen silence where both of us processed what I had just said. The woman stared at me in disbelief before turning and walking away. Next to me, Jack muttered, "Jesus Christ."

Oh God—did I really just say that? To one of Joe's biggest donors, no less? I was mortified. It's not that she was overweight (if she were, I would never have hit that nail on the head), it's that I took the bait, and in doing so had stooped to her level. I had to tell Joe. God only knows he'd hear about it, anyway.

"Don't worry," Joe said when I told him. "I blow somebody off every day—you're entitled to one." He kissed me on the forehead. "Now, let's get back in there and finish this up."

As the campaign went on, I found that, just as it had for Joe, my home life was getting strained. Not in an emotional sense—everyone was on board, everyone was okay. But there was only so much of me to go around; even though Jack and Mom were there to support me in every way possible, we still needed help. With more than a little reluctance, I set about finding someone to watch the children full-time.

I'd never considered hiring a nanny. The teenage girls in the neighborhood—Connie Piazza, Mary Thomas, the Riley sisters, and the Garrett twins—had been all the babysitters we'd ever needed. This time around, I needed a woman, not a girl who was still in school. A woman who could love my children and teach them, play with them rather than parking them in front of the television.

As interview after interview didn't work out, my distress grew. Then, as is often the case, a friend of mine, Sue Canning, made a suggestion: She knew about a young woman who worked with small children recovering from cancer or major surgery at the Children's Hospital in Philadelphia. Her name was Colleen Quinn.

Sue said that Colleen was burning out—too much sadness—and she needed a break. She thought she had the answer for both of us in my three children, ages ten, seven, and four. So I arranged to interview Colleen at Mom's house, which is where I did all first-round interviews. When Colleen walked in, she reminded me of a girl right out of the Talbots catalog: pert, cheerful, and confident. In addition, she'd been raised in an Irish Catholic middle-class family with three younger sisters, which suggested she was culturally in tune with our family values.

She knew about Joe and his run for President and was completely supportive. She had her own house, her own car, excellent experience, and great recommendations from the Children's Hospital. My mother immediately loved her—I didn't. She was overqualified. With her education, would she want to stick around doing laundry, making sandwiches, running a house that was not her own? My kids would get attached to her, and then she'd get bored and leave. In the interview, I kept harping on all the unpleasant aspects of the job—the drudgery, the repetitiveness—when Colleen finally looked me square in the eye, smiling a little ironically, and said, "Mrs. Owens—"

"Call me Valerie."

"—Valerie, you're making this all sound pretty awful. Is there any part of this job that you think I *would* like?"

I hesitated. I was being pretty hard on her, and in retrospect, I guess I was trying to scare her off. "Look," I said. "To do this job, you have to do everything I do—except sleep with my husband."

"Oh, for God's sake, Valerie," my mom interjected.

Colleen's cheeks colored a little as she laughed. She raised one hand: "I understand! I promise I won't."

Part two of the interview was to meet Jack after his work. Colleen lived in the city, so she met us at a restaurant called the Greenery on Market Street. I was there first; Colleen came in, and I asked her if she wanted a drink. I saw her eyes flick down to my Coke. A teetotaler, she must have thought. She ordered a ginger ale.

When Jack arrived, he sat down, said hello, and promptly ordered: "I'll have a Johnnie Red on the rocks. Easy on the ice."

Colleen's hand shot up. "I'll have the same."

We talked for another forty-five minutes or so. Jack loved her and thought she was perfect for the kids. I still felt she was overqualified and would get tired of washing our clothes and grocery shopping and driving the kids around. But we agreed: overqualified or not, we needed her. She was leaving the hospital and we had to get her right away or risk losing her to someone else. We agreed to pay her a lateral salary—whatever she made at the hospital, she would make working for us. She turned out to be a godsend. The children grew to love her. She never overstepped her boundaries, and we never second-guessed her.

The other person who became an invaluable asset around this time was Hollis Brookover. Hollis was a young Smith College graduate who was intent on working on the campaign as my assistant. I said no at first, but she was persistent, and thank God she was. She traveled with me in those days and anticipated what I needed before I knew I needed it. Wherever we landed, wherever we went, from Podunk to Portsmouth to Provincetown, she knew a Smith graduate on the ground. Her network extended seemingly to every corner of the known universe. The only downside of working with Hollis was that she always had so much more luggage that I ended up carrying her bags.

Despite all the madness, and despite Joe's own misgivings, the campaign gained real momentum. He was striking a chord, and his message appeared to resonate with people. At the time, Joe loved to quote a speech by the then–UK Labour Party leader Neil Kinnock that elegantly testified to ordinary citizens' need for a "platform on which to stand." It became a stump speech standard, and it worked brilliantly until it didn't—one time in August of 1987. He was at the Iowa State Fair, the biggest campaign event yet, and he failed, just that one time, to properly credit Kinnock. The time was short. He realized it when he got offstage: "Jesus, I didn't credit Kinnock." And our Iowa director at the time said, "Senator, they know that speech by heart. You've done it in all ninety-nine counties. Everybody knows that."

"Should I go back and clarify it?" He was anxious, exhausted.

"Nah." So Joe let it go.

That was Joe's mistake—no one else's. But a whirlwind of bad press followed. First, there were a flurry of stories accusing Joe of "plagiarizing" the speech, despite the fact he'd cited it at least twenty times prior. The nationwide press picked it up, and once that story got a foothold, it was followed by others; suddenly, Joe found himself having to answer for improper citations in a law school paper. The attacks had their intended effect: we were knocked sideways, and where we'd spent the last few months pulling into the lead, suddenly we spent every moment on the defensive.

To see my brother maligned on the one thing that had always been his calling card—his integrity—was devastating. Because he had spent all those years commuting back and forth between DC and Delaware, there was nobody on the Hill who could really speak for him, no one to hold up a hand and say, "Hold it, now, we know Joe, and this just isn't him." The people of Delaware knew him, but outside the state, he was an unknown quantity. The negative stories just barreled ahead with no brakes.

Ted Kaufman was bullish: "We can fight this," he said. He believed that if we addressed the controversies head-on, people would see just how flimsy they were and we could regain our front-runner status. It all seemed so transparent and fleeting. But there were other, larger issues looming.

A month before the Kinnock controversy erupted, Reagan followed through on his promise to nominate an extreme conservative to the Supreme Court. He chose Robert Bork, a federal appeals court judge who was known for an originalist interpretation of the Constitution. In Bork's reading, the Constitution was about as flexible as a business contract. If it wasn't spelled out in the language of its framers, you couldn't argue for it as an essential right. A worrisome number of fundamental

American rights seemed to fall under this definition—everything from Civil Rights, to women's reproductive rights, to the right to privacy. Because of his leadership position, Joe had the responsibility of conducting the Judiciary Committee meetings on Bork's nomination.

The summer of Bork—specifically, the August congressional recess—was a hot one, literally and figuratively. The stakes for the hearings were high, but Joe didn't want to attack Bork based on his honor or character. He wanted to demonstrate to the American public how Bork's narrow reading of the Constitution might affect their lives. I was in the room during the preparations, and I saw firsthand just how hard that would be. How do you conduct a debate about national jurisprudence and scholarly interpretation without putting the entire country to sleep? We needed something that would make sense to someone in a Wilmington grocery store—something that prompted a reflexive head nod, not a confused squint.

The key was to focus on a fundamental right that mattered to everyone, and then drill down on how Bork's reading of the Constitution might imperil it. In hours of discussion with constitutional scholars, researchers, and Senate staffers, under the direction of the lead counsel on the Judiciary Committee, Mark Gitenstein, Joe circled around privacy. In interviews about his constitutional philosophy, Bork questioned the Supreme Court's 1965 *Griswold v. Connecticut* decision, which helped establish a fundamental right to privacy. He called it legally suspect, and even allowed that he might revisit it.

I listened and tried to understand what this had to do with my life. The legalese was way above my pay grade, so I just kept asking myself, *What does that mean? Why should I care?*

One afternoon, after many frustrating hours of discussion, Joe turned to me and said, "Valerie, do you have *any idea* what these guys are talking about?"

I didn't. "If I'm watching this hearing on TV from my home, I don't care about *Griswold v. Connecticut*," I said. "I just want to know: How does that impact me? What does it mean I can do, and what does it mean I can't do?" Mark, Joe, and a few others batted this question around for a moment. Then, slowly, I said: "It sounds like it means that the government could enter our bedroom and tell Jack and me that we couldn't use contraceptives."

Joe looked from me to Mark. "Is that right?"

"Well, yes," Mark said.

"Well, then for Christ's sake, Mark, why didn't you just say that?" Joe turned to the experts and said, "Did you hear that? Write down every damn word of what she just said. We're going with that."

Sometime during that long, miserable August, I traveled to Seattle for the convention of the National Organization for Women (NOW). On trips like these, I often took one of my children with me. Since this was the National Organization for Women, I decided to take Missy, who was twelve years old. Shortly after we walked into the hall, in the two seconds I wasn't watching her, a cadre of reporters descended on Missy. "What do you think about your uncle's campaign?" My respect for the press sank to an all-time low—kids were off-limits.

To put it politely, I had long been wary of the media. So it was with tremendous trepidation that I eventually agreed to speak with David Broder, the preeminent political reporter for the *Washington Post*, about the state of the campaign. At that moment in time, I would have sooner stuck my head in an oven, but I had to summon my courage. John Marttila had thought Broder, if informed, might be convinced to write something more fair, more favorable about Joe, and Broder promised John that our conversation would be off the record. He'd written a few pieces early on that reinforced the prevailing perception of Joe in the political press: that he was young, callow, and maybe had gotten a little out over his skis.

Finally, we met for lunch. "You want to know about my brother?" I said. "Okay, let me tell you about my brother."

We talked for about an hour. I didn't mention policies. I wasn't sure what good would come of that conversation, but it seemed as though Broder was listening to me. "I had no idea who your brother was, thank you," he said when we parted ways.

The Bork hearings were set to begin in the fall. As the hearings neared and media scrutiny of us intensified, our Democratic opponents piled on and were as aggressive and negative toward us as the Reagan White House war room. It became increasingly clear to all of us that something had to give. Our candidacy was taking on water. Joe still had to make it back to the Senate floor for important votes. We were spread dangerously thin. How could we soldier through the campaign, honor Joe's duties as a Senator and a father, and prepare for the Bork hearings at the same time?

We gathered our close "campaign family" and our blood family together: Jill, the boys, me and Jack, Jimmy, Mom and Dad, Ted Kaufman, John Marttila, Mark Gitenstein, and a few others. The decision was wrenching, but the choice was clear-cut: we had to drop out of the race. There would be time to set things right. Joe would rebuild after this character assassination. The Bork hearings were Joe's first professional duty, and to stay in the race would imperil the proceedings. Joe's job was to be a US Senator; his aspiration was to be President. His first obligation was to do his job.

After we settled on the decision to drop out, Jack and I went for a walk to get some air and clear our heads. Walking along a hedge-row, I spotted three separate tea-leaf-sized pink rosebuds poking their way through. I've always looked for signs and symbols. *Ah, it's Saint Therese*, I thought. She always sends a rose to let you know that she has heard your prayer. I picked up each one and held it in my palm. I looked at Jack and said: "We're making the right decision."

Joe held a press conference announcing his withdrawal the morning of September 23, 1987. Immediately after, he walked back into the Bork hearings to get on with his work. Just days after he ended his candidacy, Bork's nomination was defeated. It was the most re-sounding rejection of a Supreme Court nominee in history, and Joe had helped to make that history. Despite his personal loss, he had still found a way to deliver on his sense of purpose.

But me? I was a different story. I'd had the wind knocked out of me. I could barely get out of bed in the morning, couldn't get food down my throat. I was devastated—not because we lost the nomination, but because it was excruciating for me to witness the orchestrated assault on my brother—an honorable man defined by his character and in-tegrity. They wanted to break him.

Instead, they nearly broke *me*. Soon enough, though, Jack prevailed: it was time to get up.

There's no accounting for what life dishes out for you. There's only accounting for how you deal with it.

My faith has given me courage. And my courage has given me strength—to get back up and to keep moving forward. That's what raw power is: pulling it together when every fiber of your being feels as though you can't.

And you know, life has a way of unfolding. . . . You just have to stay open. That doesn't mean sit back and take it, and "What will be will be." It means you keep working to be the best you can. And then, when the opportunity arises, you try to make things happen.

You have to trust in yourself. And you have to have some confidence that while not everything works out the way you think it's supposed to, you know you'll find a way.

12

TRANSITIONS

We were all a little raw from the campaign, but Joe was up and going. He began accepting invitations to speak again. David Broder, it turned out, sat down with Joe in early January and wrote an honest, generous piece about him, praising his handling of the Bork hearings, and concluding that if he wasn't presidential material yet, he would be one day.

Meanwhile, Joe's persistent headaches were intensifying. Worse, he was getting shooting pains down his body and dizzy spells. He finally saw a doctor, who diagnosed him with a pinched nerve, ordered him to wear a cervical collar, and sent him to a pain clinic.

Then, in early February 1988, after speaking at the University of Rochester, he went back to his hotel room and collapsed. When he woke up again, hours later, he was on the floor. With the help of his staff, he made it back to Delaware—he wanted to be home. The next morning, Jill called me as she left to teach at Brandywine High School. "Joe won't get out of bed," she said, alarmed.

After I dropped the kids off at school, I went over. Snow was already piling up outside. Joe's room was pitch black when I walked in. "How are you feeling, Joe?" I asked, sensing something was very wrong.

"Mmph," he answered.

I immediately called our family pediatrician, Dr. Borin (who is far more than a pediatrician to us), who diagnosed him over the phone. "Valerie, this is serious," he said. "This is an aneurysm."

I called Jill at school and said, "Come home." I called Jimmy. "Jimmy, something's really wrong. He's really, really sick, and it's not a pinched nerve."

Either Jill drove Joe or the ambulance did—again, at a crucial moment, memory eludes me. But we wound up back at Saint Francis Hospital—the Bidens have spent an inordinate amount of time in that hospital—while the snowstorm thickened. I had to pick up the kids from school and stayed home with them waiting for updates. Jack went to the hospital after work and called me. "Valerie," he said, "why don't you come down and see Joe?"

I said I couldn't. I had to feed the kids dinner, they had homework, and the weather was terrible.

"No, I really think Joe would like to see you," Jack said.

Again, I insisted that wasn't necessary. Jack was trying to keep things light, and I either wasn't catching his drift or didn't want to.

Finally, Jack's voice dropped low: "Val," he said, "get down here right now."

A neighbor came over until Colleen could get there, and I drove through the storm. By the time I got to Saint Francis, Joe was on a gurney, being wheeled out to an ambulance, which was taking him to Walter Reed Army Medical Center, just outside DC. Jimmy had checked out all the best doctors and decided that the Chief of Neurosurgery there was one of the best practitioners alive at performing the complicated surgical procedure Joe needed.

I grabbed his hand and kissed him. For some reason, amid all the other lost memories, I remember thinking my breath smelled like pizza, which I'd eaten for dinner with the kids. I didn't know this yet, but apparently a nurse had brought a priest into his Saint Francis hospital room to read him his last rites. Jill had run the priest out of the room, insisting, "You're not giving him the last rites. He is not going to die."

Jill went in the ambulance with Joe, and Jack and I got in the car with Mom, Dad, and Beau. Hunter and Frankie drove down to Washington together while Ashley, who was still very young, stayed home with a sitter, like my kids. The weather was worsening, and the state police stopped us at the Maryland border to tell us to turn back. Beau, who was nineteen years old at the time, got out of the car and spoke to them, and we wound up with a police escort the rest of the way.

The doctors at Walter Reed said the aneurysm was at the base of the brain, and it was bleeding. They would need to cut open his skull, lift his brain slightly, and repair the vessel that had burst. The good news was that he was likely to survive. The bad news was that he might lose his ability to walk, or to speak. We didn't know. It was the first time I had ever heard the phrase *morbidity versus mortality*.

We were fortunate that Joe survived, but recovery would take months, and we had to settle in for a long haul.

The Sunday after the operation, Jack and I went home to our children. Nothing had been normal for weeks, and we were anxious to get back on a schedule and a routine that would reassure them. I had given Missy a Christmas gift of a mother–daughter tennis lesson. But that Sunday morning, I was having trouble holding up my head, let alone a tennis racket. So I said to her: "You have been such a good girl, I want you to have this lesson all to yourself." All I wanted was to get a cup of coffee.

When I walked into the diner, it was very crowded, because Mass had just let out from the church across the street. At the foot of the U-shaped counter, only one stool was empty. I slid onto it and ordered my coffee. At the far end of the counter sat a man who was pontificating about the headline in the Sunday-morning paper that read something like: JOE BIDEN'S HEAD CUT OPEN—HE IS ALIVE. I heard him say, "Surprised they found anything in it. Too bad he didn't die." Everyone in his little group laughed loudly. They were such good Christians, coming in to get their coffee and doughnuts after celebrating Mass.

I felt as if I were having an out-of-body experience. I left my seat, took my cup, and started walking over to this group. The outspoken man was sitting on his stool. The others were gathered in the corner, surrounding him. As I approached, they must have sensed something strange about me. They parted, and I went up and tapped the man on his shoulder. He half turned to look at me, and I said: "I am Valerie Biden Owens—Joe's sister. My family and I certainly appreciate your kind words and overall goodness." Then, slowly, I turned my cup upside down and poured the remainder of my coffee in his lap. I put my cup down on the counter, and there was dead silence as I walked back past that long, curved counter to the front door. I went to pick up Missy, and we drove home together in silence. When we got home, I collapsed into Jack's arms and sobbed for a full hour. "I've done something very, very wrong," I kept saying. "No, you did something very right," Jack replied. "If I had been there, I would have thrown him through the plate-glass window. Now, *that* would have been wrong."

The role of serendipity cannot be discounted: If Joe hadn't dropped out of the race, I firmly believe he would have been traveling in a little airplane in Iowa or New Hampshire for the primaries in early February, trying to secure the nomination, and he'd be dead. If not for the awful, dispiriting Kinnock debacle, we might not have him with us anymore. So often, the full picture emerges only in retrospect.

Joe returned to the Senate in 1988, after seven months of recovery. His colleagues gave him a standing ovation, and he was moved to tears.

In the 1990 Senate race, our opponent was a woman named Jane Brady. She ran an ugly campaign, and in the last few weeks, she took it to another level, launching smears and attack ads on TV and radio. Her campaign also mailed manila envelopes containing cassette tapes to every Republican and Independent in the state, attempting to rehash the tired, refuted Kinnock controversy.

Needless to say, we couldn't stay silent. I got on the phone with our media team and tried to figure out how we should respond. They kept coming back to me with attack radio spots that went for the jugular—the classic mudslinging approach. That wasn't how I ran a campaign, and it wasn't how Joe lived. We disagreed with our opponents, but we never took cheap shots. This was not only contrary to our principles, but beyond that, it was tone-deaf—an ineffective way to reach our constituents. An eye-for-an-eye ad would be jarring, off-putting to our voters, and would wind up hurting Joe. Each time I reiterated my feedback, the media consultants dismissed it, coming back repeatedly with something completely wrong. This went on for the better part of twelve hours.

Finally, at 3:00 a.m., the guy I had been working with called and said, "We've got to pull the trigger here." This was how it worked back then: Our media team would produce a cassette of the ad in a studio in Washington, then send it to Delaware on the earliest Amtrak train. A staffer from the campaign office would meet the train, grab the cassette, and hand-deliver it to the radio station so the station could air it during early-morning drive time. It was an incredibly tight schedule. I said I wouldn't run their response. It did not reflect my brother—not the way he thought or spoke, not the way he campaigned.

We had a standoff. If I didn't approve, he said, we would have virtually no response for the last five days of the campaign. Did I want to shut down and risk losing the election? "Because we will lose if we don't do this," he said.

"So we're gonna have to lose," I said. I was not putting that garbage on the air with my brother's name on it.

"I'm going to have to call my boss and have him call your brother," he said.

"What do you mean? You're going to tattle on me? You're going to call my daddy? Here, this is Joe's number, I'll save you the trouble of looking it up. Have your boss call him."

So at 3:30 a.m., his boss did indeed call Joe, who was in a dead sleep. He answered in a panic. "What's wrong? Is everyone okay? Is Mom okay?"

The man assured him his mom was fine. "The problem," he went on, "is with your sister."

"Oh God," Joe said. "What's happened to Val?"

Nothing's happened, the guy clarified. "She won't let us go ahead with this ad, and we want to run it by you because we think it's important that you hear it."

"I don't need to hear it," Joe said. "If my sister said no, then it's no." Then he hung up and went back to sleep.

And that's why I love working with my brother.

When Joe started arguing for the introduction of a federal domestic abuse bill while serving on the Senate Judiciary Committee, he was mostly alone. His fight began in 1990, when he noticed that while violence against men had fallen in the past decade, reports of violence against women were trending up. Was this because violence itself was increasing, or were women more emboldened to report it? Either way, he was troubled enough to want to learn more.

He delved into the topic, and as he always did, he quickly grasped the contours of the big picture. It wasn't pretty. I still remember the outrage and disbelief in his voice when he began telling me about what he was reading. "There was this study in Rhode Island, Val," he said. "They asked middle school kids if they thought a man had a right to force sex on a woman if he spent ten dollars on her. *A quarter of the boys said yes.*"

"And the girls?"

"One-fifth of the girls agreed."

Later on, he shared with me another shocking statistic: one in ten American males believed it was okay to hit a woman inside the home if she didn't obey him. *One in ten*—the number sent me reeling. As children, Joe and I lived sheltered, fortunate lives. We didn't know, or didn't believe we knew, any mothers whose husbands hit them. But those numbers whispered a different story.

Domestic abuse was America's dirty little secret, enabled by soft law enforcement and largely ignored by society. I began to wonder about the couples I had known over the years: Had any of those women been concealing something out of fear, misplaced loyalty, or embarrassment? The thought turned my stomach.

When something shocked Joe's conscience, he quickly became unstoppable, and that's what happened next. He scheduled Senate hearings to bring awareness to a 98 percent male Senate, inviting women from both parties and all socioeconomic backgrounds and ages to testify about their experiences. When the meetings weren't well attended, he harangued his fellow Senators into showing up. He was relentless, and when he came up against apathy, his resolve only grew.

The bill Joe authored attacked the domestic violence problem from every angle: It established a hotline to make reporting abuses easier, and it forced states to recognize out-of-state restraining orders. Most important to Joe, the bill classified certain kinds of domestic abuse as Civil Rights violations and gave survivors the ability to go to civil courts and seek justice. Were the law passed, the quiet scourge of violence against women would no longer be "a private matter" or "a family affair," as it had been for generations. It would be a federal crime.

Joe's bill fell mostly on deaf ears in 1990. His colleagues, with few exceptions, were either unaware, hostile, or some combination of the two, and the VAWA (Violence Against Women Act) languished for a few years. Even several of the women's groups were not supportive of the act; they were focused on a woman's right to choose and did not want to fight for two causes at the same time.

"I feel like I'm in the wilderness, Val," Joe admitted to me.

Both of us remembered Dad's admonition: "It takes a small man to hit a child or a woman." Dad was a grand soul, all the grander for how quiet he was. But on this topic, the abuse of power, his voice was loud and clear. So, once Joe learned about this issue, taking it head-on wasn't a choice—his response was automatic, second nature.

Passing the bill finally became a possibility in 1993, after Bill Clinton became President and Joe saw an opening with the new Democratic majority. Joe urged his staff to compile reports from the rape crisis centers and shelters from across the country, and the result was a slim and bleak twenty-page report titled *Violence Against Women: A Week in the Life of America*.

The report was both matter-of-fact and unsparingly detailed. Domestic abuse, it became clear, was a full-scale American epidemic. As with other epidemics, it crossed social, economic, geographic, and political lines. You could be the wealthiest woman in the world or the poorest: as long as there were incapable, incomplete men who needed to hurt others to feel powerful, and as long as those men felt certain they would not face consequences for their actions, the cycle would be perpetuated on every rung of society. "Hurt people hurt people," as the saying goes, and boys who watched in horror as their fathers slapped their mothers across the face often found themselves resorting to the same behavior when they grew up.

Many factors can keep someone from leaving an abusive relationship: some are emotional; many are structural. Financial dependence is a terrible trap I've seen too many women of my generation fall into. I've said I didn't know women who were physically abused—but *emotionally?* Yes. It's the reason I was adamant my daughters pursue careers. But before the Violence Against Women Act, the legal system offered little to no recourse for victims of abuse. No single bill can repair a broken system, but when President Clinton finally signed the Violence Against Women Act into law in 1994, four years after my brother first began his offensive, Joe was as proud as I've ever seen him.

As for me, I've often wondered about something I might have missed—a mute signal, an averted gaze—in women I've known. It seems too unlikely, given the statistics, that I've never known a woman who had been abused. But the power of secrecy can create its own trap.

I remember a terrible scene I stumbled across once in Wilmington, about twenty-five years ago. I was driving through downtown when I saw something out of the corner of my eye. A couple was walking along the road—a man and woman, the woman very pregnant—when suddenly the man reared back and punched her in the head. She fell forward, on her stomach. I wrenched the wheel, U-turning across Greenhill Avenue in a squeal of tires. They both turned to me in alarm—the woman from the ground, and the man standing over her. I leaned over and popped open the passenger-side door, hollering, "Get in, get in, get in!"

I was reacting instinctively, and when she met my eyes, she did the same. She ran into the car and shut the door, and I pulled away as the man ran after us, shouting.

I gave her a second to catch her breath, then said, "Let's go to the police. Let's report this. Has this happened to you before?" She nodded.

"Okay, then, let's go do this. I will protect you. I will stand up. I will testify. I saw what happened. I will help you. I will put you in touch with services that can protect you if you don't have a place to stay." She nodded again, mute, and a single tear escaped.

She looked all of nineteen, twenty years old. I didn't even ask her name. As we pulled up, I told her to get out and wait for me for two minutes while I went and parked. Then we'd go in together. I'd be with her every step of the way.

But when I glanced back over at her, I saw something had changed in her expression. "I can't do it," she said. "I can't."

"Come on," I said. "I'll support you." But her eyes were frightened; she had gone someplace where a well-meaning stranger like me couldn't reach her. I tried and tried, but she wouldn't go in.

"No thank you," she said quietly. "Please just let me out here."

What else can you do? I never saw her again.

Yes, the Violence Against Women Act has moved us light-years ahead of where we once were, but too many women and men still suffer at the hands of someone they love. (If you are in an abusive relationship and you need help, please contact the National Domestic Violence Hotline at 1-800-799-SAFE [7233] or text "Start" to 88788. You are not alone.)

The fall of 1996 marked our fifth campaign for the Senate. It was also the year I welcomed a delegation of young friends of Beau and Hunter into our campaign family. They had completed law school with the boys at either Syracuse or Yale and were raring to go.

Hunter stepped up and took the lead. In late May, as the campaign began to kick into gear, my office became *our* office. We took on every campaign management decision, no matter how major or minor, together. "Aunt Val, what do you think of this?" "Hunter, can you take care of that?"

Our opponent was Ray Clatworthy, and he was the picture-perfect Republican candidate—Naval Academy graduate, military service, avowed Christian, small business owner, family man. I told Joe we needed a new media consultant. The previous consultant's work product was okay, perhaps even good for a different campaign, but this time I wanted to hire a firm that saw the world the way we did, and was more willing to listen.

Joe said, "Okay, Val, you take care of it." He was not going to fire our old firm. So I did it. When I called our former guy to tell him we were parting ways, he was in disbelief. "You're not serious," he said. But I was, and after viewing seventeen demo reels from prospective firms, I selected Joe Slade White.

Joe Slade White was able to emotionally translate strategy onto film. He got Joe; he understood my brother. He also understood that the emotion from an ad should come not from the ad but from the viewer. This model is called the responsive chord. The ad that sold me was a graceful clip for Senator Ben Nighthorse Campbell. In two minutes, a dusky-voiced, avuncular orator laid down the lines of Campbell's life story over a parade of vivid, simple images. It was warm, it was clean, and it was powerful. I knew he understood on an instinctive level how to communicate to voters, and that he had the same style as Joe and I. That began a working relationship that would last until Slade White's death in May 2021.

Slade White was a savant and a classic character, in the best sense. He chose whom he wanted to work with, and he wrote every single word of his ads; there was no kid cutting his teeth in the back room. If you liked the ad, you knew whom to praise; if you didn't, you knew whom to blame.

Every word Slade White wrote was worked, reworked, and then given a final signoff by me and Mike Donilon, who was an essential voice in every one of my brother's decisions. Slade White had a healthy ego, in the sense that he didn't mind where good ideas came from. He took criticism well and used it to create something better.

Joe also knew how to wring results out of ad buys for a fraction of the cost. His ads were so good, so resonant, that people never forgot them once they saw them. You didn't need to see the same blaring ad nineteen times for the message to sink in. He was a virtuoso of being heard amid the noise.

In 1996, the first election Slade White worked on with us, Clatworthy hit us with a barrage of negative ads. It was a multimillion-dollar media buy—waged on all platforms, including radio, TV, direct mail, and paid press—an eye-popping sum for a Senate race in 1996. It was timed for a knockout blow, running only a matter of days before the election. We knew we were in trouble. We had to respond quickly and effectively—on Philadelphia TV.

Philadelphia TV, at the time, was the fifth-most-expensive media market in the country. Northern Delaware had no TV market of its own. So if we wanted airtime in New Castle County, our most populous county, we had to buy it through Philly. It was a tremendous investment of money and resources with an uncertain payoff—95 percent of the ad's viewership would be people living in Pennsylvania—but it was our best option at the time.

That year was also a presidential election, and the airwaves were bombarded with political ads for your Congressman, for your Senator, for your Governor, for Clinton or Dole, for your county dogcatcher. The theory was that you had to buy at least 1,000 Gross Rating points, which, in 1996 currency, meant coughing up nearly $200,000 per week, bare minimum, to ensure the average person would see the ad at least twelve times. Anything less, the conventional wisdom went, and the ad simply wouldn't stand out. We didn't have that kind of money, nor did we have the time to raise it. We hadn't been planning to use television at all, but Joe and I got on the phone with Joe Slade White. "What's the plan? What do you have in mind?" Joe asked.

"I don't know," Slade White said truthfully. "But I'll know in the morning." No matter what, he said, he would come up with an ad that cut through the clutter so effortlessly that people would only need to see it once, and they'd never forget it. He assured us he could do that with buying only 550, maybe 750 Gross Rating points.

After Slade White hung up, Joe said to me: "You know, if I didn't trust that son of a bitch so much, I'd swear he was trying to sabotage us."

The next morning, Slade White called me. "I've got it," he said. We had to list Joe's accomplishments. "We have to introduce Joe Biden to the state of Delaware as if it were the first time he was running." There would be no words, he said. Just text, enumerating everything Joe had accomplished in his time in the Senate. The idea didn't sound that inspiring to me, but the total confidence in his voice swayed me to leave it with him. (The initial description of this ad was the cause of Joe's momentary fury described in the introduction.)

In the final cut of the ad, there was no voice-over. The thirty-second spot was in black-and-white, and astonishingly, Joe's name was never mentioned. Instead of the usual canned music, Slade White opted for strings. Over the fanfares, a list of Joe's accomplishments appeared in kinetic white text against a black background. Key legislative achievements moved slowly on the screen in a captivating way: "Authored the Violence Against Women Act . . . $10,000 Tax Deduction for College Costs . . . Balanced Budget Bill." I called it the *Star Wars* ad. At the end, with a close-up of Joe's face, a message appeared calling on voters to trust in Joe's accomplishments. It was stunning. The responsive chord at its best: their values were Joe's values. I had chosen Slade White for a reason, and this ad was proof of his genius should anyone ever need it.

The first morning it ran, Joe was downstate, visiting with farmers. "Hey, Joe, I saw that new ad of yours. It didn't say a goddamn thing, and you didn't say one goddamn word, and it didn't even mention your goddamn *name*. What were you thinking, boy?"

When Joe called me, I could hear the steam coming out of his ears. "Tell me this isn't true," he said. "Our one ad on Philly TV doesn't even mention my name?"

"Well, Joe, it is true," I said. "I told you we were doing this—"

"I'm coming right there," he said, his voice sounding strangled.

He must have driven ninety miles per hour, because he made the two-hour trip in record time. When he showed up at headquarters, he stormed into my office with a look that I'd seen before, though never directed at me: angry grin, vein popping in his neck. He put both hands on my desk and leaned toward me. "Valerie, why the hell would you approve something like that?"

"Joe, Joe," I interrupted. "I've got the ad right here. Why don't you take a look at it? It's all teed up."

"First, just tell me what the hell were you thinking!"

"I was thinking that it's the best ad that I have ever seen," I said calmly.

He took one big step back. After a beat he walked around the desk, bent down, and kissed me on the forehead. "Why didn't you say that in the first place?"

"Because I didn't have a chance," I said. "Do you want to see it now?"

He waved me away. "No, I don't need to see it. If you like it, it's great." He left without seeing the ad.

It's moments like this that reaffirm for me what loyalty and trust really mean. Joe has said before that he can hear any criticism from me because he knows it comes from a place of love, and it's true. People tease me sometimes about my unswerving loyalty to my family, but my loyalty is not blind. Sometimes I could wring my brothers' necks. But even as I tell them what I think they need to hear, they also know that I'll lie down on train tracks to protect them. It's true of every one of us. But occasionally, I have to admit, we get carried away.

Margaret Aitken, who was Joe's press secretary from 1997 to 2008, is an honorary member of our big, extended family. Joe says she reminds him of me, and I consider that a great compliment.

Margaret likes to tell a story about when we were walking into a memorial service. Someone who knew her passed by and said hello, and asked if she was still working for Joe Biden. Margaret said yes, and then somewhat hesitantly introduced me to him as Joe's sister. "Good thing I didn't say anything bad about him," the man quipped, and I shot back, without batting an eye: "Yeah, because I'd hate to have to punch you in front of the church."

We might shake our heads or roll our eyes when we tell these stories—usually it's "Dammit, Jimmy, you said *what?*"—but it's always with fondness. All Bidens have the same understanding about family loyalty, and we made sure to pass it along to the next generation.

In 2006, I watched with pride as such a torch-passing moment occurred. Beau ran for attorney general of Delaware that year. He was young, smart, inspiring, a man with years ahead of him and miles to go. Missy had just graduated from law school and taken her first job at a big law firm in New York City.

One morning, Beau called me and said, "Aunt Val, I need to talk to you. It's about running for AG, and about Missy. Can I ask her to be my campaign manager? Will you be upset? I know she just took a new job and moved into her new apartment, and she'll have to move home. I can't pay her much. I know it sounds pretty selfish, Aunt Val, but I need her."

"I don't call that selfish, Beau," I said. "I call that family."

Beau was right to want Missy by his side. She was her grandmother's child—full of grace—as well as her father's—full of purpose. I have long joked that Missy was born a responsible citizen: I could have left her at a bus stop when she was two years old and she would have said, "Don't worry, Mom—I'll get home."

To this day, she has an unfailing internal compass—a great sense of direction (as in north and south), and, more important, a keen intuition of right and wrong. She is, as they say, always ahead of the curve: she can figure out how to *solve* your problem before you even know you *have* one. On top of that, she is the most selfless person I know. Without a moment's hesitation, in ways large and small, she steps up to take care of whatever or whoever needs attention. Not simply because she's my firstborn, she is my heart.

When they were younger, Cuffe and Casey looked to Missy first for everything, and she was infinitely patient. I remember having to lay down the law: "Missy, Cuffe has to learn to tie his shoes for himself now."

"But why, Mommy?"

"Because, honey, he's going to kindergarten soon, and you won't be there to do it for him." There is no end to the profound depth of her generosity. The Jimmy of her generation, she is the one all the kids and cousins call when they don't know what to do; she's the one who figures it out, no matter what the "it" is.

Joe and I watched with gratitude and joy as Missy and Beau teamed up. They were two cousins who grew up together in each other's homes, in campaign headquarters, at rallies, speeches, parades, and debates; they grew up often in the glare of harsh lights, but always with the security of family. They were two cousins holding one baton.

Just like the campaign trail, parenthood forces you to think on your feet. Each day brings a new challenge, and it's never the one you expected. The specs keep changing, even as the goal remains the same.

When they're babies, your job is to clear their path. Once they start moving, you remain one step ahead—locking the oven door, gating off the stairways, securing bookcases to walls.

As they get older, though, you have to start teaching them how to live in the world without you. So you start letting them fall. Otherwise, they'll never get back up on their own. It's the hardest part of the job.

Just like me, Cuffe hadn't yet hit his stride by the time high school started. When he was in tenth grade, he was just barely taller than me, at five feet five inches, and nearly the same weight. But just like every-one else in the family, Cuffe loved football, and he didn't let his size stop him from playing. He was quick, he had a great arm, and he could catch anything. Not only did he make varsity, but as he had hoped, by his junior year he became the starting quarterback. I still remember seeing him run out of the locker room and down to the football field for his first game with those pads on. He looked like the smallest quar-terback in high school history.

Cuffe did his best, but it was a tough year for the team. The of-fensive line dissolved the second he got the ball, and he was just clob-bered, over and over and over again.

From the bleachers, I felt as if I were taking every hit. I said Hail Marys and every novena I knew; I couldn't help myself. But I also knew that sometimes the best thing to do as a parent is to let your kids make their own choices and take their own hits. Watching him get flattened game after game, I wanted to run down and hug him as he stood on the sidelines between plays. But that wouldn't have been right.

So Jack and I sat up at the very top corner of the bleachers, where we could focus on Cuffe and where he could look up and meet our eyes when he needed to. Jack would encourage him in a way that shielded his pride—with a slow, nearly imperceptible nod of the head. *It's okay. You're doing what you can. Keep going.* No one else watching us would even have noticed, but Cuffe got the message. We were bearing witness: what he was going through was painful and discouraging.

It truly took courage to suit up, game after game, when he knew with near certainty what awaited him. Playing quarterback that year wasn't cool, it wasn't fun, but he wasn't going to give up; he was going to figure out how to play better, despite the odds.

That is Cuffe. He is more committed to being a better version of himself than anyone I know. He is a warrior, and he is gentle. He is a deep reservoir of feelings, a razor-sharp mind, and a quick fuse. He is thoughtful, a man of nuance who at times can almost taste your anguish while at others can miss what is written in bold print right in front of him. He does not brook fools—he is without guile. He is genuine, honest, and loyal. He is a mimic and very funny. He can also be brought to laughter by almost anything I say. He is my soul. He forgives with generosity and grace. Actually, all our children do. They love me and their dad in spite of ourselves.

Parenting, like politics, was also a family affair for us. Hunter and Beau were our collective first children—Joe shared them with all of us, and we never questioned each other's love or reprimands of them. When Jimmy, Frankie, and I had our children, the same trust held true. We treated one another's children the same way we treated our own. We spoke freely together about one another's children, and with the children themselves. Somehow, we never stepped on each other's toes.

Perhaps because each of our connections were so strong across traditional nuclear family lines, we seemed to appreciate the unique and important role we had to play.

That's certainly how it was with Hunter and me. When Hunter was in eighth grade at Friends School, long after Jack and I had our own home, the powerful intangibles of our bond became, well, tangible. Hunter was on the football team that year, and the team held practice at the end of the school day. They'd suit up and hustle out to the field around 2:30 p.m. One rainy fall afternoon, I happened to be driving past Friends when suddenly everything in my body tensed. My heart started beating faster, my mouth went dry. My mind flooded, disorienting me for a moment, and then everything snapped into place: Oh, my God—Hunter is hurt.

I drove into the parking lot, searching for a spot. I couldn't see the field from my car, but knew in my bones that Hunter was out there. Finding nowhere to park, I did the next best thing: I left my car in the middle of the road that ran parallel to the school, with my hazard lights on, windshield wipers still going, and ran up to the field. When I crested the hill, I saw muddy white helmets and blue jerseys crowded into a huddle. I ran onto the field and pushed my way through the huddle. Hunter was lying on the ground. He looked up at me and said simply, "Aunt Val, I knew you would come."

We waited while the coaches called an ambulance. I rode with Hunter to the hospital, where Joe and Jill met us. Hunter had a dislocated hip, which required him to stay in the hospital in traction for three days. I got a ride back to Friends, where someone had moved my car into the parking lot. Thankfully, they'd left my keys in the ignition.

When Jimmy married Sara Jones from Kentucky, I was just as fortunate as I had been with Joe. He, too, wed a woman who would become my friend. Frankie, again the matchmaker, introduced Jimmy to this raven-haired beauty, a top-tier lawyer who worked on the Hill for Democratic Senator Wendell Ford, and slowly the dance began. It was joyous to see Jimmy come alive with her—just as Jill had awakened Joe to new possibilities and renewed love. Sara was the youngest of four girls. Jill is the eldest of five. I obviously had never had a sister myself, so I had some catching up to do. But they were both patient and tolerant with me as I learned the rules of sisterhood.

There were only two moments I remember in those years when one of us got a little carried away. I was the perpetrator the first time. Before Jill, during my full-time Aunt Val days, I packed the boys' school lunches every day. Each of the boys had chosen his lunch box with serious deliberation. Beau chose one that pictured the Fonz, a cool dude on TV, while Hunter picked what he called a workingman's lunch box—a black box with a rounded lid like all the construction men carried. Each lunch box came with a thermos, which was made of glass material in those days and would easily break if you dropped it.

I developed a little running joke with the boys. While they were getting ready for school, I would sometimes slip outside unnoticed and hide in the bushes. When the boys came out, I would jump out from behind them and roar. They would squeal and drop their lunch boxes on the driveway, usually cracking or shattering another thermos along the way, and then I would hug them and we would laugh. Like all good running jokes, it got funnier the longer it went on.

Well, one morning, Joe got a peek at this routine, and he was less amused. I slipped out to find my hiding spot while the boys were having breakfast. Joe was home, but he was always the last one down the steps—usually by the time Joe was ready, the boys were already waiting impatiently in the car.

But this morning, Joe came out first and got in the car, oblivious that his sister was crouching a few feet away in the bushes. I waited until the boys came out and pounced. The boys screamed, but Joe swore, "Dammit, Valerie, what the hell are you doing?"

The boys tried to convince him: "No, it's okay, Daddy. Aunt Val plays this game with us all the time," but he was not having it. "Well, it's the last time on my watch." He took the boys to school in a huff, hustling them to the car as if to protect them from my warped sense of humor.

Another time, it was Joe in the doghouse. He was visiting our house and telling ghost stories to Cuffe and Jimmy's son Jamie. Well, he might have gotten carried away, because next thing I knew, he was piling them into a car to go out at night to visit "the haunted grounds." By the time he dropped them back home, they were nearly numb from fear. Bed was out of the question—they had to stand guard against the evil beings that roamed in the night.

That's when I called Joe and said, "What the hell did you do to those kids?"

"I was just playing, they're fine," he answered.

I said that they were definitely not fine, and Joe had to come over to straighten it out right away.

"I made it all up, boys," he said. "I was just having some fun."

I gave his line back to him: "Well, Joe, that's the last time on my watch."

The funny thing about raising kids is that if you do it right, they leave you. If you imbue your kids with confidence and a sense of self, if you encourage them to push themselves and teach them to build resilience, if you convince them that with a little grit and determination they can accomplish anything—well, then one day you find yourself packing up your youngest child's belongings into clear Tupperware tubs, loading them into the back of your Chevy Suburban with the seats folded down, and carting them off to college.

By the time Casey went to college, I'd had practice sending off Missy and Cuffe. But that didn't mean I'd gotten used to it: Casey and Cuffe teased me gently that I never stopped setting the table for five after Missy left. And Casey was the baby: when I got back in the car with Jack after dropping her off, I would be a mother bird with an empty nest.

I held it together on freshman move-in day: finding Casey's dorm, Quincy House; helping make her bed; meeting her roommates; wandering around and exclaiming over everything on campus. When Jack and I waved goodbye and got in the car for the nearly six-hour drive home, we felt eerily lighter. We mused about all the excitement ahead for Casey, reflected on the two nice girls across the hall. We wondered how Fall Ball lacrosse would go for her. We marveled that we had a child at Harvard. (She was the first person I ever really knew who went there.)

But after the adrenaline wore off, somewhere around the New York state line on I-95, that lightness began to feel more like . . . emptiness. We realized, as we drove in silence, that we'd always be holding our breath a bit until she came home for Thanksgiving.

The next day, I did my best to go about my errands. I picked up the dry cleaning, headed to Janssen's Market to get the grocery shopping done. I wore my darkest sunglasses inside, hoping no one would see my eyes. I didn't feel like talking to, or being seen by, anyone.

The trouble is, normally I talk to everyone, wherever I go. My kids tease me about this, calling me Little Miss Friendly Foot. I tend to greet strangers even in an elevator, much to my children's mortification—I just can't help myself. Perhaps I drew more attention to myself by saying nothing, to the point that the grocer asked me in a kind, quiet voice, if I was okay.

I managed a curt, tight-lipped head nod, but the minute I did, it was like everything shook loose. I broke down right there, standing in the grocery line. "No," I cried. "My kids are all gone."

That's what parenthood does: you love someone so helplessly you wind up being consoled by a kind grocer on a bright fall afternoon.

Casey and I had spent a lot of time together, just the two of us. I'd spent almost the entirety of my pregnancy with her confined to bed, and when she was born healthy and strong in May 1983, I considered her a true gift from God. I cherished her. When we brought her home to her big brother and sister, they, too, greeted her with unbridled affection.

After being down for the count for the better part of a year, I had a lot to make up for. With Missy and Cuffe already in kindergarten and preschool, Casey and I were free to get up and go in my new Chevy station wagon. In hindsight, maybe we did *too much* going: to this day, she hates to ride in the car—and when she does, she keeps you posted as to the level of her discomfort.

She is the Little One—the one who, when I would kiss her awake every day, would whisper with a smile, "Good morning, Mommy"— and thereby make it so. She was my sidekick, my laughter, my soft landing on a rocky day, and still is today. She is joy and light, strength and grit. She is a beacon of empathy, just like her namesake, my mom. She is a healer who can recalibrate me to calm, and as I begin to breathe more easily, she is a sponge who absorbs my emotions. I can almost feel her taking on my worry, as if to say, "Mom, you're doing a great job—I am proud of you." I know I am not the lone recipient of her goodness. She is not just my last child—she is my only Casey, and I would be a lesser woman, a lesser mom, without her. She is my spirit.

The job of being a mother never ceases. When Cuffe's beloved dog passed away just this summer, he called me immediately, his voice abject, and I yearned to reach out over the phone and hold him close, as though he were still a little boy. But the physicality of be-ing a mother—kissing bruises, scratching backs, remembering kids' gym shorts, packing lunches, cheering at games, sitting through four showings of the same not-very-good theater production, setting the table—defines your day-to-day existence until, one day, it suddenly doesn't.

This was a churchgoing woman if ever I had seen one. She could have come right out of central casting.

She belonged to the local parish, helped decorate the church for its celebrations, and always put some money in the collection basket every Sunday when she attended Mass.

She was small in stature, modest, and earnest, but her opinions were outsized, robust, and provocative. She was either for you or against you.

She was an Iowa caucusgoer who would help determine who the next Democratic presidential nominee would be. She wielded power.

She looked me up and down and asked me what I could do for her; how could I better inform her, engage her, and ultimately persuade her that my candidate should be her candidate. She politely told me to "bring it on."

I thought I had a shot.

So, I did bring it on—but what ensued was a debate, not a discussion. In our dialogue, there was no Um *or* Oh! I see. Only But *and* Now, hold on a minute.

Our exchange, intended to be cordial, quickly devolved into a contest— who could win, not who could listen; who could advance, not who could understand.

We mimicked the politics of today—combat not conversation—even while espousing the principles of our Catholic social doctrine to honor thy neighbor as thyself. We talked the talk but didn't walk the walk—even though we had just walked out of church.

13

TO THE WHITE HOUSE

Joe had considered running for President in 2000 and again in 2004, but both times decided he wasn't ready yet. When we passed on the chance in 2004, he said to me, "Val, I wanna be ready in four years." So we were.

In 2008, everyone agreed that the principal concern before voters was foreign policy—the war in Iraq, the war in Afghanistan, al-Qaeda, Osama bin Laden. By anyone's measure, not just his sister's, Joe was a true statesman on foreign policy. There was arguably no one on either side of the aisle who had amassed Joe's experience and authority. He knew the players and the field exceedingly well.

First, I reached out to Luis Navarro, a longtime Democratic Party operative. We'd been understaffed and spread too thin for our 1988 run, and I wasn't about to repeat that debacle. Luis and I divvied up the responsibilities. This time, he would become the campaign manager while I became campaign chair—hairsplitting designations in title only. What it boiled down to was that we'd have twice the horsepower. Luis was in charge of the budget, and budget dictated strategy. I was principal surrogate and handled all media, and I was in charge of Joe. We trusted each other.

We set up our national headquarters in Delaware, and I immediately headed to Iowa to set up "Biden for President" headquarters outside Des Moines. Traveling back and forth from Delaware to Iowa that year was a bear, especially during the colder months. I stopped counting how many hours I spent on the tarmac at the Philadelphia International Airport waiting for my plane to be deiced, only to find that the flight had been canceled. You really had to want to go to Iowa.

By 2007, when we launched the campaign, I'd spent decades as Joe's surrogate. It came naturally. We don't share one mind, Joe and I, but I know what he would say, and I know what he stands for. I traveled over 1,100 miles each week so a Biden could meet as many of the ninety-nine county chairs and caucus activists as possible. We needed to forge the bonds that would lead to support.

Danny O'Brien had been Joe's Chief of Staff, but he left the Senate to take over our Iowa operation because he understood the process better than any of us. Upon his departure from the Senate, Danny turned the reins over to Alan Hoffman, who had previously held that position from 1998 to 2003. Alan stepped back in and never missed a beat, like the true champion that he is. When Danny and I took off on our statewide travels together across Iowa, headquarters was a ship without a captain. The rudder was unmanned. We needed a full-time, statewide campaign director. We needed an experienced hand to help us navigate the Iowa caucuses. One of our supporters had passed along a recommendation for someone who might fit the bill, and we quickly set up an interview. While we weren't impressed with the candidate—nor he with us, it would turn out—we felt we had no better alternative, so we hired him.

Big mistake. He was arrogant, incompetent, and deceitful—in way over his head and unable to admit it, more concerned with covering his own backside than working for us. He revealed himself to me one day on a conference call. The call was contentious, and after it was over, he forgot to disconnect. I was treated to a torrent of invectives directed at me. I was the idiot, the token relative, the sister who needed to be pushed aside, a challenger to his authority, and several other choice words. He was going to take me down, he declared, and I listened quietly as his little cohort cheered him on: "Yes, sir, let's get her."

I'd had other moments in my career like this, so I barely blinked. I could have interrupted him at any time: "Hey, big guy, I'm still listening." Instead, I let him rant until he realized belatedly that he was still connected. I didn't make a sound. He hung up, confident that he hadn't been overheard. *Sleep well, bully,* I thought. *Your secret is safe with me, until I decide to reveal it.*

How satisfying it would have been to tell him off and fire him on the spot in front of his sycophant. So why didn't I? At that critical juncture, the campaign was more important than my ego. There was work to do, and the campaign could not afford internal sabotage. I could sustain the hit—for now.

By August, though, Luis and I decided it was time for him to go. We fired him. Meanwhile, I moved to Iowa full-time. We had a small but loyal group of volunteers, staff, and family spread across the state: my niece Caroline; my daughter Missy, who was by then a veteran of the Clinton White House and the Kerry presidential campaign; Danny O'Brien; and Annie Tomasini, our Iowa press secretary, another "adopted" Biden, who had already moved there in May. They were eager for me to join them full-time.

The 2008 primary was truly an embarrassment of riches, with three principal candidates—Joe, Barack Obama, and Hillary Clinton. We underestimated the potency of people's desire for change over experience. The only solace that it gave me is that we lost with the knowledge that either Barack or Hillary would win, and each would make a great President.

Soon after Obama was nominated, he reached out to Joe. Would he be interested in the vice presidency? *I don't need you in order to win*, Obama told him. *I'm going to win. I need you to help me govern.*

Joe was hesitant. At that time, he had the best seat in the house, no pun intended, as Chairman of the Foreign Relations Committee. Could he do more with his current position than he could as Vice President? Traditionally, Vice Presidents didn't really do anything. He would have to report directly to a superior for the first time in decades.

What finally did it? Mom. She said: "We have the chance to elect the first African American as President, and you have to even *think* about it?"

After much debate, in August 2008, Joe told Obama yes, with one condition: that he be the last person in the room with Obama before the big decisions were made.

They had a handshake deal, but it seemed there was one last piece before it could be finalized. The Davids needed to sign off: David Plouffe, Obama's campaign manager; and David Axelrod, his strategist.

Since Joe's house was under constant media surveillance, given the VP speculations, it was decided that this meeting would take place at our house. The Davids flew into New Castle County Airport, and Beau and Jill picked them up—baseball caps and sunglasses adding to the intrigue. Joe had already arrived at our home, waiting for them down by the pool, where there was privacy. It was hot, but it was still early enough in the day that it was not uncomfortable to sit under the big awning. When Beau drove in with our guests, Jack and I met them and escorted them down to the pool. As promised, we left them alone: no pictures, no distractions, no chitchat.

After everyone left, Jack and I went down to clear away the soda glasses. Three chairs were pulled away from the table, two facing the pool and one facing the stairs that led back to the house. A still life.

Jack and I wanted to take a picture of the table setting; it was history in real time. But we didn't. We had agreed, no pictures. In hindsight, that was silly. It would be nice to have that memento now.

Shortly before Joe's formal nomination, he was assigned a Secret Service detail. The White House Communication Agency (WHCA) instructed that detail to work with Joe to pick a code name. Code names are serious business: they allow the agents to communicate with one another succinctly about the safety of their protectee. Joe, Senator Biden, the Senator, and so on would not do. There would be one name—constant, clear, and unique to Joe.

One morning, we had gathered in Joe's kitchen in Delaware, some family, some staff, and a few Secret Service agents, our perpetual coffee and doughnuts spread out on the table. "I don't know, talk to my sister," Joe said when a junior agent asked him about his preference for a code name. The agent approached me.

"Ma'am, according to the WHCA, Senator Biden must choose a name that begins with the letter *K*," he said.

I nearly choked on my sugar raised doughnut. Well, how many English words can *you* think of that start with *K*? I could only think of one, and there was no way in hell I was going to give my brother the code name King.

Thus began the first round of bureaucratic negotiations. "Ma'am, the Senator has been assigned the letter *K*—that's how the WHCA system operates. It goes by alphabetical order, and *K* is the current letter up for use."

"Well, what do you think, gentlemen? Do you think we can change the system for the future Vice President of the United States?" I knew he wanted the letter *C*, for *Celtic*—a nod to our Irish roots. I drove the poor agent crazy, and he, in turn, drove his superior, Jim Helminski, crazy in getting the change in protocol finally approved.

When all was said and done, I thanked the agent for his patience. "Now, let's settle on my code name. I was thinking, Celestial Spirit," I said with a grin. I was teasing him, of course—I knew that only the immediate family were assigned Secret Service code names. "Ma'am, you don't get a code name," he said seriously, before a sly smile played across his face. "Besides, we already have your code name."

"What! What is it?"

"Hurricane."

"Hurricane?"

"Yep—Hurricane. When we see you coming, we relay to our fellow agents, Category One, Two, Three, Four, or Five."

Once Joe was on the ticket, it was back to the campaign trail. Joe's debate with Sarah Palin on October 2, 2008, in Saint Louis, was the last time I sat in the audience for one of Joe's debates. That night, I sat in the front row next to Jill, and as usual found myself envying her poker face; it was painful for me to hold still and keep from grimacing. I was uneasy that night for two reasons. For starters, Beau was heading to Iraq the next day. Both he and Hunter were with Joe backstage in the waiting room, and his sons were the last people to speak to him before he walked out onto the stage. "Home base, Dad—remember home base" was Beau and Hunter's counsel to their dad.

I was also uneasy because I recognized Sarah Palin as a worthy opponent. She wasn't qualified to sit next to the leader of the free world, much less to take his place, but as a purely political animal, she was a force. She looked like apple pie and sunshine, but she wasn't that tasteful. She would and did draw first blood, but we knew she would label Joe a bully if he responded. She reminded me of Jane Brady, Joe's opponent in the 1990 Senate race, who took a similar no-boundaries approach. Joe had to be careful lest he draw comparisons to Rick Lazio, the man who ran against Hillary Clinton in her first NY Senate race in 2000. During their first debate, Lazio demanded she sign a pledge to reject "soft money," going so far as to leave his podium and shove it in front of her, invading her space. In that moment, Lazio became the face of misogyny. My guess is that Palin's strategy was to provoke a similar moment from Joe.

"May I call you Joe?" she asked when she walked onto the stage. Joe smiled graciously and said of course. We learned later that she asked because she always slipped up and called him "O'Biden." From my vantage point in the front row, I thought she did pretty well. She ignored the moderator's questions, but that was her entire strategy. "I may not answer the questions the way that either the moderator or you want to hear," she declared, "but I'm going to talk straight to the American people." She was feisty, and she understood that people might be rooting for her just because she was the underdog.

Afterward, I went backstage to find Mike Donilon grinning. Joe had won, he said. He was sure of it. I wasn't so sure, but it turns out I was wrong—the difference between watching a debate from the front row and on the television screen turned out to be enormous.

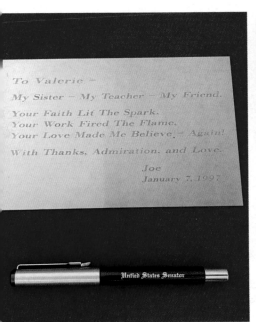

To Valerie —

My Sister — My Teacher — My Friend.

Your Faith Lit The Spark.
Your Work Fired The Flame.
Your Love Made Me Believe — Again!

With Thanks, Admiration, and Love,

Joe
January 7, 1997

gift from Joe after the 1996 Senate victory.

My sister-in-law Sara and me at the Democratic
National Convention in Los Angeles in 2000.

Beau congratulates his campaign manager, my daughter Missy, after his successful 2006 Delaware Attorney General race. (Photograph by AP Photo/Pat Crowe II)

Working with the Women's Campaign International in Liberi in 2009. (Photograph | Sue Goldstein-Rubel)

Second Lady and Vice Sister, a.k.a. Jill and Valerie, attend a summer afternoon event in Washington in 2010. (Photograph by Brad Glazier)

Joe, as Vice Presiden led the US delegatio to Rome to attend th inauguration of His Holiness Pope Franc on March 19, 2013. He invited me to joi them. (Photograph b *L'Osservatore Roman*

In Selma, Alabama, on March 3, 2013, I accompanied Joe to the Bloody Sunday Remembrance March. Photograph by Melina Mara/*The Washington Post* via Getty Images)

I was a Resident Fellow at Harvard Kennedy School's Institute of Politics in 2014. I loved every minute of teaching my seminar, "Up Close and Personal," a class filled with students hoping to pursue careers in public service, politics, and policy.

"That's it, no more questions," I tell the Vice President following his remarks to Harvard students at the Institute of Politics in 2014. But, as usual, he kept on going. (Photograph by Catherine McLaughlin)

My "campaign staff" of Harvard students at the Institute of Politics in 2014. Clockwise from me: Cybele Greenberg, Rohan Pavuluri, Madeleine Gearan, Faith Jackson, Mary Grace Darmody, and Ryan Pallas.

In 2015, as a Senior Advisor to United Nation General Assembly 71, I delivered an intervention on human rights on behalf of the United States.

On International Women's Day in 2015, I was honored as one of fifty "Women Inspiring Change." Joe, Jimmy, and Ashley surprised me by joining Casey, Jack, and Missy to hear my keynote address that day at Harvard Law School.

It was an emotional moment for all of us when Joe and Jill returned to Wilmington after the Vice Presidency. At the welcome-home rally on January 20, 2017, I spoke about Joe's roots in Delaware, his long years of service, and his coming home. It had been a long journey filled with many shared memories.

Missy, Cuffe, and Casey in 2017—clearly my best work

Casey married Chris Castello on July 1, 2017. *Left to right*, the extended Owens family joined the bride and groom: Missy, Christine, Jack, Jackson, Thomas, Casey and Chris, me, Jade, and Cuffe. (Photograph by Michael Connor of Connor Studios)

On Iowa caucus day, February 3, 2020, these eagles stood as sentinels along the road as Missy and I campaigned. "Ah," we thought, "Beau sent them." (Photograph by Missy Owens)

On the 2020 "Soul of the Nation" bus tour through South Carolina with actor, fellow Biden supporter, and Delawarian Sean Patrick Thomas. He made the trip a lot more fun. (Photograph by Michael Holahan/USA Today Network *The Augusta Chronicle*)

Speaking at a campaign rally in North Augusta, South Carolina, in January 2020. God love the people who came to hear me talk about my brother on that chilly, windy day. (Photograph by Michael Holahan/USA Today Network, *The Augusta Chronicle*)

The day after Joe selected Kamala Harris to be his running mate in August 2020, she came to Wilmington. Before they began their formal schedule, Joe invited me to have lunch with the two of them. (Photograph by Adam Schultz)

Ron Klain, Mike Donilon, Joe, and me in the holding room immediately before a presidential debate in 2020.

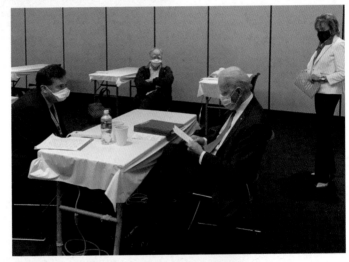

Four days after Election Day, Joe was finally declared the winner of the presidential race. At the boisterous victory celebration in Wilmington on November 7, 2020, Joe points to me and shouts, "Val! We did it!"

What a moment. On November 7, 2020, after the victory speech had been given, the celebration had ended, and nearly everyone else had gone home, Joe and I huddled together at the Chase Center in Delaware to watch as TV networks recapped the highlights of the day. It was a time of quiet reflection and awe. (Photograph by Adam Schultz)

Walking the White House colonnade with my brother, President Joe Biden, in spring 2021. (White House photograph by Adam Schultz)

Steve Schmidt, senior advisor to John McCain's 2008 presidential campaign, has since become a friend of mine. He is a good man, and he knows both when to fight and when to make amends. He played a major role in selecting Sarah Palin as McCain's running mate and has since said that it was the worst mistake he'd ever made, not only torpedoing McCain's chances of winning, but also delivering a terrible blow to the United States, which he holds so dear. Palin was supposed to reignite McCain's campaign; instead, however, she turned out to be a stick of dynamite that not only exploded in his hand but worse, inflamed a culture of ignorance and bigotry.

Election night 2008 was in Grant Park in Chicago, where a crowd of hundreds of thousands were pressed closely together for as far as the eye could see.

It was November 4 and unseasonably warm—we didn't even need our winter coats. Joe's motorcade, filled with extended family, pulled up to the entrance of the park, where we were quickly led down a cordoned-off narrow curvy pathway, which snaked around the back of the stage and led us to the designated outside area that was secured for the family.

People cheered and clapped when we entered. It was dark at this point, and the anticipation in the air was palpable—our first African American President, Barack Obama, and my brother, Vice President Joe Biden.

When Obama first walked onto the stage to thunderous applause with Michelle and their children as America's next First Family, there was such joy, goodwill, and hope. We all believed we were on our way to an even better tomorrow.

"If there is anyone out there who still doubts that America is a place where all things are possible; who still wonders if the dream of our founders is alive in our time; who still questions the power of our democracy, tonight is your answer," Obama declared when he took the stage. When Barack finished his remarks, Michelle returned onstage with Joe and Jill at her side, followed by their children. But the best moment—from a sister's point of view—was when Joe turned back to get Mom. As she approached then President-Elect Obama, she reached out her hand to him to walk with her and Joe to the front of the stage—but not before she whispered to both of them, "*I told you.*" She was beautiful in her new coral suit, radiant, and proud of the two strong men at her side. As soon as our family left the stage, they Skyped Beau, who couldn't be there because by then he had deployed to Iraq.

That night, I watched Michelle hold her brother's hand. I, too, held my brother's hand, and smiled. We were fortunate women. Michelle's older brother, Craig, was her "protector," the person who understood her, even when she didn't always understand herself. The bond that immediately drew me to Michelle was that of sisters who were lucky enough to have older brothers who loved us as much as we loved them.

There was never a time I saw Michelle Obama that she did not greet me like a dear friend. Her hug is a total immersion, and as warm as her smile. Over time, I came to appreciate that during the primary campaign, what I had taken as aloofness was likely the classic reserve of a brilliant and beautiful woman confronting an unfamiliar and often hostile environment. That night, she stepped into the role of First Lady with confidence, grace, and determination. And she looked like a natural.

Before we joined our family's tent, Jack and I stopped by the President's, where he was gathering with his family, friends, and staff. One of the people we spent time with was Valerie Jarrett, one of the Obamas' closest advisors and friends. At the Democratic Convention that year, Valerie had let me and Jack in on some news. "You know, Barack told me he wanted your brother to be his VP right after the last primary debate," she said. "I told him, 'Okay, Barack, you can pick him. But we've got to do this the right way. Let's look at the other good people out there, and then you can make your choice.'"

"You know, Valerie," I had replied with a laugh, "you could have saved me a whole lot of worrying."

My brother was Vice President now, which meant there wouldn't be any campaigns to run for a good long time. I've been asked multiple times why I've never gone on to run someone else's campaign. My record suggests I could help propel a career from obscurity onto the national stage. But I was never trying to build a résumé. I just wanted to help my brother. I knew Joe better than anyone else in the world did, and I knew what he had to do to both stay true to himself and to win. I understood, even when some professionals did not, that the two goals were one and the same. Being true to himself was the only way for Joe *to* win. You can't fake authenticity.

Looking back on my track record—fifty years, seven Senate campaigns, one County Council race, three presidential elections, God only knows how many dinners and phone calls and mailings and fundraisers and arguments about ad copy—I can boil down what I know about how to run a successful campaign and an enduring candidacy into one simple idea: if you win the heart of the voter, the rest will follow. There's an old saying, "No one cares what you know until they know you care," and it is never more true than in the political field. This isn't the only way to win an election, of course, but it is *our* way.

When a member of your family becomes Vice President, everyone's life changes somewhat, but no one's changed as directly or completely as Jill's. In the years leading up to Joe's selection as VP, Jill was a self-proclaimed and avowed nonpolitical spouse. She was a team player, to be sure, but her mantra was "I am an educator. Val's the political one. Let her make the speeches."

This dynamic changed after Joe was sworn in as VP, and Jill became Second Lady. Jill has Joe's sense of purpose and resolve, but happily for all of us, her sense of humor and joie de vivre are all her own. Even before they moved into the Naval Observatory, the VP residence, Jill began outlining her policy priorities and forming a team that would build her platform as Second Lady in a way that reflected both her passions and her personality.

Her first love is teaching, and it is in heralding and promoting community colleges that her fire burns brightest. She has always said that community college is the best-kept secret in our educational system. And to this day, she is a full-time professor. Second, she has devoted herself to advocating for military families. She understands that while families do not wear a uniform, they, too, serve and sacrifice.

While I never made a move to Washington, I also never stepped away completely from Joe's world. I was still his sister, and we talked constantly—about his triumphs, his concerns, his frustrations. The Republican Party, shell-shocked by the magnitude of their loss in 2008, regrouped and decided to devote themselves to making Obama "a one-term President," in the famous words of Senator Mitch McConnell. For Joe, I know there was some disappointment in watching those who had been his colleagues for decades resort to cold obstructionism. Compromise, which had always been the prize of the Senate, had become a dirty word. Every decision in government, including once-routine procedures like lifting the debt ceiling, became showdowns. The era of bipartisanship, of colleagues working across the aisle to find common cause, seemed if not dead, then more remote than ever. It saddened him.

Mitt Romney, who ran against Barack and Joe in 2012, was no one's idea of an extremist. He was a moderate, running against an incumbent in a time when his own party was racing rightward, away from the center that Romney stood for and believed in. I didn't agree with a lot of Romney's positions, but I respected him. When I saw the documentary about Mitt that came out years later, I was struck with the realization that if something like that had been released during the campaign, he would have had a better chance of winning.

President Obama was true to his word: Joe was always at his side, always the last person in the room with him. They had a spectacular partnership, and each brought something out in the other. Like any long-term relationship, it deepened over time. There was sometimes a tendency in the press or the pundit class to compare the two—the cerebral Obama and "working-class Joe." Sometimes it made Joe feel as though they thought he just fell off a turnip truck carrying a lunch pail. He was, of course, proud to be a supporter of working people, but he had other strengths, too—representing all Americans. And over time, everyone saw them.

As I said, it's not easy raising an older brother, but after Joe became Vice President, my work felt, well, done. I decided to embark on a journey to add some new chapters to my career, and in doing so, found myself in unexpected places—from the floor of the UN General Assembly to the halls of Harvard. At every step, I marveled at the turns a life can take.

First, though I had done so for more than twenty years, I began traveling more frequently as a volunteer with Women's Campaign International (WCI). WCI was founded by my friend, former Representative from Pennsylvania Marjorie Margolies, to enact meaningful change worldwide by supporting women who are mobilizing their communities. WCI believes, as I do, that more women need to get involved in politics if this world is ever going to change for the better.

Mom taught me and her sons that every issue is a women's issue. When one of us is discounted, disenfranchised, disrespected, when one of us is sold, battered, belittled, then we are all less. As is written in Matthew 25:40: "Whatever you do unto the least of my brothers, you do unto me."

The women with whom we met during my travels with WCI so often wanted the same things that American women want: a better life for their children, a brighter future, and a say in the matter. They came to our training sessions despite the risk of backlash in their countries because they believed that in the face of struggle, a better life was possible.

Another common thread that struck me during my travels—from Liberia to Venezuela, Taiwan to Romania—was that so many of the incredibly accomplished women I met battled impostor syndrome. I'm no psychologist, but just as I would be marveling at a particular woman's courage, resilience, and creativity, she would confide in me about her total lack of confidence, or her inability to own her achievements. *I'm not even that smart. I don't belong here. I have no idea what I'm doing. One day, they'll realize I'm a fake.*

Coined by psychologists Pauline Rose Clance and Suzanne Imes in 1978, the term *impostor syndrome* refers, loosely, to the negative self-talk and feelings of inadequacy that high achievers occasionally suffer from. I know this feeling. I sometimes fought it during my career as campaign manager.

To be any kind of leader, you need a hell of a lot of confidence. Confidence is the number one prerequisite for success in life. But to be a *woman* leader—to make tough decisions while often facing discrimination, disrespect, and doubt—you occasionally need a booster shot. I think that because of my parents and my brothers, I was lucky to have been given that booster shot. Joe told me that I could be anything I wanted to be, and he told me frequently enough that I eventually believed him. My husband Jack continues to reaffirm that.

I'd venture to say many women don't have the same experience, so I've tried to pass on that booster to those who might need it. That's in part why I founded Owens Patrick Leadership Seminars in partnership with my dear friend Michele Pollard Patrick, a certified protocol officer and business etiquette consultant. Our work focuses on coaching women to develop and project confidence in a business environment, as well as in more formal social settings. While confidence is sometimes innate, more often it comes as the result of practicing new skills, just like anything else.

In 2014, I was invited to be a Resident Fellow at the Harvard Kennedy School's Institute of Politics (IOP). It was just one semester, but teaching my seminar there remains, without question, one of the happiest and most rewarding professional experiences of my life.

That fall, Jack and I loaded up the car, merrily reenacting some of the very steps we had taken with Casey thirteen years before, when we prepared to send her off to Harvard. ("Did you already put the comforter in?" "Do you think I need this winter coat, too, or will three warm jackets be enough?") I was in a state of total disbelief and wonder. If you had asked me whether Casey could be successful at Harvard, whether her mind and her spirit belonged at a place like that, I would have told you, without a moment's hesitation: absolutely, yes. But if you had asked me whether I ever thought I belonged at an Ivy League school (let alone Harvard), whether I really and truly thought I deserved a seat at that table, I would have answered just as quickly: no. A stubborn remnant, I'm sure, of that old Catholic school chip on my shoulder. Georgetown, Holy Cross, fine—those Jesuit schools were places for Bidens—but not Harvard. Mom would have been disappointed in me if she could have heard my internal dialogue.

I had Jack and the kids to thank for helping me realize the error of my ways. When Missy, Cuffe, and Casey were applying to colleges, Jack had one rule: they could go wherever they wanted, but they had to apply to at least one Ivy. To my surprise, I had found myself wanting to object. A resistance welled up in me that I struggled to contain, and I felt discouragements coming to my lips, which I had to suppress. What I felt myself wanting to say to Jack was *Why would you make them apply somewhere they might never get in, and where they may never feel comfortable?* The fact was, they were exceptional students, and there was no reason they couldn't get in.

When Jack and I first approached campus to drop Casey off in 2001, it was—as I now refer to the brightest, most sparkling days—a Harvard-blue-sky day. I remember looking out the window at students running around the Charles River, seeing the crew team out rowing, their oars cutting one long thin line through the water in coordinated strokes. It was magical.

This time, in 2014, eager to alight from the car after a long, congested drive, we sped through the final stretch from Boston into Cambridge. And then we got pulled over. "Dammit," Jack whispered under his breath.

The officer approached the window, assuming his role, Boston accent and all. "Do you know why I pulled you over?" The whole thing.

Jack, as he often does with strangers, tried to make a bit of polite, friendly conversation to lighten the mood. He explained that we were so excited to head off to Harvard that he simply hadn't realized he was speeding.

The officer stared at him for a beat, then at me, and then looked to the back seat. "If you're going to Harvard, where's your kid?"

Jack and I couldn't help but laugh. Jack looked at me with raised eyebrows and said, "Can I tell him?" I nodded. "My wife is going to teach a seminar. Can you believe it!"

The cop, despite himself, couldn't help but ask a few follow-up questions. He sent us on our way with a ticket, yes, but also with a smile.

When we finally made it to campus, I felt a rush of happy memories, remembering days spent watching Casey play lacrosse, or having dinner with her teammate's mother, Robin Sproul, now a dear friend. And now, here I was, following in my daughter's footsteps.

My course, "Politics: Up Close and Personal," was a compendium of the insights I'd garnered from fifty years of campaigning. I showed them the Joe Slade White ads; I invited guest speakers to talk about polling, paid media, the free press; I even invited my brother, who at the time was Vice President, to speak to the class. But my seminar was also a glimpse into the story of my life: how my stomach dropped whenever Joe was attacked; how we regrouped after the 1988 campaign fell to pieces; how we navigated every 3:00 a.m. phone call, dispiriting new poll, and near miss. There had been no distinction between politics and "real life," because politics, at its highest level, *is* real life. Real campaigns are fought and won with heart, soul, and trust, and all the same ironclad rules that govern relationships are just as true of good campaigns: Listen more than you speak. Reflect the dreams and ambitions of others back to them. Don't lie.

The unexpected bonus of my going to the IOP was that I also got to know Cathy McLaughlin, who had been executive director of the IOP for the past twenty-two years. Cathy is an exceedingly capable, savvy, loyal woman who knows all the ins and outs of what it takes to run such an incredible institution. (The politics of academia are even more intricate than those of the Democratic Party.) The following year, Cathy planned to retire to Cape Cod; she wanted to go to the beach.

I interrupted her plans. "Cathy, I think your future has a *B* in it, but it's Biden, not the beach." I asked her to come to Delaware to help us set up the Biden Institute at the University of Delaware, and with the help of Hunter and Ted, she agreed.

I lived on campus for the duration of my time at Harvard, which lent it extra preciousness. Each Resident Fellow had undergraduate students who served as interns for the semester. I called them my "campaign staff." They took me to their classes with them, introduced me to their favorite professors, and invited me to their dining halls for dinner. It was such a kick to walk into Cambridge together and eat at all the little restaurants, talk about the news of the day, what the plan was for our next class, and wander back to campus late in the evening. It was a safe, warm community. They couldn't get enough of my stories, and I couldn't get enough of their hopeful, inquisitive, genuine spirits.

Every Monday, they came to my apartment for spaghetti dinners. I am not a creative cook, but I make the best sauce ever, and during those dinners, the students let me into their lives as I had let them into mine. We talked boyfriends, girlfriends, current and national events, and just plain, *What am I going to do with my life?* We talked a lot about confidence. These were Harvard students, the cream of the crop, and I saw that they often felt lost despite their prestigious education. Like many of us, they seemed to think of confidence in the abstract, as something you either have or lack. Confidence is real, but it is as fluid as water: sometimes it flows, sometimes it freezes, sometimes you can feel it trickle right out of you. Like any inner resource, you can build it with time and practice.

By the end of the semester, my interns and students had become like a little family. When I put on my running shoes and ran on the path around the Charles, I felt so alive, full of energy and hope. The students had given that to me. I will never forget it.

All through his childhood, Joey fought a stutter. The sounds would stick in his throat, and his face would redden with anger and confusion as kids laughed. For years, he fought the bitter taste of embarrassment that landed on his tongue instead of a word.

He wasn't going to be defined by the stutter—this other voice that lived just beneath the surface and could override any utterance at a moment's notice. But it took him years to subdue it.

In high school, some kids called him Dash, but not because he was fast—although he was, and a star player on the football team. They called him Dash because to them, he sounded as if he were speaking in Morse code.

But there is only one victim in this story here, and it is not that boy. The victim was the stutter itself—which the boy spat out with defiance and resolve, reciting poetry and speeches into the mirror until he had mastered them.

And there is only one champion here: the boy, who would one day become the next President of the United States.

14

RUN, JOE, RUN!

Mom told us that out of every tragedy something good will come, if you just look hard enough. And I've seen that to be true throughout my life. But what good could possibly come from Beau being diagnosed with the deadly cancer glioblastoma in the prime of his life? None that I have found.

No words gave comfort, and the grief in those early days was so overwhelming that it seemed to blot out every good thing in my vision. It stripped me bare and harrowed my soul. I had never before been so horribly angry at God.

But grief proceeds as mysteriously and inexorably as love. Grief may descend like sickness, but it moves through you like a cure. Grief—grief so profound you can taste nothing else—must seep into every fiber of your being before it can begin to wash over you and cleanse you. It is crushing, complex, hollow, silent, and blaring. It is everything and nothing. At night, I tried to will myself to sleep.

I waited for the darkness to pass, prayed that it would, though I wasn't sure to Whom I prayed. The family endured while Beau prepared, living his last days with the utmost dignity and grace.

Finally, it was time. On May 30, 2015, Beau was "Gone, gone, gone," as Father Leo O'Donovan said at his funeral Mass.

So, too, was a piece of my heart, of the heart of each member of the family.

Why? Why Beau? I heard no answer from God, only a deafening silence. When I expressed this frustration to a dear friend, she responded gently: "Because, Valerie, Beau can be even more powerful where he is now." I mulled that over. Perhaps.

But the words that gave me the most solace came from a poem that Vicki Kennedy sent to Joe, which he shared with me. It is called "Gone from My Sight" by the Reverend Luther F. Beecher, and this section of it pierced me so deeply that I have kept it on my desk ever since:

> I am standing upon the seashore.
> A ship at my side spreads her white sails to the morning
>   breeze,
> and starts for the blue ocean.
> She is an object of beauty and strength,
> and I stand and watch her until she hangs like a speck of
>   white cloud
> just where the sea and sky come down to meet and mingle
>   with each other.
> Then someone at my side says: "There! She's gone!"
> . . . .
> And, just at the moment
> when someone at my side says: "There! She's gone!"

there are other eyes that are watching for her coming;

and other voices ready to take up the glad shout:

"There she comes!"

Beau was brave in the face of death. He wasn't afraid of dying—
his concern was for the living: his wife, Hallie, and their two children, Natalie and Hunter, whom he would be leaving behind. He also
feared that his own death might break his father—not only his heart,
but also his spirit. That's why Beau made his dad promise him that
he would not turn inward, that he would not quit. Beau knew if his
dad gave him his word, he would keep it. Joe gave him his word, and
despite the pain of his loss, or perhaps because of it, Joe kept moving
forward.

We were picking ourselves back up as a family when Donald
Trump was elected President. Like millions of Americans, we were
appalled. If ever there was a force of anti-empathy in the world, it
is Donald Trump. He is a bully, pure and simple—a narcissistic,
incompetent, and incomplete man. He is the embodiment of resentment. His power comes from tapping into our baser instincts.
After eight years, it was a blow for Joe and President Obama to
turn the White House over to a man whose team was hell-bent
on undoing everything they had accomplished. But as we all know
President Obama said, "Progress isn't always a straight line or a
smooth path."

When Joe and Jill moved out of the Vice President's residence in
DC, they rented a home outside the capital so Jill could keep teaching at Northern Virginia Community College for the remainder of
the school year. It was from this house that we put together the
chapters that we thought the rest of Joe's public life would comprise:
the Biden Foundation, the Penn Biden Center for Diplomacy and

Global Engagement at the University of Pennsylvania, the Biden Institute for Domestic Policy at the University of Delaware, and the Biden Cancer Initiative.

Joe embarked on a lecture series in which he spoke about everything from foreign affairs to the issues facing middle-class families. During that time, he was also writing his beautiful memoir *Promise Me, Dad.* The book offered an intimate glimpse into the last year of Beau's life as he fought glioblastoma. I had been closely involved with Joe's first book, *Promises to Keep,* but *Promise Me, Dad* was entirely Joe. He said it was cathartic, and that writing it was cleansing. He wanted to show the world what a magnificent man Beau was, and he didn't need anyone's help to do that.

During the *Promise Me, Dad* book tour, it was clear to me that those who came to hear Joe saw something compelling in him and his story. The chants of "Run, Joe, run" at book events felt deeper than cheerleading: this was a collective expression of need. People needed an empathic leader, craved one in their souls. That primordial call was hard to shake.

Only a few months earlier, white supremacists and neo-Nazis had stormed Charlottesville in the so-called Unite the Right rally. Watching unrepentant racists with tiki torches parade through the city chanting slogans was horrifying; hearing the President of the United States defend them was even worse. Everything Trump had campaigned on—to get rid of NATO, build a wall, blame all your problems on the Other—appealed to our lowest common denominator, which could only assist us in destroying ourselves. Joe was shaken to his core. He penned an op-ed about how Charlottesville represented a battle for the soul of the nation. It was a defining moment. Unless the tone of the country drastically changed, I knew he would run.

Soon after that, I started waking up early in the morning, well before the sun had risen, my brain crackling. It was a sensation I knew all too well. I could see a path before me, littered with spent casings, attack ads, ambushes. It was the campaign trail. It was calling, for better or for worse.

As the years of the Trump presidency wore on, bringing fresh degradations almost every day, Joe just couldn't tolerate what he was seeing. With Nixon, we saw the mechanics of governance do their job: they checked and expelled an agent who was trying to overstep his bounds. Trump didn't just represent policy failure or erratic personal behaviors; he represented something darker, more primal, more insinuating, striking deeper into the heart of what made us who we are. It seemed that for the first time in our lives, democracy was in peril.

Even more troubling was watching Joe's old colleagues at best do nothing or at worst, participate. Joe was never a Washington insider, but he was a Senate man, and he had strong relationships with people on both sides of the aisle. The Republican Senators Lindsey Graham, Richard Lugar, and Arlen Specter each came to Delaware when Joe was a Senator to participate in the Biden Seminars and talk about the bipartisan legislation that they worked on together. Senator Alan Simpson of Wyoming was another friend who spoke of Joe's character and integrity. Joe had an especially strong bond with Senator Chuck Hagel, who was one of his closest friends in the Senate. Joe and Senator John McCain had a deep, abiding friendship—Joe gave one of his eulogies, and Cindy McCain endorsed Joe for President in 2020.

What puzzles me is this: What happened to Lindsey Graham? After John McCain died, perhaps a part of Senator Graham's soul died as well. The man is unrecognizable to me today.

A particular interview in 2015 by the *Huffington Post* with Senator Graham sticks with me. He talked about Joe, and with tears in his eyes said: "The bottom line is if you don't admire Joe Biden as a person—you have a problem. You need to do some self-evaluation. . . . He is as good a man as God ever created."

Also in 2015, Graham spoke to CNN about Trump as a candidate for President. He called Trump "a race-baiting, xenophobic, religious bigot," and went on, "He doesn't represent my party, he doesn't represent the values that the men and women who wear the uniform are fighting for."

Fast-forward to 2016, when Trump was elected President: Graham went from the foregoing statements to making character-assassinating comments about Joe and our family. Even worse, he became sycophant in chief to Trump when the very underpinnings of our democracy were being threatened. This is incomprehensible to me.

Finally, Joe made peace with a simple fact: if he turned a blind eye to Trump's demagoguery and vileness, he might never again be able to look at himself in the mirror. He knew that Beau would have expected him to have courage and do the right thing. He remembered Mom's saying that bravery lives in every heart, and at some point, it would be summoned.

For as long as Joe and I have worked in politics, I never doubted for a minute that he should run in each of the races he entered. Even in 1972, when it looked impossible.

But I didn't feel that way this time. Not because I didn't think he was the best candidate. Not because I didn't think he could win. Not because I didn't think it was important. I had the same fears for the country that Joe did when it came to Trump. I just thought the price was going to be too high.

Every time I closed my eyes, I could see the campaign Trump would run. It was as vivid as a movie. Brutal. Crass. Classless. And every time I saw that movie, I would feel sick. Physically ill. Trump would do and say anything to win. And he would spare no one. And I didn't want to go through it. I didn't want the family to go through it. I was worried the family *couldn't* go through it. I worried about Hunter. The grandkids. And Joe. I knew the family had voted and said they understood the risks and still wanted Joe to run, but it's one thing to say you understand what's going to happen, and it's another thing to live through it. Maybe because I had run so many campaigns, I was already living in my mind what was about to happen.

But Jill, Hunter, Ashley, and the grandchildren all wanted him to run. Jack agreed. "Joe, you've got to do this," my husband said. Former Majority Leader John Boehner, whom I got to know after the 2016 election, told me to advise Joe *not* to run. "He's a good man and he has served his country well," Boehner said. "He should just enjoy his life. They will eat him alive. Politics now is a blood sport." Part of me wanted to say to those urging him on, *Look, he's done enough. Leave him alone.*

Now, I knew Joe was not the Messiah who was going to cure the country with the laying on of hands. But the values he's always represented best—civility, basic decency, kindness, empathy—were the precise traits most lacking in American discourse. That's why I believed Joe was the right person at the right time to lead our country. Whereas Trump is vulgar, Joe is gracious. Whereas Trump is mean-spirited, Joe is kind. Whereas Trump is vindictive, Joe is healing. Joe understands that you can't lead unless you can heal. Joe was speaking to the heart and soul of America.

So on April 25, 2019, Joe formally declared his candidacy. He was going to do this, one last time. And the rest of us were all in behind him. Joseph R. Biden Jr. was a candidate for President of the United States.

In the early stages, we had some hard decisions to make. Running for President means being willing to meet the moment, and when Joe announced his candidacy, a woman's right to choose was under unprecedented attack. For decades, Joe had held the same position: He felt he had no right to impose his religious beliefs on the rest of society. Over more than fifty years in the Senate, he never voted to curtail a woman's right to choose. However, he had consistently voted against federal funding for the procedure through Medicaid.

Now it was clear to us that the landscape had shifted. We could no longer sit in the middle of the road on the issue, since the middle of the road was rapidly disappearing.

Like many women, I harbored complicated feelings on the topic. I'm pro-choice, but I remain convinced that Democrats chose the wrong term for our side of the issue. We should have been pro-life, for we are the ones advocating for a better life, a life in which a mother gets to determine her future and that of her child. Sometimes, I even accidentally say I'm pro-life, because that's what it feels like the pro-choice position should have been called.

Despite this, when it came time for me to face down my own choice, I had a great deal of difficulty. All my pregnancies were challenging, but my third was the hardest. I was bedridden for eight months, and I went to the hospital three times because of premature labor.

It turned out that my body hadn't gotten the memo that I was pregnant, and my system kept trying to flush the pregnancy out.

There was a large, grapefruit-sized mass in my uterus pushing against the baby. We didn't know what the problem was exactly, because I couldn't get an ultrasound until the six-month mark. My doctor did the next best thing he could do—he gave me his professional opinion. He came into the hospital room and told me and Jack that there was a good possibility that our baby was going to be "a bad baby" (his exact words). He went on to say that if I were his wife or his daughter, he would tell me to terminate the pregnancy. He said, "You're young enough, you can have another."

He went on to explain that if I didn't do anything, I was almost certain to miscarry in twenty-four hours. If I wanted to keep my pregnancy, he would give me hormone injections, but he couldn't guarantee what sort of effect they would have on the baby's development.

Jack and I talked about it. We wondered if we had the capacity to raise a child who might be born with severe impairments. The hormone injections were supposed to be fine, and had been around for a while, but the doctor had been frank in saying that there were unknowns. "Whatever you decide," Jack said, "I'm with you, one hundred percent."

I was a tangle of ambivalence, trying to sort through my various feelings and fears. Nothing about our situation was simple—for me, for Jack, for our family. It was messy and full of intersecting lines. I didn't want to hold on to what Nature was telling me was a nonviable pregnancy, nor was I certain about taking the hormones the doctor described. When my mother was pregnant, women were given the natural hormone thalidomide to maintain their pregnancies. However, the effects were sometimes devastating. Children were born without limbs. I had too much information, which is often a dangerous and confusing thing. The doctor was right, of course: I was still young and could have another baby, and he had been pretty straightforward in his recommendation.

In the end, we decided to continue my pregnancy. It's hard for me to say why, exactly, other than that it was the right choice for me. Even so, my heart was troubled every single day. I prayed that I had made the right decision. I prayed to Saint Gerard, patron saint of safe deliveries, and especially to the grandmother of a friend of mine— a woman whose strength and courage in life were an example to me. Her name was Hannah, and though she died before I could meet her, I felt as though I knew her and she knew me. She held me close as I talked to her the night before the birth.

During the cesarean, I closed my eyes and imagined a gift package—a dark blue box with a white ribbon. I pulled the ribbon, lifted the lid, and in my mind, there was a healthy baby in there, with all its fingers and toes. That was the very first question I asked when the doctors finished the operation: "Does my baby have a full set of fingers and toes?" The doctor and nurses didn't answer. No one said anything to me. I repeated the question once, and then again.

It turned out our baby had swallowed amniotic fluid—that's why I didn't hear a cry. The medical team couldn't answer me, because if they said "Everything's okay" and it wasn't, they would open themselves up to liability. They rushed the baby out of the operating room, heading for the NICU, and Jack moved to follow them. He stopped abruptly, looked back at me, then to the baby, and back at me again.

"Go," I said. Before I even learned if my baby was okay, they put me under to finish the operation.

When I woke up in a haze of alarm and confusion, Jack was by my side in the recovery room. I could tell by his face that we were okay. We had a healthy, beautiful baby girl. I felt a flood of such awe and gratitude, even as beneath that, I still felt the tremor of fear brought on by a near miss.

We were lucky. We rolled the dice and got the prize. But I had everything I needed to feel secure in taking this gamble: first of all, I had Jack. Second, I had financial resources. Third, I had a full-court-press emotional support system ready to activate at a moment's notice. And finally, I had health care, and a family ready to help however they could. And it was still one of the scariest times in my life.

I have seen countless young girls and women who had none of these resources, yet were nonetheless expected to make such pivotal decisions. There is just no way—under the auspices of the pro-life movement or otherwise—I could imagine wagging my finger at those who made a different decision than I did.

Under Trump, the Republican Party was actively dismantling access to abortion, passing restrictive laws in forty-five states; as a nation, we were poised to return to an era where millions of women would no longer have any options. I argued that it was time for Joe to drop his support for the Hyde Amendment, which prohibited federal funds to be used for abortion services. Especially for low-income women and women of color whose only option for care was through the Affordable Care Act, voting to oppose federal funding for abortion was, in reality, voting to curtail a woman's right to make her own choice. If we wanted to preserve the spirit of the ACA, the Hyde Amendment had to go. I know how hard Joe wrestled with the decision, but ultimately, he agreed.

This behind-the-scenes role as Joe's confidante felt right to me in 2020. I was finished with full-time campaign management. I didn't want to be waking up at 3:00 a.m., worrying about everything I could control *and* all the things I couldn't: social media disinformation, fundraising, and security (both physical and virtual). I was ready to clear out of headquarters, as was Greg Schultz, who had set up and managed the campaign from its inception years earlier. We both took on new roles, so it was with confidence that in early spring 2020, Jennifer O'Malley Dillon assumed the role of campaign manager with Kate Bedingfield as her deputy. Greg and I gratefully passed the torch to these tough, brilliant women.

We had chosen Philadelphia, Pennsylvania, as our national campaign headquarters. Pennsylvania was critical in defeating Trump, and such a pivotal state in our own lives that it felt like the right thing to do. We had roots in Scranton; we always felt like we belonged there. The feeling was mutual—many Pennsylvania Democrats called Joe their third Senator.

Nonetheless, we didn't want to neglect our Delaware family. We launched the campaign with a rally in front of the Rocky steps in Philadelphia, but later gathered our longtime supporters in Wilmington to lay out the road map to victory. I told the crowd, "You will determine the outcome of this election, just as you have so many times before. You continue to be the wind beneath my brother's wings, the whisper in his ear, the roar in his commitment, the steel in his backbone."

After the campaign was up and running, I was asked by a reporter what it felt like not managing this final campaign, and I said: "Damn frustrating." It was, because for the first time ever, I had to convince a new team *why* I thought something was a good idea, instead of just saying *because I said so.*

But the second half of my comment (which was not reported) more accurately reflected my thinking: "Thank God. Now I can focus on what I like to do best: meeting voters on their home turf, and representing Joe." I had not hung up my spikes, as the sporting analogy goes—instead, I had laced on combat boots. I was hitting the road.

To send me on my way at the start of this, our last epic battle in the fight for the soul of the nation, Jill gave me a red leather journal with the following inscription: VALERIE, CHARACTER SHOULD DETERMINE DESTINY ON THIS JOURNEY . . . WHO BETTER AT HIS SIDE THAN YOU? WITH LOVE, JILL. When I read her inscription, I thought, *Right back atcha, Jill.* She and I are our own version of a power couple. We divide and conquer, and we flank Joe, emotionally and physically. On Super Tuesday, when a protester rushed us onstage during Joe's victory speech in LA, Jill, fierce as ever, beat the Secret Service to the mark, stepping in front of Joe to intercept the protester before he even saw it coming.

My official title was National Co-Chair of "Biden for President," but titles never meant anything to me. My most important title was one I had worn all my life: sister. I was always amazed at and humbled by the number of people who came out to meet me and hear about my brother. I went to so many places—big cities in Texas and California, small towns in Iowa and Nevada, countless communities in South Carolina that were stops along the way on the "Soul of America" bus tour.

One day during the South Carolina tour, I was going over my remarks en route to a local event when I heard staffers and volunteers mention the Wrecking Crew. What was that, a rock band? They explained that it was a group of predominantly African American community leaders who had backed Kamala Harris for President. Kamala had recently withdrawn from the race, so I wondered, *What's the Wrecking Crew up to now?* I asked the staff if they could set up a time for me to speak with them. Soon, I was talking on the phone to a woman named Bernice G. Scott. I asked her if she would meet me at the next stop.

When the doors of the bus opened and I stepped down to greet her, the first thing I heard was, "Oh Lordy—look at those legs. I want to get some of those fancy stockings, too." That was Miss Scott—a powerhouse of a woman whose teasing put me at ease immediately. I said I had expected to be greeted by a rock band, and she said: "Honey, we are the *Reckoning Crew,* not the Wrecking Crew, but we do rock—the system, the structure, the goalposts. And we will help you do it, too." She helps me to this day—with her energy, prayers, and goodness.

As our journey continued, I made our case. I spoke about bullies, a resonant subject when the Commander in Chief was swaggering around the Oval Office as if it were his own private playground. I reminded them of how roundly Joe was mocked for his childhood stutter—both by his fellow students and even sometimes by the teachers—and how that experience taught him a basic lesson: he could survive by stooping to their level, or he could accept that we were all in this together and hold tight to empathy.

"He chose empathy," I said. "He knows the gut-wrenching truth that we all eventually face—everyone's life is an incredible act of bravery." Above all, the message was distilled in Joe's oft-repeated words: this was a battle for the soul of America.

Even if you've run a hundred campaigns before, you're never quite prepared for the next one. Sure, you can apply all the tactics and notes that helped you win the last one, but each election is a new contest and a fresh referendum. Ask any good campaign manager, and they'll tell you—every campaign is the first one, and each one could be your last.

Even so, we knew that running against Trump would be totally unlike every previous election. He stopped at nothing to attack his enemies, and he cared nothing about norms, civility, or truth. He had the mind not of a President, but of a vengeful dictator, and running against him felt almost degrading. To put this man on the same stage, in the same league, as my brother—to present *this guy* as an alternative to Joe Biden—was nauseating. As a sister and as a citizen, I was appalled.

I didn't buy into the conventional wisdom in the press that people already had made up their minds about this election. I was itching to get in front of voters and see for myself. I knew I'd find the skeptics. Give me an hour with someone who doesn't understand what kind of man Joe is, and I'll often give you a convert, or at the very least someone ready and willing to give him an honest shot. It was always worth a try.

During our previous presidential campaign in 2008, we had visited a small rural town in Iowa where I had gone to meet potential supporters. It seemed to be miles from anywhere, but it was home to the folks who gathered in the back room of a local restaurant to hear me talk about my brother. When I entered the room, an older man had his back to me. He was talking loudly about how he didn't like Biden, not one little bit.

He was fond of hearing himself talk, and as he went on, I tapped him on the shoulder. "Hi, my name's Valerie, and I'm Joe Biden's sister. You know, I think you have my brother pegged wrong."

The guy drew himself up taller. No, he didn't, he declared. He added a few more choice words about Joe, concluding, "I will never vote for him—period."

"You know, I don't think our mother would like what you just said about her son," I said. "I'm going to call her—maybe you'll listen to her."

"Hell, call her," he said. "I'll tell her the same thing." The guy seemed to be enjoying the attention.

So I called Mom on my cell phone and handed it over to him. At first, he was disdainful. "This isn't Joe's mom," he scoffed. But after he got over his bluster, he grew quiet. I watched him listen, and when he spoke again, it was an entirely different register. "I'm sorry, Mrs.

Biden," he said. "He must be a fine young man from what you say. Yes, ma'am, I'll check him out. Thank you."

I had this memory in mind when I returned to Iowa in 2020. It was the earliest test of our mettle, and when I got there, the ground game was in disarray. We didn't invest enough money in hiring, and we had a worthy opponent in Pete Buttigieg, the young Mayor of South Bend, Indiana, who came in and organized a humming machine. With some urgency, I set about talking to local party chairs, trying to whip up as much support as possible.

In Waterloo, I tried to convince a legislator in a very conservative district to caucus for Joe. As I talked, the man kept nodding. He agreed with Joe's positions on everything and thought he was a good guy.

"So you'll support us?" I pressed.

He shifted uncomfortably. "I'll do everything I can in the background," he said, "but I don't want to come out to support him publicly."

"So you want to kiss me in the dark, but when we go out, you won't even hold my hand?" I shot back.

The night before the caucus itself, I spoke at a packed rally; I was the first speaker, meaning the lowest on the totem pole. But I whipped up the crowd, and over the roar that came back to me, I thought, *If this were a primary, we'd sweep the state.*

The Iowa caucuses are a strange beast, subject to arcane rules. When you find your caucus location, you must be inside the room, or at least lined up outside, by 7:00 p.m. No one can get in after that, and what's more, you are committed to stay until 9:00 p.m. If you're a parent who has to pick up kids; if the freezing, often-brutal winter weather, with its subzero temperatures and black ice–coated roads keeps you away; if the babysitter you lined up is ten minutes late—oh well. It's a tough slog for these caucusgoers; they are committed and determined advocates. This process is not for the faint of heart.

As always, the Biden family's sense of shared purpose kicked into high gear. When we were campaigning in Iowa, my son, Cuffe, took a leave of absence and drove from LA to Iowa for the month of January to campaign for Uncle Joe. Jimmy's son Jamie came out for a couple of weeks, and my son-in-law, Chris Castello, came in from Seattle. Missy took all her vacation time just to travel with me in Iowa.

As we went from place to place, Beau was never far from my mind. Seeking solace, I realized that the caucus took place on Beau's birthday—February 3. I found that thought soothed me, so I kept the thread going. Hunter's birthday was the very next day—he was born on February 4, 1970. February 1970—2/70. Ah! The number of electoral votes that would put us over the top was also 270, so that must mean that this February would be good for us. Flimsy, I know, but it put a smile on my face, and stoked the fire I needed to keep going. Sometimes you just have to find something bigger than yourself to believe in.

The night before the results came in, I was charged with nervous anticipation mingled with dread. It was like the night before Christmas inverted—Santa was coming, but no matter how good you'd been all year, you might wake up to no presents and an empty stocking. You just never knew.

The results the next day were delayed thanks to chaos—Trump-supporting trolls teamed up to clog the phone lines, attempting to disrupt the results, and a smartphone app designed to make it easier for Iowans to vote reliably did the opposite. It was a dismaying beginning to the 2020 election season, but the picture only got worse when the results started to come in.

We were shellacked: fourth place. It was a dismal showing, and the memories it summoned—of 1988 and 2008—were unwelcome. I'm an extremely competitive person. Ask my children what it's like to play minature golf with me. Jimmy won't even bowl with me. But while I don't *like* losing, I can stomach it. What's harder for me is watching Joe take a hit. But that evening, just before he left, I could see he was still standing tall.

There was little time to stew over our loss. We had only a few days to prepare for the New Hampshire debate, which took place days before the February 11 primary. On debate day we flew from Delaware to New Hampshire at 2:30 p.m.: me; Joe; Mike Donilon; Beau's wife, Hallie; as well as their daughter and son, Natalie and young Hunter. Jill was already waiting for us in New Hampshire. We were running late, and on the drive to the airport, the weather was wild, unpredictable. In the car, we were lashed by heavy rain, only to be greeted by brilliant sun at the airport, which turned again to dark clouds when we boarded.

Before we took off, the pilot fixed us with a wry look. "Buckle up, and I mean *buckle up*," he said. "This could be very bumpy." Indeed.

An hour and a few Hail Marys later, we landed in New Hampshire. We had maybe an hour to get to our hotel and then to the debate site. At the hotel, Joe nicked his earlobe shaving, and worried it would not stop bleeding in time for the debate. He was holding tissue paper to his earlobe on the ride over, and I watched, praying blood wouldn't drip on his white shirt. He was preparing himself, and sitting behind him, I knew to be quiet. Jill and the kids had already left to be seated in the auditorium by the time we arrived.

Whenever I bumped into other candidates, they were unfailingly respectful and cordial. "Your brother's a good man," Bernie Sanders said to me when I walked past him with his wife and two sons. When I tried introducing myself to Amy Klobuchar, she cut me off, smiling. "I know who you are!" she exclaimed. "I see you all the time. You take good care of your brother. Good luck." It was such a relief to be work-ing in an atmosphere like that, free from the poison of the national discourse.

When Joe prepared to go onstage, he became very focused. No high fives, no chest-puffing—that just wasn't his style. As for me, the most I'd ever get from him was a quiet "I'm glad you're here." It was all either of us needed.

Ron Klain, now Joe's White House Chief of Staff, was his debater in chief then. He ran debate prep and assembled the policy team before each event. My role, though informal in title, as always, was clear: be Val. Ron was vocal in his desire for me to speak up: "You have great instincts for how to connect with people, and above all, you're not afraid to tell him when you think he's wrong." I was good with that arrangement.

I often have comments for Joe—always during campaigns and, to a much lesser degree, once he is in office. They usually take the form of critiques, refinements—sometimes a criticism if he lost his temper or was a wise guy. Or I'd make some sort of crack, about things he might want to put another way. One time I told him, "Jeez, Joe, if you say it like that onstage, even I wouldn't vote for you." That usually drove the point home.

I am generally reluctant to correct him in public, but when I see or hear something I don't like, I always tell him. I just wait until we are alone. The question inevitably comes: "What do you think, Val?"

One thing you can always count on with Joe is that he will either be writing or redrafting a stump speech en route to his next event. Between every venue, he tweaks his remarks. "How does this sound, Val?" And every time, it sounds better, although somehow it is never delivered as written. Because at each event, he has an innate feel for what to say.

Sometimes this causes a problem, such as when he tries to pack ten pounds of information and inspiration into a five-pound bag. Or, more precisely, a thirty-five-minute speech into fifteen minutes. He never takes it very well when his staff signals him to wrap up—it only seems to instigate him to further extend his point. I am often the one who calls out from the side or taps him on the shoulder and says, "Joe, we really have to go. We're keeping these people too long."

In small group gatherings, though, it's a delicate balance. While people want to have a less scripted discussion, they don't generally take it well if Joe delivers a monologue when they were promised a conversation. I recall a particular dinner for prospective donors that took place at a private home in New York City. I could feel the mood shift from interest to resentment as Joe went on and on. The guests there wanted to be heard, too. It's hard to practice the art of conversation and answer detailed questions at the same time. I told Joe we had to figure out a better formula. My refrain to him was "Leave them wanting more."

During the 2020 debates, I never sat in the audience; I couldn't take it. I stayed in the greenroom, watching the debate on TV with Ron and Mike, and sometimes Campaign Chair Steve Ricchetti. The worst person to watch one of Joe's debates with—by far—is Ron. By the time he's finished with his expletives, I have become absolutely sure of two things: (1) we are going to lose, and (2) the entire world is going to implode.

Not that I was any better. During those primary debates, my nerves were tight as a drum. I knew how Joe would answer his questions—I'd heard him answer them a hundred times in the past. But I knew if he misspoke even a little, there would be no mercy for him.

To help ease my anxiety, I carried my red clutch bag, which I kept with me as a talisman. It has a white owl imprinted on it. One night, driving back to Joe's house from debate prep, I'd spotted a white owl sitting on Joe's fence post. It was on the left side of his driveway. I yelled "Look at the owl!" to everyone's disbelief.

"What owl?" Joe said without even looking up.

When I pulled out of the driveway to go home, that owl flew right in front of my windshield—almost as if it had been waiting for me. I couldn't wait to get home to look up what it meant. Was it like a black cat crossing your path? I discovered it was a sign of wisdom and endurance, of protection and power.

Funny thing is, that handbag had been in the back of my closet for more than a year. *No longer,* I said, *you're coming with me,* and it became my companion throughout the campaign. Superstitions have a way of spreading, and soon, the first question the traveling staff asked me was not "How are you?" but "Did you bring her? Do you have the owl?"

Under the very best of circumstances, debates are nerve-racking. But the 2020 primary debates were particularly messy. Candidates repeatedly spoke over their allotted time, and the moderators failed to rein anybody in. It was more of a spectacle than a debate, each presidential hopeful ignoring the rules of engagement in single-minded pursuit of their defining ten-second sound bite. I was exhausted watching it; I can't imagine how it felt to participate.

Joe, God bless him, was as calm as ever. There's a silence, a stillness about him—a deep internal reservoir of confidence. In those difficult early primaries, I watched him with something close to awe as he kept pushing forward. On to the next contest, he said. We're not finished yet.

When it became clear that we would lose in New Hampshire, Joe and Jill boarded a plane to go to South Carolina. They needed a jump start on campaigning there to stop the bleeding. I was left with former New Hampshire Governor John Lynch to deal with the non-victory "victory party." It was considered bad form for a candidate to leave while the results were still coming in, and our supporters were still gathering. Some people were insulted: "I can't believe he just left town." But the consensus was that it was too important for them not to move to the next stop, and I was left to explain.

"The press is ready to declare people dead quickly," Joe said. "But we're alive and we're coming back and we're going to win. Now we're going to go to South Carolina and take this back."

South Carolina was the lifeboat. Neither of us said it out loud, because we didn't need to. If the results of that one didn't go our way, that was it. Joe's path to the nomination would be all but closed off. He would never become President of the United States.

The tension en route to Charleston for debate number ten was unbearably high. There was simply too much to do, and too much at stake not to do it well. Joe was still on a whirlwind—seven or eight events a day, fundraising calls, press interviews, and nonstop debate prep. He didn't have time to eat or, more important, to think. *It's too much to expect of anyone to do all this right,* I thought.

Joe's South Carolina team was concerned. They said we had a poor ground game, no concise message, no elevator pitch that said what we meant and what we stood for. We should be aware, they continued, that the philanthropist billionaire candidate Tom Steyer had cut into some of our support.

"You're Catholic," Congressman Clyburn said when we met with him. "Speak in threes." Every answer Joe gave in the debate should respond to the following: (1) What's in it for me? (2) What's in it for my family? (3) What's in it for my community?

I called John Della Volpe, the director of polling at the Harvard Kennedy School Institute of Politics. We'd gotten to know each other in 2014, during my time as a Resident Fellow.

John and I had become friends, and during Joe's 2020 run, John said he wanted to help in any way he could. I called him because I wanted a summary of what he'd learned recently while doing polling at the College of Charleston. When it came to youth polling, John was the best, and I valued his insight.

The gist of his report was that Joe needed to recalibrate his relationship with young voters. One-half of them were all in for Bernie, but that left the other half looking for an alternative, someone who would recognize their views. When Joe ran with Obama, the relevant national mood was optimism and opportunity. Not so anymore for kids born after 9/11. For them, *fear* was the operative word. Fear of crushing debt and lack of affordable housing, fear of assault rifles and mass shootings, fear of the failures of the criminal justice system. And, of course, overwhelming concern for the health of the planet. Their personal health came in second to the earth's. They might be invincible, but Mother Earth was not.

None of this was news to us. It reaffirmed what we were hearing in our own polling and reinforced our gut sense of the electorate. Even in the face of our dispiriting early results, I firmly believed Joe was made for this moment. I hoped South Carolina primary voters felt the same.

As the date drew near—February 25—I was holding on to a secret hope. Beau's birthday had fallen on the Iowa caucuses, and while that hadn't panned out the way we'd wanted, I was convinced that Beau was playing a role up there somewhere. Congressman Clyburn's wife,

Emily, was also in heaven, and I envisioned that she and Beau were going to make themselves known. How, and in what way, I didn't know. But my faith was unshakable: Joe's son and Clyburn's wife would help us right the ship, not only keeping us afloat but also retooling us for rougher seas ahead.

That intervention arrived, I believe, in Congressman Clyburn's moving and inspired endorsement speech. Clyburn's endorsement of Joe didn't just track along policy and principle; it was personal, exquisite. Clyburn reminded his supporters they knew who Joe was—they had seen his heart and soul for decades. But more important, the Congressman said, Joe knew them.

We won every county, in every demographic, with a larger voter turnout than in 2016. In the next big contest on March 3, known as Super Tuesday, we went on to sweep the South, winning in nine states. "Joe Biden Shocks the World," read one headline. *Thank you, Beau.*

The following day I was riding high on our victory, still speaking in front of big crowds gathered to support Joe. Our team was monitoring the news for new developments in the disease that the World Health Organization had officially dubbed COVID-19 on February 11, only three weeks earlier. There had been some worrisome signs—nursing homes in Seattle were overcome by it, and Governor Jay Inslee had just declared a state of emergency. "If—and this is a big if—there is a social-distancing strategy that becomes necessary, the emergency declaration would give us some legal authority," Inslee said. Cases were beginning to pop up on the East Coast, too.

But the nine days following Super Tuesday ushered us into a new reality. By the time Joe's next debate with Bernie Sanders rolled around—scheduled for March 15 in Arizona—the CDC had officially designated COVID-19 a pandemic; and on March 13, President Trump declared a national emergency. Travel restrictions had begun. Owing to concerns about air travel, CNN relocated the debate to Washington, DC, and closed it to a live audience. Only five people were allowed to accompany Joe to the CNN site. I attended along with Ron, Mike, Annie Tomasini, and Ashley Williams, who was leading the Advance team, which helps coordinate travel on behalf of the campaign.

Joe won that debate. Three weeks later, Bernie Sanders officially withdrew his candidacy.

After that, everything came down like a row of dominoes—the quarantines, the sequester-in-place orders, massive death tolls making the front page. We scrambled to make sense of new protocols and upended norms. The outbreak of the pandemic stopped our ground game in its tracks. Campaign events were canceled—no more rope lines, selfies, meet and greets—everything that Joe considered second nature, the lifeblood of campaigning, and a virtual source of inspiration. When he got to do that kind of work, he was the very best Joe Biden could ever be.

Everyone working on the campaign was like a duck—each stationary in our own ponds while paddling furiously underwater to keep our lives afloat. Every morning, Joe got a briefing from his top medical doctors about the pandemic and number of deaths. Joe was aware that every number was more than a statistic—it was a mom or dad, husband, wife, child.

The campaign set up a mini studio at Joe and Jill's house. The Trump administration tried to mock him for "hiding," but we were content in the knowledge that we were doing the right thing, and refused to be drawn in. Joe had been bullied before, and he certainly wasn't going to dignify the world's biggest bully with a response to explain why he was following science.

Besides, there were bigger things going on. We watched with a mounting sense of powerlessness as the President denigrated the advice of Dr. Anthony Fauci, trumpeted dubious cures, and dismissed and downplayed the dire threat even as it spread worldwide, striking down millions. Trump told people not to worry—it was no worse than the flu, and with early precautions, it would all be over soon. It was a Democratic hoax designed to make him look bad, he added, unable to help himself.

It was so absurd that it would have been comical were it not all so horribly tragic. Joe had laid out a detailed plan for what he would do to stem the tide of death if he became President—but he wasn't, and Trump was turning a deaf ear to any information he didn't want to hear.

As for Joe's campaign, we were like everyone else we knew—adapting, trying to make the best of things. Annie Tomasini, Stephen Goepfert, Ashley Williams, and Anthony Bernal created a "pod" and were the only ones physically at Joe and Jill's home to make sure everything functioned. Their efforts were herculean.

Zoom became a way of life. I preferred phone calls. On a phone call, you don't have to worry about fixing your hair. You don't have to think about lighting or what color jacket to wear or tidying the counter so that plate isn't visible in the shot over your shoulder. I did hundreds of Zoom calls on Joe's behalf. They were hard because I had to memorize my remarks cold, whereas on the phone, I could at least look down to my bullet points.

As the long summer of 2020 wore on, we began to plan for the nominating convention in August. It would be entirely virtual— the first of its kind. The theme was unity, but under the weight of

COVID-19, I felt less connected than ever before. The Fourth of July would be a holiday unlike any other in my lifetime. It was without the usual parades and thousands of small-town fireworks, hundreds of big-time exhibitions.

Meanwhile, Trump was bringing out his supporters to rallies by the hundreds—no masks, no social distancing, no precautions required or requested to inhibit the spread of the disease that was killing thousands of Americans each day. Once Trump had gathered his faithful, he entertained them with his usual menu of race-baiting rhetoric, disinformation, and cultural divisions.

The rest of us—the great majority of Americans—remained at home, in our own backyards, with our families and friends, a self-selected group who had practiced CDC guidelines for two weeks or more to be sure we were free of virus symptoms. This was still not entirely safe, but it was a reasonable chance to take if we wore masks, washed our hands, and maintained social distancing.

It was a delicate balance. We are social animals, and we need companionship, light, and laughter in our lives, or our own fire can go out. But we also recognize that we have an obligation to those around us, to keep them safe as well as ourselves.

It was jarring to discuss how to unite Americans while we all were sequestered in place, communicating through online video platforms. Our public gathering spots—the parks, the playgrounds, the restaurants and bars—were empty. That message of unity seemed both impossible to transmit and more important than ever.

In mid-March, at the last Democratic debate, Joe had announced that his vice presidential nominee would be a woman. Why? Because Joe understands that every issue is a women's issue, and if we continued to use only half the brainpower, creativity, passion, and productivity available to us, then we would continue to come up short, with only half the answers.

Joe assembled a vice presidential search committee that included former Connecticut Senator Chris Dodd, Delaware Representative Lisa Blunt Rochester, Los Angeles Mayor Eric Garcetti, and former Staff Director of the Senate Judiciary Committee Cynthia Hogan. Fourteen women were preliminarily vetted. The committee reviewed their superficial public records and interviewed them to see if there were any red flags. Each woman was tremendously impressive.

Joe and the committee were thoughtful, deliberate, and respectful in their approach to making his choice. He didn't want to trot out a list of "qualified women" as prospective running mates, only to have them second-guessed by the media. (If she wasn't picked, what was wrong with her? What secret had disqualified her?) So Joe played it close to the chest, and so did the women with whom he spoke.

Several of the women called me because they assumed correctly that Joe would speak to me about his selection. I was truly honored that they considered me to be an honest broker. I was impressed with their commitment and vision. Each was a leader, and each had an extra ingredient that catapulted her to "best of class." I listened to their reasons for wanting to serve with Joe, and the issues that they held closest to their hearts. It was a difficult decision. On August 11, 2020, Joe chose Kamala Harris.

After Joe selected Senator Harris, she came to Delaware to meet with him. Their meetings took place at the Hotel Du Pont, the same place

where we held that first victory party back in 1972. The first day of
her visit, Joe called and asked me to come down and meet her for
lunch. I arrived a few minutes before she did.

When Senator Harris arrived, Joe motioned toward me. "Kamala,
I want you to meet my sister, Valerie," Joe said, introducing me to his
new running mate again, although of course we'd seen each other on
the campaign trail before. "She's been my best friend all my life, since
I was three years old. She rode around the neighborhood on my handlebars. She's taken care of me all my life. And I should warn you up
front," he added with a laugh, "if you ever cross me or come after me,
she'll come after you."

"I understand completely," said Senator Harris. "I have a sister,
too."

Joe grinned. "Not like this one, you don't."

In the Roman Catholic Church, every day is named after a saint.
Joe was scheduled to debate Trump on September 29, so I checked
to see what saint landed on that day. Turns out, it is the Feast of the
Archangels—Saint Michael, Saint Gabriel, and Saint Raphael. The
archangels drove Lucifer out of heaven—Michael was the leader, Gabriel represented strength, and Raphael is most often associated with
healing and acts of mercy. Leadership, strength, healing—everything
that Joe was running on.

On the day of the debate, I sat across from Joe on the plane as we
made our way to Cleveland. "I know you won't *really* listen to this," I
said, "but I want you to pay attention and not brush me off."

That got his attention.

I told him about the Feast of the Archangels, and the meaning
behind each one. I could already see him dismissing it, so I raised my

eyebrows and held his gaze. "Look, Joe, you say the rosary, right?" I knew for a fact he had his rosary beads in his pocket.

He nodded.

"You still talk to Beau, right?"

"Yes," he said.

"Well, then believe this. Because you can't believe those two and not believe this one. They've got your back."

He thought about that for a second, and then grinned at me. "I love ya, kid," he said.

We had our usual debate team around to prepare for Trump, which we all expected to be a totally different experience from any of Joe's past debates. This was a man who literally could say anything and nothing at the same time.

Ron, as usual, ran the show. Anita Dunn, who was a close advisor to Joe, played the role of television moderator in our rehearsals. She understands the media as well as anyone and knew that some moderators would try to formulate gotcha questions that would yield great ten-second sound bites. She worked hard to flummox Joe.

Equally adept was Bob Bauer, who played the role of Trump. Bob was a master. He showed us how devastatingly effective a smart, controlled Trump could have been. In fact, if Trump had followed Bob's playbook, there's no doubt in my mind he would have done a much more credible job. Bob really knew Joe, and knew how to get under Joe's skin.

The Trump who came out on the debate stage that night was even worse than our worst caricature: heedless, reckless, ignorant, cruel.

But in contrast to Bob Bauer, he was neither focused nor smart. He interrupted nearly every time Joe opened his mouth, in a clear bid to shake or rattle Joe. In the absence of any kind of strategy or message of his own to promote, he came to throw banana peels and hope that Joe slipped on one of them.

He didn't. One of the only moments when Joe lost his composure was also, maybe, the most satisfying of the entire debate. Fed up with the constant interruptions, Joe turned to Trump to say, "Will you just shut up, man?" It might not have appealed to our better angels, but I wanted to pump my fist all the same.

November 3 was unlike any election night in history. No crowds, no chants, no cheering—and no results. Because of unprecedented numbers of mail-in ballots, the process had slowed to a crawl, and multiple states were still being tallied. But as the votes piled up, the path for Trump to remain President all but vanished. The country was on edge, but we were calm. Trump supporters were yelling, "Stop the count!," but we knew nothing would. Once the votes were counted, we knew we would win. All we had to do was wait.

There was only one little problem: We'd rented the Chase Center in Wilmington for Joe's victory speech for the night, and had set up the stage outside to meet COVID-19 protocols, and now we had to hold on to it—indefinitely. Apart from the stage setup, the TV crews and trucks, the tents, security, cranes, fireworks, drones for the light show, and a small army of people there to manage it all, we also had a fleet of Jeep Wranglers on loan so my brothers, Jill's sisters, and all our children could safely gather while maintaining social distancing. Holding the rental space was like lighting money on fire by the tens of thousands on a daily basis.

Joe took the stage to urge all of us in the crowd and across the country to let the process take its course, to be patient. "Sometimes democracy is messy," he said. We weren't going to declare victory prematurely. Meanwhile, Trump tried to sabotage the only American political norm left open to him: the peaceful transfer of power. We expected it, but it was still a kick in the gut to see it happen. I went to bed on November 3 unable to stay up to watch the results trickle in any longer. I woke up around two in the morning, only to turn on the TV and see that Trump had claimed he won. I turned the TV off in disgust.

Surely it will be over soon was the thought that got me through that night and the next day, but then another day rolled around without a clear result. How long could we sustain it? Should we dismantle everything, find a plan B, or wait it out?

We decided to stay put. The Jeeps sat dark in the field, facing an empty stage with an unmanned lectern. Meanwhile, in Arizona, Pennsylvania, and a handful of other crucial swing states, election officials did the hard, grueling work of counting, one ballot at a time, while the storm raged around them.

At no point were we afraid that somehow Joe wouldn't become President. Trump couldn't stave off the inevitable, no matter how hard he tried. But he was going to do everything he could to discredit and vandalize the process before he was removed. It was a sobering reminder of just how deep the fissure went in American politics, and how much Trump had done in his four years to deepen it.

When the news finally broke on Saturday, I was with my daughters, Missy and Casey, and my seventeen-month-old granddaughter, Jean—the namesake of my mom. We were at the Westin Hotel, getting our daily COVID-19 tests. As we were coming out, we saw reporters beelining toward us. A jolt ran through me. I knew what that must mean.

Someone stuck a microphone in my direction. "Your brother was just declared the victor. How do you feel?"

"This is great news for us, and it's even better news for our country," I replied.

We hopped in the car and turned on the radio. As we pulled out of the parking lot, we heard it for ourselves: the AP called it. The three of us looked at one another and, for the first time, let out a hearty cheer. We felt like warriors standing at the end of a long battle, triathletes after a punishing physical ordeal. There was as much relief in the moment as there was joy. Pulling out of downtown Wilmington, we saw people in their cars honking their horns in celebration. The joy radiated.

I called Joe immediately.

"Come over," he said. Joe and Jill had been there for days, quarantined together with their kids and their spouses and their grandchildren. When we arrived, everyone gathered on the porch for a socially distanced victory toast. It was a warm, beautiful day, and while we would have been justified in jumping up and down and shrieking with joy, the mood was pleasant and happy, but much calmer and more subdued than one might imagine. How could we really celebrate with all that was going on in our country at that very moment? Jill gave the briefest of toasts—there was just too much to say, and too little that really needed saying, so she kept it light—and we all clinked glasses. We were one glass short. Adam Schultz, now the chief official White House photographer, didn't get one, so Joe, who had noticed, passed his champagne over to Adam to enjoy. Then, the moment commemorated, Joe and Jill went inside and immediately began making calls to thank those who helped turn the tide in our favor.

Because of all the turmoil, it was hard to salvage a single clear, triumphant moment from the process. The waters were too poisoned by COVID-19 and Trump, the invisible toxin and the visible one. Because of disease protocols, we couldn't have a full family gathering, let alone a public one. What I felt instead was a quiet validation. *Let them count the votes,* I thought, as Trump fumed and did all he could to delay or discredit the results. *We won this fair and square.*

Mike Donilon said it best: "More people voted in this election than had ever voted in American history and they did it in the middle of a pandemic."

It began to sink in. *Joe was going to be President of the United States.* The task at hand was daunting. Joe began preparing immediately. There was no honeymoon, not a day off. Even as the transition formally began, the reality was difficult to accept. Months afterward, I would still walk past the television and hear the words "the President of the United States said," and my immediate thought was *What did that ass do now?* It would take me a minute to realize my mistake.

When I told Joe this story, he laughed. "I think that sometimes, too," he said. "And it's me."

I didn't have a game plan, but I always knew I wanted to be in the game.

EPILOGUE

Everything I had feared about the 2020 campaign came true. It was as brutal and vulgar and dishonest as I'd imagined it would be, especially to Hunter. Trump and his henchmen spared no one in their attempts to draw Joe's integrity into question. Trump spent his entire campaign in the gutter. Thank God America's better angels were triumphant.

It was no surprise to me that Donald Trump wouldn't show up at Joe's inauguration. A small man does not rise to the occasion. But I was so grateful to see other leaders from both parties in attendance. I approached former President George W. Bush and former First Lady Laura to thank them both for coming. "It's important," I said. President Bush, in his usual way, made a warm joke, something to the effect of "Where the hell else would I be?"

Joe had asked me my thoughts on the inaugural address. His question prompted me to reflect on a Ken Burns documentary I'd seen that included lines from a song called "American Anthem." The song speaks of the long journey to a singular moment in time—the centuries of labors, loves, loss, heartbreak, and hope that lead us to one day. And it challenges us to consider our legacy: What will we leave behind when we are gone?

I thought about our country, what we are now, and how far we have come. And I thought about the man, my brother—the soon-to-be President of the United States—and his own journey: the labors, love, loss, heartbreak, and hope that led him to this very place, at this very moment. I suggested Joe include a few lines from the song, and he did. The song asks "What will our children say when we are gone?" When it came to my brother, this was a profound question with a simple answer: he gave us his best.

Later that day, when Joe and Jill moved into the White House, the family joined them there. I watched with joy as the new President and First Lady walked up to the front door of the People's House—and then laughed when, unbelievably, the door wouldn't budge. Somehow, it was locked. There was an awkward beat and a brief scurry while someone inside fixed the malfunction. The door opened and then the family followed Joe and Jill in.

I wanted a moment alone with my thoughts, so I stepped into one of the rooms in the family quarters. Soon, Jack and Jimmy joined me while the rest of the family was being given a tour.

A little later, Joe poked his head back in the doorway. He looked at me and Jimmy and beckoned us over to him. "I wanna show you something," he said.

We got up to follow him.

"Where's Frankie?" he asked.

I told Joe that Frankie had gone back to the Blair House, where we were all staying, to check on one of the kids who didn't feel well.

Before we knew it, the three of us were walking down that famous colonnade and into the Oval Office.

We looked around, taking it all in. Jimmy had been here before. Joe had tasked him with redecorating the Oval Office with the help of our friend, the Pulitzer Prize–winning historian Jon Meacham. Jimmy had picked the rugs, the sofas, the decorations. He replaced Trump's chosen portrait of President Andrew Jackson with one of President Franklin D. Roosevelt and added busts of MLK, Cesar Chavez, RFK, Rosa Parks—all of which reflected Joe's understanding and reverence for the soul of this nation. Already, the Oval Office had begun to look more like the United States.

We tried to get FDR's Oval Office desk—I wanted everything Trump had touched out of there—but to this day, the desk resides at FDR's family home in Hyde Park. There is a replica of it in a warehouse somewhere, but we didn't want the replica. Thus, the desk Trump had sat behind remained. It was the *Resolute* desk—the same one used by Presidents Kennedy and Obama, so that was certainly good enough, and went a long way toward exorcising from my mind the repugnant image of its previous occupant.

But today, it was only the three of us—and it was Joe's desk. We were silent. Words were unnecessary.

"Thanks," Joe said to us.

My thoughts quickly returned to Jack, whom we'd left back in the family quarters. When I went to find him, I told him that we'd just visited the Oval Office. "I'm sorry I didn't bring you," I said.

Jack shook his head, reminding me yet again why I love him so. "No, no," he said. "This was a brother–sister moment."

It was that. We kids had come a long way together.

Fate has delivered both crushing blows and dizzying good fortune in my life, and in every period of flux, the only way I've found to respond is to try to remain open and alive to the possibilities.

In 2016, I was appointed Senior Advisor to the United States Mission to the United Nations 71st General Assembly. I lived in an apartment three blocks from the UN Headquarters in New York City. Every morning I walked to work so proud to be even a small part of that august organization: the majesty of its mission, the dedication of its delegates to the execution of its goals, and the leadership of our Ambassador at the time, Samantha Power. My job was to represent the United States at various events both on and off the UN Headquarters campus. It was the honor of a lifetime, but there are no words to describe the feeling of absolute awe and humility I felt when I stood at the dais of the United Nations and addressed the world on issues of global significance. The following year, after Obama and my brother left the White House, the University of Delaware established the Biden Institute in his honor. I serve as Chair. Joe, Jill, Jimmy, and I all back at our alma mater.

My experiences at the Institute of Politics at Harvard are ones I want to replicate for our students at the University—which is why having Cathy McLaughlin by my side is a godsend. Her experience, reputation, and vision immediately put us on a fast track. Because of Cathy, we did not have to learn on the job. I want to have a hand in creating many future Joe and Josephine Bidens. In 2018, the University renamed its School of Public Policy and Administration the Joseph R. Biden Jr. School of Public Policy and Administration. It is a top-ranked academic institution, but to my family, it is so much more. It is a legacy to my brother's character—his commitment, decency, and resilience.

Edith Wharton, a renowned American author, wrote that "there are two ways of spreading light": one is to be the candle, the other the mirror that reflects it.

It would be easy to assume that my brother Joe has always been the candle—and that I've always been the mirror reflecting his light and working to make it shine brighter. Oftentimes, yes, that is true. And, of course, it's still true, even today, that women in leadership are often relegated to being mirrors, advancing the work of others. But my brother made sure that never happened with us—the light traveled back and forth between us and spread by means of the work we've pursued.

Joe was the light for me when I was a little girl. I gave light to Joe as his campaign manager, his sister, and as Aunt Val to his children. Jack, Missy, Cuffe, and Casey have shone brightly for me countless times over the course of our lives together. And, in my own small way, I tried to offer some light to those students at Harvard and at the Biden Institute at the University of Delaware.

This is what good leaders do. This is what Joe has always done— as a brother, a lawyer, a Council member, a Senator, a Vice President, and a President. It's what my mother, the beacon, did when she counseled us to pay as much attention to what someone *didn't* say as to what they *did* say.

Looking back over the years, our family's faith in one another has been our true north. When Mom and Dad began their final declines, our approach was much the same—hold on to one another.

First, Dad's health faltered—a series of ministrokes, starting in 2000, that weakened and diminished him. When it was clear that Dad was not going to recover, he and Mom moved temporarily into the first floor of Joe and Jill's home, where we could provide better care for them. We all got to spend time with Dad in those last weeks. Frankie was living and working in Florida at the time, but he was able to be there at the very end. We took turns with Dad, sometimes just sitting and holding his hand, telling stories. We instinctively knew how to behave because we had watched Mom do it for our grandfather, Pop Finnegan, when he was dying.

On what turned out to be Dad's last day, September 2, 2002, he passed at 5:55 a.m. with Jimmy at his side. We were all sleeping over at Joe's, and Jimmy came to wake us. Dad was done fighting. He died as he lived: with elegance and dignity, with grace—no complaint, no bitterness. We all spent that night and into the early hours of the next morning talking about Dad. Jimmy knew so many more stories than the rest of us did—and we pieced together a fitting eulogy for our father, which Joe delivered with eloquence and love.

After Dad died, Mom moved back into the Woods Road house, and things were good for a while. But then, little incidents began to add up: a trip on the stairs, a slip on the rug, a fender bender in the grocery store parking lot. Her routine—daily Mass at noon at Saint Joe's, weekly hair appointment at Lorie's, food shopping—was unraveling. She lost weight and began to lose interest in just about everything. She missed Dad more than we knew.

A couple of years went by before she agreed to leave Woods Road. But it was to be on her own terms, in her own place—a cottage on Joe's property that was only two miles from her old home. It was familiar territory to her. We all pitched in and furnished the place for Mom. Joe and Jim created the perfect home for her. Jill, Sara, and I only got to pick out the dishes and new bed linens. For a while, things were good again. On the morning Joe was announced as Senator Obama's choice to be Vice President, Mom stood at the edge of the driveway and waved goodbye as we left to attend Joe's first event with the Obamas. Later, in 2008, Mom made the trip to the Democratic National Convention in Denver, to election night in Grant Park, Chicago, and did not miss a minute of the inauguration in January 2009.

But later that same year, 2009, Mom seemed to be holding on to some precious but dwindling reserve of energy. Then, she fell and broke her hip—and began her final decline. I fought it every inch of the way.

Instead of being sympathetic, I grew domineering. "Mom, cut it out. You can walk three steps, for God's sake." I knew that if she didn't fight harder, she would die. And I could not accept that. My brothers were more gentle with her, but Beau, Missy, and I were having none of it.

It took some help from a close friend to bring me to my senses. Frank Farmer sent me a chapter from *Crossing the Creek*, a book by Michael Holmes about the body preparing for death. The essence is that it takes the human body nine months to prepare for birth and, under ordinary circumstances, months to prepare for death. So that was what Mom was doing. I cried and felt a little bit ashamed. My own need for Mom was just too great, but I had to learn to let go. This was Mom's journey, and I was either going to help her on her path or stand in her way.

After that, if Mom didn't want to eat, I stopped trying to force her. If she commented about someone speaking to her, I did not correct her by saying that no one had spoken, that we were alone in the room.

My sister-in-law Sara, who loved Mom very much, wordlessly took over much of the logistics for my brothers and me. She scheduled Mom's home care appointments, trips to the doctor, haircuts at home, prescription refills, and finally, hospice. You name it—Sara had already done it.

On January 8, 2010, Mom was in her home. Her children surrounded her—Frankie on her right side, holding her hand, Jimmy on her left, and Joe and me at the bottom of the bed, touching her legs—while the rest of our family gathered in her living room. Here is where *Crossing the Creek* helped me again. "Joe," I said. "Leave the room so Mom can die in peace. She will not die with you here. She won't let you down."

He wasn't sure, but he believed me and did as I asked. Joe let go of her leg and backed into the bathroom that was directly across from the foot of the bed. Mom took her last breath within minutes. *Take care of each other.* That was Mom's mantra, and it continues to echo in our minds. We listen.

There is a Kierkegaard quote very close to my heart: "Faith sees best in the dark." I think the same could be said of empathy. When life is hardest, our ability to suspend judgment and reach across differences shines brightest. Empathy is also a kind of faith—the faith we have in one another.

When I look back on my life, I see it as one long trust fall into the power of empathy. The concept never leaves me for very long. It's a fancy word with a pretty basic meaning. Simply put, it means "to feel"—not as in "to touch" or "to experience," but as in "to absorb." With empathy, we are more open to understanding, at some basic level, the emotions of another soul. It is the connective tissue of our humanity.

It is clear to me that tragedy chisels the character more deeply and more lastingly than do the spoils of victory. My brother's tremendous compassion as a man, his tenderness as a father, his devotion as a husband, his commitment as a brother, his wisdom and vigilance as a leader, have all come in large measure from his losses and have created an emotional reservoir from which he invites others to draw.

Today, I think there's an epidemic of declining empathy in this country. Not so much on an individual level—there remains as much within the lone human heart as there ever has been—but on a societal level.

Even before the pandemic, we found ourselves living more isolated lives. Increasingly, we are more in our heads, gnawing away at our own anxieties and preconceptions, less engaged in our communities. Isolation can become insulation—it's easier not to acknowledge what you cannot see or feel or touch for yourself. What you don't see, you don't notice.

Moreover, the impact of the Trump presidency—a manifestation of a complete lack of empathy—continues to be profound. It called forth the darkest shadows harbored within the soul of our nation, revealing just how divided we have become. Our connections have been broken; some are shattered. Our character and integrity as a nation hang in the balance. This isn't an indictment so much as an observation.

But I believe good will prevail. During the fall of 2021, I had the opportunity to meet with His Holiness, Pope Francis, in Rome. "I pray for your brother every day," he told me, and gave me a rosary to take back to Joe. I found great solace in that. I believe the Pope is pulling for Joe, and I believe he is pulling for our country. He is the first Jesuit to serve as the Holy Father and he took his name, Francis, from the Franciscans, who represent compassion in the Catholic faith. We could all use more compassion in our communities today. The Pope declared 2021 the Year of Saint Joseph, and I don't believe that to be a coincidence.

To be sure, our country is in turmoil, and every person is experiencing it to varying degrees of intensity. The ground keeps shifting underfoot, throwing people, communities, and institutions off balance. But we can and must trust one another. We are all in this together, though, from time to time, we may wish otherwise. Simple acts of kindness take the measure of a person—a phone call, a visit to the housebound, asking "How are you?" and truly waiting to hear the answer.

Kindness reverberates. What you say and do matters. That is what I learned—growing up Biden.

ACKNOWLEDGMENTS

My thanks to:

My publishing team at Celadon (Deb Futter, Jamie Raab, Christine Mykityshyn, Randi Kramer, Rachel Chou, Anne Twomey, and Jennifer Jackson), for believing in this project from the outset and giving it wings;

Jayson Greene, a talented writer who worked with us to put this book together;

My agents at javelin, especially Robin Sproul, the initiator, the instigator, and my friend, who is an endless source of encouragement, and Matt Latimer, for his total commitment and patience;

Mary and Luisa McDonough, who nourished my body with healthy food and my mind with Charcoal Pit milk shakes;

Margaret Aitken, for her humor and irreverence;

Samantha Power, who can taste the power of words;

The Buccini family, for their friendship and their faith;

Ted Kaufman, our wise man;

Jade, Christine, and Chris for their unflinching loyalty and love;

Missy, Cuffe, and Casey, who guided my pen and my spirit—to the very last sentence;

My brothers, Joe, Jim, and Frank, for supplying the raw material;

My husband, Jack, for being my anchor.

ABOUT THE AUTHOR

Valerie Biden Owens is the first woman in US history to have run a presidential campaign—that of her brother Joseph R. Biden Jr. She also led his seven straight US Senate victories and has been his principal surrogate on the campaign trail.

Valerie is chair of the Biden Institute at the University of Delaware and a partner at Owens Patrick Leadership Seminars. Valerie sits on the advisory board of the Beau Biden Foundation for the Protection of Children. For twenty years, when Valerie was not managing or advising President Biden's campaigns, she served as executive vice president of Joe Slade White & Company, a media consulting firm. She has worked extensively with Women's Campaign International, teaching women how to organize and develop communication and political skills. Valerie has also served on the national board of the Women's Leadership Forum of the Democratic National Committee and has served for thirty-five years on the board of the Ministry of Caring. She is a graduate of the University of Delaware. She is married to Jack Owens, an attorney and businessman. They have three children.

CELADON
BOOKS

Founded in 2017, Celadon Books, a division of
Macmillan Publishers, publishes a highly curated list
of twenty to twenty-five new titles a year. The list of
both fiction and nonfiction is eclectic and focuses
on publishing commercial and literary books and
discovering and nurturing talent.